REWRITING THE NATION

BRITISH THEATRE TODAY

Aleks Sierz FRSA is Visiting Professor at Rose Bruford College, and author of *In-Yer-Face Theatre: British Drama Today* (Faber, 2001), *The Theatre of Martin Crimp* (Methuen Drama, 2006) and *John Osborne's Look Back in Anger* (Continuum, 2008), and most recently co-editor of *The Methuen Drama Guide to Contemporary British Playwrights* (Methuen Drama, 2011). He also works as a journalist, broadcaster, lecturer and theatre critic.

Methuen Drama

Methuen Drama, an imprint of Bloomsbury Publishing Plc

3 5 7 9 10 8 6 4 2

First published in Great Britain in 2011 by Methuen Drama

Methuen Drama
Bloomsbury Publishing Plc
50 Bedford Square
London WC1B 3DP
www.methuendrama.com

Quoted material on page iv © Ziauddin Sardar.
Reproduced, with permission, from *The A to Z of Postmodern Life: Essays on Global Culture in the Noughties* by Ziauddin Sardar (London: Vision, 2002), p. 97

ISBN 978 1 408 11238 0

A CIP catalogue record for this book is available from the British Library

Available in the USA from Bloomsbury Academic & Professional, 175 Fifth
Avenue/3rd Floor, New York, NY 10010. www.BloomsburyAcademicUSA.com

Typeset by SX Composing DTP, Rayleigh, Essex
Printed and bound in Great Britain by Martins the Printers, Berwick-upon-Tweed

REWRITING THE NATION

BRITISH THEATRE TODAY

By Aleks Sierz

Methuen Drama

In British identity, power and territory are expressed in hierarchies of race and class. It is a little too glib to argue that British identity had the luxury of seeing race as external, the definition of difference beyond its shores. But the exercise of power that created an empire on which the sun never set, and a notion of class that defined and shaped modernity and was not a stranger anywhere in the world, are essential attributes of what it is to be British. Without it the British could not be simultaneously xenophobic, internationalist and parochial – the sort of people who go on Spanish holidays to eat fish and chips and drink warm bitter ale. British identity is based on an assumption of authority that makes the world a familiar place, a proper theatre in which to continue being British.

Ziauddin Sardar, *The A to Z of Postmodern Life: Essays on Global Culture in the Noughties* (London: Vision, 2002), p. 97

CONTENTS

ACKNOWLEDGEMENTS

First, my main thanks as always goes to my partner Lia Ghilardi, who has been brilliant from the beginning until the very end: for discussing the initial idea, for numberless and impassioned disputes about the plays, and for always pointing out, with her sociologist's eye, the bigger picture. Second, many thanks to Mark Dudgeon, my publisher at Methuen Drama, who has been exemplary in his enthusiasm, knowledge and support – as have all the staff, especially Suzi Williamson, Jennifer Key and Neil Dowden. My work has been considerably enhanced by my discussions, in some cases over more than a decade, with several academics, notably Elisabeth Angel-Perez, Mireia Aragay, Peter Billingham, Susan Blattes, Nicole Boireau, John Bull, Maria Delgado, William Dixon, Rebecca D'Monte, Helen Freshwater, Stephen Lacey, Michal Lachman, Martin Middeke, David Pattie, Dan Rebellato, Graham Saunders, Peter-Paul Schnierer, Jean-Pierre Simard, Merle Toennies, Liz Tomlin, Ken Urban, Clare Wallace and Pilar Zozaya.

With a book such as this, playwrights have helped me enormously by sharing their knowledge of, and insights into, the new writing system in Britain, so special thanks to Hassan Abdulrazzak, Kay Adshead, Bola Agbaje, Howard Barker, Mike Bartlett, Sarah Beck, Richard Bean, Alistair Beaton, Gurpreet Khar Bhatti, Michael Bhim, Adam Brace, Moira Buffini, Gregory Burke, Leo Butler, In-Sook Chappell, Lin Coghlan, Ryan Craig, Martin Crimp, Tim Crouch, April De Angelis, David Edgar, David Eldridge, Georgia Fitch, Tim Fountain, Fraser Grace, James Graham, debbie tucker green, David Greig, Sarah Grochala, Tanika Gupta, Charlotte Jones, Dennis Kelly, Fin Kennedy, Lucy Kirkwood, Kwame Kwei-Armah, Chris Lee, Doug Lucie, Duncan Macmillan, Nicola McCartney, Chloe Moss, Anthony Neilson, Chris O'Connell, Joe Penhall, Mark Ravenhill, Philip Ridley, Atiha Sen Gupta, Ashmeed Sohoye, Simon Stephens, Colin Teevan, Laura Wade, Steve Waters, Joy Wilkinson, Roy Williams, Sarah Woods, Michael Wynne, Alexis Zegerman.

Additional thanks for all kinds of help to Vicky Angelaki, Lily Ash-Sakula, Tom Atkins, Knut Ove Arntzen, Suzanne Bell, Andreia Bento, Paul Bourne, Jack Bradley, Mike Bradwell, Katarina Ciric-Petrovic, Anthony Clark, Jo Combes, Dominic Cooke, Christopher Corner, Sarah Dickenson, Elyse Dodgson, Kate Dorney, Anna Evans, Philip Fisher, Anne Fuchs, Kate Gambrell, Christopher Gatt, Lisa Goldman, John Goodfellow, Ramin Gray, Annette Max Hansen, Andrew Haydon, Ian Herbert, Paul Higgins, George Hunka, David James, Clare Jepson-Homer, Caroline Jester, Simon Kane, Gene David Kirk, Hildegard Klein, Alice Lacey, Ruth Little, Charlotte Loveridge, Howard Loxton, Alex Mangold, Sam Marlowe, Anne Mayer, Jorge Silva Melo, Jonathan Meth, Julian Meyrick, Katie Mitchell, Enric Monforte, Abigail Morris, Lucinda Morrison, Laura Myers, Margit Nordskov Nielsen, George Osgerby, Roger Owen, Andrea Pitozzi, Petra Pogorevc, Nancy Poole, David Prescott, Michael Raab, Paula Rabbitt, Ian Rickson, Becky Sayer, Roxana Silbert, Paul Sirett, Rob Swain, Jaime Taylor, Ewan Thomson, Jenny Topper, Graham Whybrow, Philip Wilson, Agata Witczak, Charlotte Woodward. And to anyone I might have inadvertently omitted.

I would also like to sincerely thank colleagues, especially Nesta Jones, Michael Earley and Jayne Richards, at Rose Bruford College, where I am a Visiting Professor, for their moral, intellectual and financial support. I'm also conscious of a debt to the editors of all the academic journals that have printed my articles over the past decade: David Bradby and Maria Delgado, Simon Trussler, Dan Rebellato, Ted and Adele Shank, Bonnie Maranca, Caridad Svich, Darren Gobert, and Josh Abrams and Jennifer Parker-Starbuck. And, likewise, many thanks to the editorial staff, too numerous to name individually, of newspapers and magazines such as the *Daily Telegraph, Independent, Independent on Sunday, New Statesman, The Stage, Sunday Times, Tribune* and *What's On in London*. Similarly, I'm grateful to all my fellow theatre critics for all their insights into new plays. A heartfelt thanks has to go to Dominic Cavendish, founding editor of the theatreVOICE website, who gave me the chance to interview so many playwrights and directors. Finally, a special acknowledgement to all the excellent staff of Boston University's

British Programme in London and to the very many students who have taken my courses in Modern British Drama and Experiencing London Theatre. My accounts of some of the plays that appear in this book owe more than a little to the class discussions I enjoyed with all you guys. Rock on.

Aleks Sierz
June 2010

ABBREVIATIONS

All references to plays are to the editions in the Bibliography.

The following abbreviations have been used for producing theatres or companies, and while simple co-productions list both producing theatres, complex co-productions, where more than two theatres are involved, are abbreviated by 'etc.'.

ATC	Actors Touring Company
Bromley	Churchill Theatre, Bromley
Contact	Contact Theatre, Manchester
Coventry	Belgrade Theatre, Coventry
Dundee	Dundee Rep, Dundee
EFF	Edinburgh Festival Fringe
EIF	Edinburgh International Festival
ETT	English Touring Theatre
Frantic	Frantic Assembly
Gate	Gate Theatre, Dublin
Hull	Hull Truck
Ipswich	New Wolsey Theatre, Ipswich
Live	Live Theatre, Newcastle upon Tyne
Liverpool	Liverpool Everyman and Playhouse
Manchester	Royal Exchange Theatre, Manchester
Menier	Menier Chocolate Factory
NTS	National Theatre of Scotland
Paines	Paines Plough
Plymouth	Theatre Royal Plymouth
RSC	Royal Shakespeare Company
Sheffield	Sheffield Theatres
Stratford	Theatre Royal Stratford East
Suspect	Suspect Culture
Watford	Palace Theatre, Watford
WYP	West Yorkshire Playhouse

INTRODUCTION

3rd Historian   The truth is, every country is invented.
                         (David Edgar, *Testing the Echo*, 59)

This book looks at new writing for the theatre in Britain during the
first decade of the new millennium. This was the New Labour era: the
nation was led by prime ministers Tony Blair and Gordon Brown, and
the state funded the arts with a rare generosity. Under New Labour,
theatre got more money than ever before and there was more new
writing than ever before. At a very rough count, there were some 3,000
new plays produced during the 2000s, more than double the amount
of the previous decade. The implications of this bonanza will be
explored and questions about the quality of the work will be addressed
throughout the book. But its central theme is national identity. It
argues that theatre is part of a widespread conversation about who we
are as a nation, and where we might be going (clearly, that word 'we'
is contentious). As Professor S. E. Wilmer succinctly says, theatre is a
public forum which offers a 'particularly effective means of conveying
notions of what is national and what is alien'.[1] Most playwrights not
only reflect and refract the reality around them; they sometimes
anticipate and second guess the future. As they write and rewrite our
notions of what it is to be British, they might stumble upon new
conceptions of who we really think we are, and what we could
become. At a time when the idea of national identity was being hotly
debated, British theatre made its own contribution to the continuing
argument by offering highly individual and distinctive visions of
Englishness and Britishness.

All this happened in a fresh, if often problematic, political context.
Following a landslide victory in the general election of May 1997,
New Labour confidently proclaimed the arrival of a New Britain.
Within a couple of years, this was realised by means of a constitutional

settlement involving devolution for Scotland, Wales and Northern Ireland. New regional assemblies, each with different powers, were set up for these nations. Clearly, the resulting decade of devolution had an impact on theatre outside London. Generally speaking, New Labour's financial generosity meant that all cultural institutions, including theatres, had to deliver on social policies: their mission was to create wider audience access, greater ethnic diversity and more innovative product. In May 2004, Culture Secretary Tessa Jowell published 'Government and the Value of Culture', an essay in which she argued that 'Culture has an important part to play in defining and preserving cultural identity – of the individual, of communities, and of the nation as a whole.'[2] Not only did British theatre have to be a social worker, opening doors to new audiences and soothing the pangs of social exclusion, but it also had to tell us about ourselves.

At the same time, the tensions resulting from social fragmentation, cultural segregation and increasing migration in the United Kingdom as a whole became more evident. From such change comes conflict: so on the one hand are ranged the forces of tradition, of Middle England, of conservative visions of one nation; on the other come new ideas about cultural hybridity, a sense of multiple identities, of identity as a work in progress. When there is a tension in British theatre between its native traditions and foreign imports, it is possible, argues Professor Steve Blandford, for new work that 'reads against the grain' of public opinion to suggest new 'hybrid identities' at a time when identity is in flux.[3] Or, as the popular comedian Eddie Izzard puts it: 'We should be proud to be English because we are so cosmopolitan' – the nation is 'the mongrel dog that's really wily and clever and steals all your biscuits and sells them to the local kids. The pedigree [ethnically pure] dog is kind of pretty but thick as two short planks and he chokes on the biscuit.'[4]

On stage, such hybrids take many different forms. For example, Oladipo Agboluaje's *The Christ of Coldharbour Lane* (Soho, 2007) sported a burning Union Jack on the playtext's cover and hinted at the possibility of creating a new identity, a mix of street culture, black Christianity and traditional Englishness, as exemplified in the ecstatic exclamation at the end of the play: 'They will see the New Jerusalem on the horizon and raise a mighty shout! For Brixton! For England! For Britain!' (81). In a more comic vein, the final scene of Robin Soans's *Mixed Up North* (Out of Joint, 2009) showed a mixed-race company joyfully performing a Bollywood parody. Similarly, the programme of David Edgar's *Testing the Echo* (Out of Joint, 2008) quotes the late Labour politician Robin Cook:

> Chicken Tikka Massala [sic] is now a true British national dish, not only because it is the most popular, but because it is a perfect illustration of the way Britain absorbs and adapts external influences. Chicken Tikka is an Indian dish. The Massala source [sic] was added to satisfy the desire of British people to have their meat served in gravy.[5]

Of course, the problem with such metaphors is that although we are what we eat, people do tend to be slightly more complicated than what is served up for them.

One big complication is globalisation, which has become such an enormous influence on daily life. And one result of such processes of change is increased concern about cultural identity. In the words of social anthropologist Kate Fox, 'Change does not necessarily mean the abolition of traditional values [. . .] Ethnic minorities in Britain are if anything increasingly keen to maintain their distinctive cultural identities, and the English are becoming ever more fretful about their own cultural "identity crisis".'[6] By articulating the concerns of various tribes, British playwrights are deeply involved in the project of writing and rewriting the nation. One key question is how far have the English, as opposed to the Scots, Welsh or Northern Irish, remained English? Are they, in George Orwell's often quoted words, 'still English': do they really have the ability to 'change out of all recognition and yet remain the same'?[7] It would not be at all surprising if British theatre articulated the tensions between English and British identity, and if it treated the whole subject as a strongly contested and contradictory territory. As Jen Harvey says, national identities can oppress or enable, and can often be 'simultaneously, in different degrees, both oppressive and enabling'.[8]

This book's subject is British theatre. Once again, this is a problematic concept, not least because most playwrights are influenced by ideas and events from all over the world. In an increasingly globalised world, the idea of Britishness is constantly being questioned, contested and qualified, whether implicitly or explicitly, by work from abroad. Ireland is a case in point. This nation's theatre plainly offers, in Clare Wallace's words, 'a powerful parallel tradition' to that of Britain's, but 'although Irish playwrights are acknowledged (though frequently only with an eye on national identity politics), where to place Northern Irish playwrights remains a perennial problem'.[9] Similarly, the notion of a British drama or an English drama remains acutely problematic: as Professor Mary Luckhurst points out, 'A major difficulty for the idea of English drama is that it has been consumed by the notion of British drama [. . .] Englishness needs redefining.'[10] Likewise, according to Krishan Kumar, because 'it is evident that for much of the twentieth century Britishness flourished alongside, and perhaps to a good degree overlapped, Englishness',[11] perhaps the new century offers a chance to change this, to create a compromise Britland. On stage, the slippage between Englishness and Britishness is well illustrated by Scottish playwright Gregory Burke's *On Tour* (Royal Court/Liverpool, 2005): when a 'Manc' and a cockney – both English football fans – first meet, they bond not by singing 'There'll Always Be an England', but by chanting 'Rule Britannia' (12). Because the main subject of this book is British identity many contemporary playwrights – Irish, American and Continental – are absent from these pages. Happily, the landscape of new writing in this country is broad enough to embrace all these kinds of work – but they are not the subject of this book.

This is a book about new writing, and mainly about New Writing Pure as opposed to New Writing Lite. So, although I mention many theatres and companies in passing, I have not dealt in detail with organisations whose primary focus is on ensemble acting, physical theatre, devised work, live art, multi-media experiments, site-specific ventures, street theatre, theatre-in-education, one-off one-person shows, circus, or whose main objective is community work, work with children, young people, prisoners or puppets. There's nothing wrong with these kinds of theatre – they are simply not the subject of the book. New Writing Pure is work which is often difficult, sometimes intractable, but it usually has something urgent to say about Britain today. It is work that, in playwright Simon Stephens's words, is 'challenging in either form or content', or both.[12] And it is work that, in Roy Williams's telling phrase about his *Sing Yer Heart Out for the Lads* (National, 2002), stages a struggle around the question: 'What kind of England do we want?'[13] Or, for that matter, what kind of Britain? So while this is a book about plays that entertain as well as instruct, it is not a book about popular light entertainment or West End comedies or commercial musicals – once again, there is nothing wrong with any of these genres, but they are not the subject of this book.

Equally, this is a book about live performance rather than just the literary text. Of course, text-based theatre is itself a good example of the Englishness of British theatre: one of this culture's characteristics is its love of words. But this book is not primarily a study of the printed word. The text, as playwright Moira Buffini reminds us, 'is only the half of it'.[14] So this is a study of British theatre as a form of performance, where the contribution of the director, designer and actors are as important to the creation of a production's meaning as that of the writer they all aspire to serve. For example, playwright Leo Butler recalls the late onstage scene change in his *Lucky Dog* (Royal Court, 2004), a play whose picture of married life seemed to suggest a sense of stasis in England:

> One of the show's highlights came right at the end of the play, when the back wall collapsed, revealing the fluorescent yellow beach on which stood Linda Bassett (who only moments before had been snarling and barking), a transformed woman in her bathing suit and shades [. . .] one of those rare occasions when the combined talents of the company come together.[15]

Suddenly the stage radiated the possibility of change, surely an allegory of national life. Other instances of powerful stage imagery are not hard to find: in David Edgar's state-of-the-nation drama *Playing with Fire*

(National, 2005), the strongest moment was wordless – the Muslim Fazal's blunt denial of the outstretched hands of two women, signalling a rejection of compromise. Significantly, a similar incident occurs in Richard Bean's *England People Very Nice* (National, 2009). And also, this time as a comic act, twice in Cosh Omar's *The Great Extension* (Stratford, 2009). Stage pictures such as these invoke a sense of who we are. Other examples abound. Isabel Wright's *Peepshow* (Frantic, 2002), whose title suggests a culture obsessed with reality TV, was set in a cross-section of a block of flats: at one unforgettable moment the bodies of the characters seemed to flow through the ceilings and floors of the building, implying that our imaginations can free us of constraints. Sometimes, such wordless moments happen outside the stage space. In Scottish playwright Anthony Neilson's extremely disturbing play *Relocated* (Royal Court, 2008), which was a dark vision of a land haunted by child killers, the audience ascending to the Theatre Upstairs became aware of a powerful smell of disinfectant, which suited the grim subject of the play: cleaning up after murder.

Experiences such as this suggest that the audience is a vital element in the creation of meaning. It's even tempting to say that the meaning of a play lies in the experience of the audience. In today's theatre, as in much of postwar culture, the audience has been largely middle-class, middle-aged and white – despite New Labour policies to broaden it. The general picture is of audiences that tend to sit quietly, and that absorb meaning in an individual rather than a collective way. All very English. But there are exceptions, some good examples of which occurred during the Royal Court's fiftieth anniversary season in 2006: Tom Stoppard's *Rock 'N' Roll*, which evokes a sense of traditional Englishness in its Cambridge University scenes, includes a speech from Eleanor, who's terminally ill, which floors her younger rival: 'And, Lenka, don't try to shag my husband till I'm dead, or I'll stick the art of motor-cycle maintenance up your rancid cunt' (60). At the Royal Court, where the audience is virtually unshockable, such lines were mutely accepted. During the play's West End transfer, by contrast, the line provoked a gasp, quickly followed by a palpable wave of sympathy for Eleanor. Incidents such as these also raise questions about whether men and women gaze at plays in the same way. For example, Terry

Johnson's *Piano/Forte* is set in an English country house, a place which resonates with ideas about upper-class toffs. But when Kelly Reilly exploded onto the stage semi-naked (without a top) it's likely that the men in the audience were more forgiving than the women, many of whom might well have asked whether this display was strictly necessary. Turning to national attitudes, young Americans found Caryl Churchill's *Drunk Enough To Say I Love You?* – a critical account of the Anglo-American 'Special Relationship' – one-sided and offensive; young Brits tended to accept it at face value. Similar differences apply to racial attitudes: in Tanika Gupta's *Sugar Mummies*, a play set in the West Indies which implied that today's sex tourism is imperial oppression in a different guise, the scene in which a privileged white woman whips an impoverished black man was experienced by a white audience as slightly uncomfortable, but by a black audience as absolutely outrageous. As Gupta remembers, the 'predominantly black audience [. . .] changed the meaning of the play'.[16] In most accounts of theatre, the audience is seen as one entity, but in reality it is always a much more complex being. For example, debbie tucker green comments on audience reactions to her *Stoning Mary* (Royal Court/Plymouth, 2005): 'Younger people might feel differently about the play to older people, black different to white, Asian different to black.'[17] Different audience members experience the same play in different ways; in the best plays, the audience is split – there is a conflict of feeling, and a feeling of conflict, in the stalls. And in the bar afterwards.

In the past, critics and commentators tended to assume that a play says only one thing (that it has just one message). It would be more accurate to say, and most observations about how audiences actually behave (whether in the theatre or on the journey home) would surely confirm this, that the most richly textured plays say several things, and usually all at once. And meaning doesn't just come from the content of a play. As Forced Entertainment's Tim Etchells says, 'The meaning of what you do *is* the aesthetic and *is* the form'.[18] Meaning comes across by means of both form and content. Similarly, the discussion of the play's message is the play's message. Conflict over what a play is saying is what it's actually saying. A good example is Simon Stephens's comment on his controversial *Motortown* (Royal Court, 2006): 'The play was at various times, by various critics, received as being a criticism of the [Iraq] war and a criticism of the anti-war campaign.'[19] But as well as stimulating, theatre can soothe. Some venues aim to provoke, but often audiences just want to be entertained. Or just feel that they are all in it together. Imagining a nation can be a comforting act of participation, flattering the lonely self with the idea of what Benedict Anderson dubbed 'an imagined community', in this case of fellow audience members.[20]

Clearly, the different meanings of a play are usually conveyed through the use of narrative. Like many cultures, the English delight in telling stories.[21] But British theatre tends to be all about presenting a story in a clear, linear and naturalistic way. Stories, of course, do a lot of hard work. As narratives, they give us pleasure by shaping reality, and they help us to enjoy the show by leading us by the hand through the labyrinth of meaning, contradiction and conflict that is drama. Narratives play to our natural desire to know what comes next, to find out what is hidden, and to our need to expose the truth in its banality as well as its revelatory power. Narratives teach us about the world: they make visible the motives of fictional characters, perhaps compensating for our inability to truly know people in real life. Sure, they make us feel that life is more manageable than it really is. In doing so, they also police us. They remind us of moral codes, the boundaries of desire and the consequences of doing wrong. They sometimes even show the good being rewarded (it is fiction, after all). They provide patterns for living, and help make sense of the world. Narratives 'R' us. As one character, in Tamsin Oglesby's *US and Them* (Hampstead, 2003), another account of the Anglo-American Special Relationship, says, 'A narrative is good' (86). Yes, and, with typical self-reflection, David Greig and Gordon McIntyre's *Midsummer* (Traverse, 2008) offers a meditation on how 'the more you tell a story the more it becomes a story. All the rough edges get worn away' (47). And David Farr's hilarious *The Danny Crowe Show* (Bush, 2001), which analysed our national obsession with celebrity culture, offers the following exchange:

Magda It's just a story.
Miles So was *Hamlet*. Some catch on. (18)

Some of the stories which catch on are about national identity. Certainly, Englishness or Britishness is a state of mind, an imaginary place, a fictional way of being, a set of stories we tell ourselves.

Like other fiction, theatre is not just a response to the real world, still less a simple reflection of it; plays also relate to other plays. A good example is David Greig's *San Diego* (Tron/EIF, 2003), a highly enjoyable fantasy which engages both playfully and painfully with the legacy of Sarah Kane. Typically whimsical, it features a character called David Greig (played by Billy Boyd, wearing a 'David Greig' T-shirt, in Marisa Zanotti's original production). In one scene, three other characters called David and one called Sarah, who all work 'in conceptual consultancy', brainstorm the idea of an airplane being a community, a 'village' (68–79). This scene is clearly inspired by Martin Crimp's *Attempts on Her Life* (Royal Court, 1997), which also satirises the chat of media folk. Greig's play even nods in the direction of Crimp's with its mention of 'message deleted' (113), an echo of the first scenario of Crimp's play, titled 'All Messages Deleted'. *San Diego* also echoes other plays: when one character says, 'You want to have sexual intercourse with my melon' (22) it is reminiscent of Joe Penhall's *Blue Orange* (National, 2000), where the troubled Christopher mentions having 'tried it with a grapefruit' (114). Greig's depressed character Laura also seems like someone who's stepped out of Sarah Kane's *Cleansed* (Royal Court, 1998) and, in her desire to cut herself, from one of Mark Ravenhill's plays. At the same time, the influences also flow the other way: Laura must surely have influenced Lisa, the central character of Anthony Neilson's *The Wonderful World of Dissocia* (EIF, etc., 2004). Greig's play, with its scene about a filmed hijacking (38–40), finds a resonant echo in Mark Ravenhill's *Product* (Paines/Traverse, 2005) and, perhaps, even in the title of Ravenhill's *pool (no water)* (Plymouth/Lyric Hammersmith, 2006) because in Greig's play one character states: 'There's a pool. But there's no water' (32). The image of women going to a well to fetch water in Greig (71) is similarly echoed in Crimp's *Cruel and Tender* (Young Vic, etc., 2004) (62). In such dizzying ways, a contemporary play can be part of a conversation not only with its audiences but also with other plays that they might, or might not, have seen. Finally, Greig's play rewrites the idea of a national culture, showing that a piece of playwriting can be Scottish without being about Scottish history or about Scotland today – theatre can define itself as Scottish by its playful attitude to theatre form and by its theatrical daring.

Another influence on the theatrical imagination of the 2000s has been a technological one: the digital world. Virtual communities and social networking sites have altered our sense of identity. As well as countless shows that mention digital gadgets, or use video screens and other electronic effects, the explosion of new media has also subtly altered the imagination of many playwrights. This is a kind of cultural osmosis. Producer Michael Kustow says of the new media, which he calls 'the wired world': it is 'a model of life, of thinking and seeing and mapping experience'.[22] To simplify what is a complex process, the effect of new digital media on the theatrical imagination has been to speed up and complicate story-telling, to widen our sense of what is possible on stage and to make our idea of communication more sophisticated. This is expressed in the way playwrights construct narratives, especially in the way these jump from scene to scene and from idea to idea or image to image, and the way they are full of short and, to use an old-tech word, 'telegraphic' dialogue. Playing with time and space, in simultaneous scenes for example, has become increasingly common. If the digital is a new language, exposure to it colours the traditional vocabulary of theatre. In some plays, such as Dennis Kelly's *Love and Money* (Manchester/Young Vic, 2006), which looked at debt culture, emails become an efficient way of storytelling; in others, such as Douglas Maxwell's *Helmet* (Paines/Traverse, 2002), characters literally live in the digital world of Playstation; others have titles which allude to video games, as with Mark Ravenhill's *Shoot/Get Treasure/Repeat* (Paines, 2008); in others, such as Complicite's *A Disappearing Number* (Barbican, etc., 2007), the speed and imaginative possibilities of the digital world have seeped into both playtext and staging. Professor Steve Dixon sums up, 'New technologies thus call received ideas about the nature of theatre and performance into question.'[23] While this is true, it doesn't do to underestimate the dead hand of aesthetic tradition: received ideas have a way of clinging on.

Theatre is all about location, location, location. More than most art forms, it is rooted in a specific time and place. Location is theatre's most exciting asset, and its greatest drawback. To experience it, you have to be there. As Tom Stoppard says, 'If you are not there, you miss it.'[24] Because I happen to live in London, this book tells its stories from a metropolitan perspective. Likewise, I am white, middle-aged, middle-class and the son of Polish immigrants. Although the feeling of national identity exerts a pull towards words such as 'we', 'us', 'our' and, by contrast, 'them' and 'their', the meaning of this varies across the social spectrum. Britishness and Englishness can be experienced in a variety of ways, some of which are highly problematic. Obviously, I am well aware that the view from other audience members and indeed other cities – whether Edinburgh, Cardiff, Belfast, Birmingham or Plymouth, to name but five – is different.

Clearly, the structure of this book is an attempt to impose a sense of order on a disorderly reality. For that reason, after discussing the definition of new writing and explaining the new writing system in Britain, I have chosen a thematic structure in order to discuss individual plays, which cover the first decade of the new millennium (2000–2009). So there are chapters on how national identity is evident in plays that deal with global issues, social issues and personal issues, followed by one on more imaginary worlds. In general, the book is not only an account of national identity as seen by some of today's top playwrights, but also a glimpse into the new writing scene, a cultural milieu dedicated to creating contemporary new plays. But if the focus is on new writing, what exactly is this cult of the new?

I. CONTEXT

1 CULT OF THE NEW?

Sarah Forget 'the edge', it's a mirage. I should know. I wasted ten years touring in a Bedford van deluding myself I was delivering 'edge' to the blunted masses. When I finally realised the edge was merely the questionable invention of a handful of psychologically suspect, self-referential literary managers and artistic directors.

(Simon Block, *A Place at the Table*, 36)

In British theatre today, new writing is everywhere. Everywhere, you can watch plays that are examples of new writing; everywhere, you can meet new writers; everywhere there are new writing festivals. Every year, more than a million tickets are sold for new plays. In fact, there is a deluge of the new. And the new bears the stamp of the contemporary. Everyone, from playwrights to artistic directors, wants to be of the moment. As Harriet Devine, celebrating fifty years of new plays at the Royal Court, writes: 'Today almost every theatre in Britain, from the National Theatre to many tiny fringe venues, offers openings to new playwrights.'[1] In 2007, one provocative blogger wrote:

From the Royal Court in London to the Traverse in Edinburgh, via Liverpool's LLT and companies like Paines Plough, it often feels like Britain is positively drowning in new writing. To the casual observer, there's a glut of theatres and programmes that specialise in new writing, especially by young people.[2]

Two years later, critic Michael Billington agreed that new writing was 'an increasingly crowded market'.[3]

If new writing is such a central feature of the theatre landscape, what are the numbers involved? According to the latest Arts Council statistics, which cover 2003–8, 42 per cent of plays in a sample of sixty-five English theatre companies were new, and 'the box-office performance of new plays showed a considerable increase on any previous figures [. . .] New writing box-office rose from 62.1% in 2003–4 to 68.6 in 2007–8', which means that 'new writing has grown dramatically as a category since the mid-1990s'.[4] As a proportion of the repertoire, new work likewise grew substantially. This boom depended on a critical mass of new writers. It's very easy to make a list of fifty new writers that emerged since the mid-1990s. In the past decade, more than 300 playwrights have made their debuts. It has also been calculated that between 500 and 700 writers make a living out of stage plays, radio plays and TV drama in Britain. These are really remarkable figures: Britain today has many more living writers than Periclean Athens, Shakespeare's England or the first postwar new wave. That's why people speak of a renaissance of new writing in the past twenty years.

But what is new writing? Well, it's a very British idea – in the United States of America, very few people have heard of new writing; in Europe, it's only sporadically glimpsed. In those countries, there are old plays and new plays, but new writing has little status, a poor profile and no history. By contrast, British new writing is special. It differs from other work in the theatrical repertoire because it is new not only to audiences but also to its directors, designers and actors. And although it can be more expensive to put on than revivals of classics, new writing is the heart of British theatre. And it has a very British history.

A partial history of new writing

British theatre has always staged new plays, but the history of new writing is comparatively recent, and has always been involved in the project of rewriting our ideas about national identity. According to most accounts, the story begins with the arrival of John Osborne's *Look Back in Anger* on 8 May 1956 at the Royal Court. One of the functions of history is to create narratives that have the power of myths, and this is what happened with May '56, and the Angry Young

Men. This mythical moment, when a new play changed the mindset of British culture, has been variously described as a 'revolution', as heralding 'a new age' and as symbolic of 'the urgent demand for change'.[5] Osborne's play had a contemporary and individual voice that spoke to young audiences, and it projected a picture of British life that was gritty and down-to-earth, contesting the idea that new plays could only evoke the fairy-tale world of stiff upper lips, French windows and posh preoccupations.

Initially, George Devine, the pipe-smoking artistic director of the Royal Court, had dreamed of leading an avant-garde theatre, on an arty European model. But after reading Osborne's play, he realised that the future lay in contemporary new writing. In March 1956, he told *The Times*: 'Ours is not to be a producer's theatre, nor an actor's theatre; it is to be a writer's theatre.'[6] And, gradually, the Royal Court became the home of new writing in Britain, introducing writers such as Arnold Wesker, John Arden and Edward Bond. From abroad, it staged work by Arthur Miller, Eugene Ionesco and Samuel Beckett. In a sense, new writing was a type of theatrical modernism. And, in those days, the Court had an international feel. At the same time, it spoke of a very British aesthetic.

From the start, new writing had a strongly naturalistic style and a social realist agenda. Professor Stephen Lacey calls it 'working-class realism'.[7] This means a view of society which depicted working-class or lower-class life in an unglamorous – and often deliberately dirty – way, while stressing the truth or authenticity of this experience. It was usually in opposition to the ruling culture of middle-class values, and emphasised social problems such as poverty and violence. More provocatively, Scottish playwright David Greig calls this theatre style 'English realism'. He points out that the most popular playwrights in the West End in the early 1950s were French wordsmiths such as Jean Anouilh rather than British playwrights. Indeed, in Kingsley Amis's *Lucky Jim* (1954), when a family organise the reading of an Anouilh drama, the novel's anti-hero Jim Dixon mutters bitterly: 'Why couldn't they have chosen an English play?'[8] Jim was in luck. Just two years later, after *Look Back in Anger*, a new genre of English drama came into being. Greig outlines its characteristics:

This English realism, this 'new writing' genre which has so thrived in subsidised spaces over the past 40 years, attempts, as one of our leading playwrights put it, to 'show the nation to itself'. It seeks out and exposes issues for the public gaze. It voices 'debates' rather like columnists in the broadsheets. Its practitioners are praised for their 'ear' for dialogue as though they were tape recorders or archivists recording the funny way people talk in particular sections of society and editing it into a plausibly illustrative story. English realism prides itself on having no 'style' or 'aesthetic' that might get in the way of the truth. It works with a kind of shorthand naturalism which says, 'This is basically the way I see it'. Distrustful of metaphor, it is a theatre founded on mimicry. In English realism, the real world is brought into the theatre and plonked on the stage like a familiar old sofa.[9]

Clearly, in the late 1950s and early 1960s, this style had a combative air. After all, national identity seemed to be at stake. Kitchen Sink Drama was the cultural revenge of upwardly mobile lower-middle-class writers against what they perceived to be an elite of snobbish, effete and Europhile dramatists. To this imagined effeminacy, they counterposed a muscular masculinity. Abstract ideals were countered by down-to-earth writing. While foreigners seemed to flirt with philosophy, English writers boasted of their native common-sense. Against self-conscious experiment, they pitted realistic narratives about ordinary people. At its worst, this required an embattled little-Englander feeling, in which English playwrights formed a bulwark against fancy foreign muck. In its rhetoric, it could easily be anti-gay and anti-female. Osborne, for example, thought Britain's problems were caused by the runaway 'female' values of passivity, conformism and absence of 'imaginative vitality'.[10]

But the new wave of Kitchen Sink Drama also introduced an exciting contemporary feel to British theatre. In September 1959, *Spectator* critic Alan Brien described the way it rewrote the image of the nation:

The settings have been unfamiliar – a Midlands attic, an Irish brothel, a new housing estate, a Soho gambling shop, a Bayswater basement. The characters have been misfits and outcasts exiled in the no-man's-land between the working class and the middle class. The dialogue has also been eloquent, bawdy, witty and concrete. The basic kick of the whole movement has been the feeling that the play was written last weekend, the exhilaration of listening to talk alive with images from the newspapers, the advertisements, the entertainments of today.[11]

The initial new wave kicked off by Osborne was later followed by other new waves. Among the myth-makers of new writing have been press officers, such as the Court's George Fearon, who came up with the Angry Young Man label, and critics such as John Russell Taylor, who documented the successive new waves, or Kenneth Tynan, the campaigning *Observer* critic and advocate of the new. Other theatre people have also helped create the story of new writing. Director Dominic Dromgoole, for example, has stated that 'it would be hard to imagine a better record of the way we live now than could be drawn from the plays of the past forty-five years'.[12] And playwright David Edgar argues that each new wave dealt with a different subject matter. So the first new wave of the late 1950s and early-to-mid-1960s was mainly concerned with 'working-class empowerment' in the wake of the welfare state. Then, 'for the generation that followed, forged in the youth revolt of the late 1960s, the questions were much more aggressively political': namely, revolution or reform? Then, in Act Three of this postwar drama, the 1980s, 'the ground shifted once more, as women, black and gay playwrights confronted the questions of difference and identity'.[13] Next, a new generation of in-yer-face playwrights, such as Sarah Kane and Mark Ravenhill, emerged in the 1990s, a decade in which the characteristic subject of the conversation between playwrights and their audiences was the crisis of masculinity. Now, after 9/11, the ground has shifted yet again with the revival of political drama and a concern with national identity being the chief characteristics of this current Act Five of postwar drama.

A brief history of new writing can't include a litany of names because this would easily stretch to hundreds, but mention can be made of some set-pieces: the classical actor Laurence Olivier agreeing to star in Osborne's follow-up, *The Entertainer* (1957); the tussle with the censor over calling God 'the Bastard' in Beckett's *Endgame* (1958); the butchering of a tramp in David Rudkin's *Afore Night Come* (1962); the outrage caused by the baby-stoning scene in Bond's *Saved* (1965); the cries of 'filth' that greeted Joe Orton's *What the Butler Saw* (1969); the National Theatre producing Trevor Griffiths's play about Marxist politics, *The Party* (1973); the collective soul-searching in rehearsals of the Joint Stock production of David Hare's *Fanshen* (1975); 'Mike's Cunt Speech' in Steven Berkoff's *East* (1975); the fuss over the representation of an anal rape in Howard Brenton's *The Romans in Britain* (1981); the innovative overlapping dialogue in Caryl Churchill's *Top Girls* (1982); the Court's self-censorship over Jim Allen's *Perdition* (1987); the amazing success of *Trainspotting* (1994); the media outrage over Kane's *Blasted* (1995); the crashing of the Court's computer system by the title of Ravenhill's *Shopping and Fucking* (1996); Martin Crimp's dazzlingly experimental *Attempts on Her Life* (1997). This quick selection of several distinctive and original voices shows just how controversial new writing often was.

But this relentless rise of the new did sometimes suffer a hiccup. In the late 1980s, for example, there was a crisis in new writing. New work dropped from being about 12 per cent of the nation's subsidised repertoire in 1980–5 to 7 per cent in 1985–90. Artistic directors saw new plays as box-office poison, and young directors avoided them. David Edgar describes how, instead of new writing, there was

> a nationwide epidemic of adaptations (up from 6 per cent of the repertoire in the 1970s to 20 per cent in the late 1980s), suggesting that theatre had lost confidence in itself and was turning to other media for validation. Then it became harder and harder to see original plays you didn't know by heart. In 1988, if you went to the theatre in England and didn't see *The Tempest* or *Gaslight* they gave you a small cash prize. In the

years following, there were major outbreaks of *Seagulls*, *Blithe Spirits*, *Doll's Houses* . . .[14]

This dismal landscape changed during the 1990s when new writing enjoyed a remarkable comeback. If, at the end of the 1980s, new plays formed less than 10 per cent of staged work in subsidised theatres, by 1994–6 the figure was 20 per cent. So production doubled. Even more important was box-office success. In the late 1980s, new writing regularly attracted audiences of less than 50 per cent; by 1997 this figure was 57 per cent, which means that new plays could outperform classics, adaptations, translations and even Shakespeare.[15] Likewise, a heavily hyped brat pack of young writers such as Sarah Kane, Mark Ravenhill, Patrick Marber, Martin McDonagh and Anthony Neilson had a major impact on British theatre. They introduced a new sensationalism: whatever you think of in-yer-face theatre – a sensibility which was characterised by explicit portrayals of sex and violence, with a fresh directness of expression, rawness of feeling and bleakness of vision – it certainly put new writing back on the map. And where these writers led, others followed. After Generation XXX came a huge variety of new playwrights, writing in a dizzying variety of styles. Without them, the current bonanza of new writing would never have happened.

But although *Look Back in Anger* has an excellent claim to being the foundation myth of British new writing, historical truth is always a bit more complicated. After all, as well as telling stories, historians have a duty to question myths. As Professor Dan Rebellato says, 'The story of British theatre in 1956 has been so often retold that its shape, its force, its power and meaning have been lost in the familiarity of the telling.'[16] For example, despite the fact that *Look Back in Anger* was constantly brought back into the Court's repertory during 1956 and 1957, the biggest box-office draw of those years was Devine's Christmas revival of William Wycherley's Restoration classic *The Country Wife* (1675). The success of this old play saved the theatre financially: not for the last time, new writing was sluggish at the box office.

The image of a vigorous heterosexual nation promoted by new

writing has also attracted criticism. In a widely quoted 1999 news-paper article, Mark Ravenhill argued that the new wave writers of the 1950s, led by Osborne, were 'straight boys' whose mission was to clear away the 'feyness and falseness' of postwar theatre, which was dom-inated by gay writers such as Terence Rattigan and Noël Coward.[17] Instead of the class terms in which the moment of 1956 is usually discussed, Ravenhill outlines the repressed sexual politics of the new wave: the clash between old and new could also be seen as that between an effete gay establishment and vigorous straight newcomers. At the heart of the nation was sexual tension.

It is also true that the Royal Court was not the only Arts Council-funded playhouse to produce new work in the 1950s. On the other side of London, the Theatre Royal Stratford East, run since 1953 by the indomitable Joan Littlewood, staged new plays in a repertoire which also included British and European classics. Her contribution to new writing ran parallel to that of the Court. In May 1956, about two weeks after *Look Back in Anger* opened, she staged Brendan Behan's play about capital punishment *The Quare Fellow*. This was followed by plays such as Shelagh Delaney's tale of dysfunctional family life *A Taste of Honey* (1958), and Behan's anti-Republican comedy *The Hostage* (1958). Littlewood's innovative rehearsal techniques, which stressed impro-visation, resulted in stagings that were more experimental than those in other theatres. She championed, but also edited and rewrote, the work of her writers. Her theatre, moreover, was mainly about one person – Littlewood herself – whereas the Court was a collective enterprise, with several directors (Lindsay Anderson, John Dexter and William Gaskill) making their contribution. Actually, the rivalry between these two theatres continues to this day. A recent historian of Littlewood's theatre, for example, complains that, 'Theatre Workshop's [financial] problems were compounded by the rise of the Royal Court Theatre as a darling of the fashionable left.'[18] Yet despite the Theatre Royal's exceptional impact, new writing was a small part of its repertoire. Unlike the Court, it was not a specialist new writing venue.

New writing depended crucially on state subsidy. The catchphrase that became associated with the Royal Court in the late 1950s was 'the right to fail': playwright Nicholas Wright says that it meant 'the right to put on one or perhaps two plays which would be financially unsuccessful' without the theatre going 'bankrupt'.[19] It meant a degree of financial security which allowed some artistic risk-taking. Indeed, by the 1980s, the Court staged about 10 per cent of new British plays. This new writing was consciously created in opposition to commercial and mainstream theatre. Because of state subsidy, it didn't have to depend on the market to succeed – and many modern classics, such as Arden's early work, were originally flops. In this opposition to the dictates of the market, Devine and Littlewood were taking up the modernist project of the independent theatres of the 1890s. At that time, which was a kind of prehistory of new writing, the Independent Theatre Society, the Stage Society and the New Century Theatre produced new work with a literary or artistic, rather than commercial, value: they were dependent on subscriptions rather than box office and, as theatre clubs, managed to avoid censorship by the Lord Chamberlain. Their activities focused on 'the search for new playwrights', and culminated in the Harley Granville Barker and J. E. Vedrenne seasons, three of which were produced at the Court Theatre in 1904–7.[20] Significantly, regional reps also helped to promote the new drama.

In the 1960s the newly established and state-funded National Theatre Company and Royal Shakespeare Company both worked hard to create a repertoire in which the classics rubbed shoulders with new plays. And gradually, over the years, the number of specialist new writing theatres expanded, as the Court was joined by new venues such as the Hampstead, Bush and Soho theatres in London and the Traverse in Edinburgh and Live Theatre in Newcastle. In the late 1970s, the Theatre Writers' Union negotiated terms and conditions on behalf of playwrights. And state subsidy enabled playwrights to survive outside London. The Belgrade Theatre in Coventry, for example, opened in 1958 and was the first venue to benefit from clause 132 of the 1948 Local Government Act, which allowed local authorities to levy a tax of up to six pence in the pound to pay for arts and entertainment. This theatre was vital in the development of Wesker's *Chicken Soup with Barley* (1958), the first play of his trilogy about a left-wing Jewish family in London's East End. Equally significant is the fact that Joan Littlewood's Theatre Workshop began its postwar life not in the capital but by touring, with bases in places such as Kendal and Manchester. Arts Council subsidy also helped Glasgow's Unity Theatre produce Ena Lamont Stewart's *Poor Men's Riches* (1947, rewritten as *Men Should Weep* in 1976) and Robert McLeish's *The Gorbals Story* (1946). All this happened before a line of *Look Back in Anger* was written. The first new wave, notes Stephen Lacey, 'had strong connections to non-metropolitan, often Northern, social experience'.[21] The nation was a much bigger place than the Home Counties.

However important, subsidy does not tell the whole story of new writing. There were plenty of commercial ventures which staged contemporary work. For example, J. B. Priestley's *The Linden Tree* (Duchess Theatre, 1947), the prototype of the postwar state-of-the-nation play, was financed by its author. It ran for 422 performances. Far less fortunate was Rodney Ackland's *The Pink Room*, a play about the condition of Britain at the end of the Second World War which conveyed the sense, in the words of Richard Eyre and Nicholas Wright, that 'a new world is dawning, one of purposefulness and common sense. Trivial people are on their way out.'[22] When it opened in 1952, it was savaged by some critics, and Ackland fell silent. He had to wait more than three decades before the play – rewritten and renamed *Absolute Hell* – was staged at the Orange Tree theatre (1988) and revived by the National (1995). Harold Pinter almost suffered the same fate when his *The Birthday Party* closed after a week at the Lyric Hammersmith in 1958. Luckily, he managed to relaunch his career. Other landmark contemporary plays, from John Whiting's *Saint's Day* (1951) and Terence Rattigan's *The Deep Blue Sea* (1952) to Samuel Beckett's *Waiting for Godot* (1955), were also commercial ventures. So were most of the poetic dramas, written by idealists such as T. S. Eliot and Christopher Fry: whatever their religious, social and political conservatism, they were dramaturgically innovative and popular at the box office during the 1950s. Nor was commercial theatre the only backer of new work: after the BBC screened a short extract of *Look Back in Anger* in autumn 1956, it was the commercial ITV that screened a full-length version. It was only gradually that, in the theatre, a split developed between work which was commercially populist (and often unchallenging) and work which was subsidised (and could be experimental).

The one type of commercial playwriting which is now viewed with suspicion is the populist comedy. One reason must be that comedy, as Professor Christopher Innes reminds us, 'is a highly conventional genre',[23] and new writing has often aimed at affronting convention. Once, however, the West End regularly hosted writers such as Alan Bennett, Simon Gray, Michael Frayn, Peter Nichols and Tom Stoppard, non-political writers that have been dubbed the 'new mainstream' by Professor John Bull.[24] For decades, the prolific Alan Ayckbourn wrote two plays a year and John Godber produced comedy after comedy. But the ready accessibility of such plays, with their comedic brio and sense of fun, have made them suspect in the eyes of new writing stalwarts. Popular comedies have not been considered serious art. Too much fun to be good, they have tended to be ignored by academia. Today, writers such as Willy Russell, Lee Hall and Tim Firth are seen as New Writing Lite. Yet the best of Ayckbourn, Bennett or Frayn exemplifies that humorous strand of the national character that claims not too take life too seriously, while, at the same time, aching deeply inside. Here, the laugh in the face of adversity hides a heart that is quietly breaking. How very English.

Another new writing myth worth questioning is the idea that it was an aesthetic monolith. In fact, from the start, it has been split between a naturalistic majority and a more experimental minority, between, if you like, *Look Back in Anger* and *Waiting for Godot*. These two kinds of writing have existed in a permanent state of tension, each challenging the other: the naturalists goading the experimentalists into being more comprehensible, with the minority challenging the majority to be more imaginative. As well as Beckett, the experimentalists have included women such as Ann Jellicoe, whose *The Sport of My Mad Mother* (1958) looks odd on the page but on stage was an early example of total theatre, and Caryl Churchill, perhaps the most consistently innovative playwright of the postwar era. In the 1990s, playwrights such as Crimp, Kane and Ravenhill developed this legacy of experiment, innovation and imagination. In writers such as these, the streams of European absurdism, surrealism and modernism wash through British theatre.

In fact, British new writing is, like the British nation, a mongrel beast. Just as, since the 1950s, British society has been influenced by American culture, as well as Continental lifestyles, taking food from France, style from Italy and design from Scandinavia, so its theatre has been influenced by American and European playwrights. So-called British theatre would be unrecognisable without its Irish writers. And, ever since the first new wave, foreign practitioners have galvanised experimental theatre. Much more recently, playwrights from Europe and beyond have been influenced by Britain's younger writers, and then passed that influence back. Others, such as Yasmina Reza – whose popular comedy *Art* colonised the West End for more than six years from 1996 – even became noticed by a wider audience.

As British new writing boomed in the new millennium, audiences liked it. In September 2001, a Whatsonstage website poll found that 78 per cent of respondents agreed that theatre is a living art form and new writing is essential for its future. Although there was more new writing than at any other time in the nation's history, this profusion of work means that no one story can be told about the 2000s. In previous decades, from the Angry Young Men of the late 1950s to the in-yer-face playwrights of the mid-1990s, there was a sense of an avant-garde breaking through and riding a new wave. Not so in the past ten years. If the 1990s were, to use a science metaphor, Newtonian, with every cause having an effect, and one thing happening after another, the 2000s were the quantum decade, with everything happening at the same time and all over the place. British theatre resembled a nuclear reactor: inside, everything is bouncing off the walls; common sense flies out the window; paradox rules okay. In the 2000s, the story is an absence of story. Instead of a new sensibility coming into its own, what you had was a flowering of various sensibilities, a whole variety of voices.

At the same time, the question was raised about how to get young playwrights to write for large stages (most were producing plays for small studio theatres). This debate was the result of writers taking matters into their own hands. In Autumn 2002, a group who'd met at the National Theatre, set up the Monsterists. Led by Richard Bean, Moira Buffini, Ryan Craig, David Eldridge, Tanika Gupta, Colin

Teevan and Roy Williams, they issued a Monsterist manifesto 'to promote new writing of large-scale work in the British theatre': desiring to liberate new writing 'from the ghetto of the studio black box', the Monsterists not only wanted to put big plays on main stages, they also demanded 'equal access to financial resources', meaning star directors and star actors.[25]

The 2000s might have been a post-feminist era, but gender equality remained a knotty subject. Although women playwrights were more visible than ever, their numbers fell short of parity with men. When Sphinx's Sue Parrish did a survey of 140 productions nationwide in January 2006, she found that, in that particular month, 62 per cent of new plays were by men and only 17 per cent by women (the rest were multi-authored). Of the decade's ten Critics' Circle Awards for Most Promising Playwright, eight went to women, although only one won the Best Play Award (Charlotte Jones for *Humble Boy* in 2001). What seems clear is that, despite women having a greater visibility, more men than women write plays, and they are more prolific. In 2009, critic Lyn Gardner summed up:

> There are plenty of women directors and playwrights with successful careers on national and international stages. But the discourse about cultural politics and feminism that was so vibrant on our stages and in discussions well into the 1980s – questioning women's relationship to cultural production and trying to reimagine the lives we want to live – seems to have largely disappeared. Sometimes I think we were so busy winning the battle that we didn't notice that we were losing the war.[26]

If one of the functions of history is to reveal truth by examining origins, then the history of the term 'new writing' is disappointing. Its origins are hazy: no one can agree on who invented it, or when. Perhaps it was originally coined simply in imitation of the various waves of new writing in postwar prose and poetry. Nevertheless, since the early 1970s, the term has become widely accepted. By 1975, the Arts Council Drama Department had set up a New Writing

Committee, and the term was being used by theatre practitioners as well as by arts bureaucrats. Gradually, in the 1980s and 1990s, new writing acquired its current identity as a particular type of new work. Today, there is even a national new writing system.

The new writing system in the 2000s

New writing not only has a history, it also has a material base. Today, it is a publicly funded nationwide industry with its own specialised theatres. 'In the UK,' says playwright Tim Fountain, 'there is a sort of "new-writing establishment", and correspondingly a new-writing ecology which is gratifyingly strong.'[27] This ecology has its own pecking order: 'Currently,' wrote critic Jane Edwardes in 2003, 'there is an unofficial ladder of development that sees first-time [London] writers going to [small theatres such as] The Bush or Soho at the beginning of their careers before moving on.'[28] In fact, the new writing system has traditionally been simplicity itself: it is composed of six new writing theatres which specialise in developing young writers and staging new plays. The big six are the Royal Court, Bush, Hampstead and Soho in London, the Traverse in Edinburgh and Live Theatre in Newcastle.

To understand the new writing establishment, the first point to grasp is that new writing is a specialist activity that requires specialist theatres.[29] When a theatre focuses all of its energies on finding, helping and staging new writing, whether by newcomers or old hands, it has a better chance of achieving a critical mass of innovative creativity than institutions for which this activity is just an add-on. Here, the key figure is the artistic director who, with advice from their literary manager, is responsible not only for the choice of plays, but for the mission and character of the venue. In its turn, new writing (which could be defined by any marketing department as plays no one knows by writers no one has heard of and about issues no one wants to hear about) needs a specialist audience. What this means is that, especially outside London, audiences for new writing have to be created, cultivated and sustained – and that takes time. And investment. So the ecology of new writing depends on two sources of nourishment: the Arts Council and the National Lottery.

Of all the many agencies which fund theatre, the Arts Council, as Professor Theodore Shank writes, has 'done the most to foster playwriting'.[30] In its latest incarnation, the historic Arts Council of Great Britain was divided into three separate bodies for England, Scotland and Wales in 1994. Thus the system of arts subsidy anticipated political devolution. Gradually, funding has been devolved from a centralised approach – with the London-based Arts Council England (ACE) ruling the country – to a decentralised one using Regional Arts Boards. In 1999, ACE commissioned cultural consultant Peter Boyden to look into regional theatre and he produced his report on the Roles and Functions of English Regional Producing Theatres in 2000. Following this, ACE distributed an additional £25 million a year of funding from 2002–3. Jonathan Meth of Writernet, a now-defunct body that supported writers, called it 'the most significant single funding increase for at least a generation' and Lyn Gardner pointed out that it was 'the largest annual increase in subsidy ever received by any art form'.[31] Such expressions illustrate the psychological effect of increased funding – gone was the old siege mentality, and suddenly anything seemed possible. By mid-2002, some London theatres were already reporting positive changes. Productions increased, salaries went up, optimism revived. In general, statistics suggest that a 10 per cent increase in funding produces a 25 per cent increase in activity; and 20 per cent amounts to an increase of 57 per cent.[32] By 2009, ACE was investing about £100 million in some 230 theatre organisations. Compared to American theatres, few of which are publicly funded, this is great. But compared to most European countries, it's peanuts.

Of course, the funding system is much more complex than this thumbnail sketch suggests, and there's something very British about such an ad hoc patchwork of subsidy. Most new writing theatres are also funded by local authorities. In addition, most seek sponsorship from business organisations, educational foundations or private patrons. Other sources of money for new writing include local festivals, other government agencies using budgets for education or health to finance theatre work, and so on. Last but certainly not least, most venues depend on box-office takings for roughly 50 per cent of their annual income. This is one result of the increasing commercialisation of British theatre since the 1980s, and clearly has had an influence on the choice of play being produced. Staging too many experimental or difficult plays can bankrupt a theatre: for most, the norm is to strike a robust balance between populist work and more demanding fare. But although increased funding has resulted in more activity, which is the story of past decade, the question is: does increased quantity equate with increased quality?

If, in common with other theatres, the big six new writing venues were recovering from a long financial famine in 2000, they were also enjoying the fruits of the Lottery bonanza. Since its inception in 1994, the National Lottery – distributed by the Department for Culture, Media and Sport – has invested heavily in theatre buildings. The upsurge in new writing in the past decade coincided with the biggest new building programme for a quarter of a century. The Royal Court, Traverse, Bush and Live theatres were refurbished, the Soho and Hampstead got brand new buildings. Large sums of money were involved, but they were not unproblematic. 'Ironically,' comments Professor Baz Kershaw, 'the influx of large Lottery grants had created instability and uncertainty for the whole theatre system in the 1990s.'[33] Likewise, in 2003 for example, playwright Penny Gold felt that 'money went towards employing extra staff [in new buildings] and so was not available to invest in new writing'.[34] The cult of the new meant new buildings, new staffing levels and new regulations. Larger grants meant greater demands from funders, most of whom have a political agenda: so the desire of new writing theatres to be exclusive and intensive clashes with the funders' requirement to be inclusive and extensive. Thus the problems of scarcity have been overtaken by the problems of abundance.

The big six new writing theatres each have a different character, which reflects their history and their leadership. In 2000, the Royal Court was led by Ian Rickson and this iconic venue's mission was the promotion of writers that 'set out to disturb, to provoke and to question'.[35] This theatre had the image of being a cutting-edge, rather daring venue which led the field in new writing, and Rickson embodied its more austere roundhead tradition – his programming was comprehensive and eclectic, mixing old and new writers. At the Traverse, Scotland's premiere new writing theatre, artistic director Philip Howard promoted Scottish writers and emphasised touring shows to the Highlands. At the tiny Bush, artistic director Mike Bradwell was a larger than life character, a canny operator as well as an excellent director. His manifesto was: 'We have to be there to be a nuisance, an irritant.'[36] At the Soho, artistic director Abigail Morris staged work by young first-time writers, and promoted the short, no-interval, ninety-minute play, and a good proportion – in some years a majority – of her output was by women. At the Hampstead, artistic director Jenny Topper described her taste as 'the well-made play that is crammed full of ideas and hides its subversive heart in a cloak of laughter'.[37] Finally, Newcastle's Live Theatre is that rare beast: a specialist new writing theatre outside London. Under Max Roberts, it has enjoyed relationships with local writers such as Peter Flannery, Michael Wilcox, Peter Straughan and Julia Darling. In 2003, local playwright Lee Hall described the theatre space as classless: 'There are no neat rows, there is no proscenium to hide behind, no them and us.'[38]

In 2007, the most significant thing to happen to four of the big six was a change of artistic director. In one of those coincidences that seem to shoulder a significance beyond their immediate impact, Dominic Cooke took over at the Court, Dominic Hill at the Traverse, Josie Rourke at the Bush and Lisa Goldman at the Soho. The old guard departed and the theatres changed direction. Cooke's announcement that he wanted to explore 'what it means to be middle class, what it means to have power and what it means to have wealth' was widely, if erroneously, interpreted as an affront to his theatre's previous devotion to dirty realism, to representing the poor and the voiceless.[39] In Edinburgh, Howard's emphasis on Scottish talent gave way to Hill's openness to English writers; at the Bush, Rourke's main contribution was innovative explorations of new theatre spaces; and at the Soho Goldman introduced a more political orientation, while also allowing in plays by veterans alongside brand-new talents. At the Hampstead, Topper had already been replaced by Anthony Clark in

2003: his mission was to 'put on what I would call more robust work with challenging content by established writers' and he defended his staging of older writers, saying that the equation of new writing with young writing is 'ridiculously ageist, and implies that new writing is purely a cult of the young. And no, it's not – that's just one stream. Nobody would say that Caryl Churchill or Harold Pinter or David Hare don't write new plays.'[40] However, Clark's taste in new work antagonised some critics, and the Hampstead's reputation fell. As critic Mark Shenton says, 'The trouble is that a bad smell has attached to the place, and it has become difficult to dispel.'[41] Clark resigned in 2009.

In theory, the big six make up the British new writing system. In practice, things are much more complex: for example, in 2008 Writernet listed more than 300 new writing production companies and estimated that there were some 25,000 play scripts in circulation at any one time.[42] Due to the boom that new writing experienced during the 2000s, with increased funds and increased local interest, the map of new writing in Britain today reveals an immensely varied landscape.

Its most outstanding features are the Royal National Theatre and Royal Shakespeare Company (RSC), the twin peaks of the country's theatre system, commanding huge resources and impressive influence. Both of their new artistic directors, Nicholas Hytner at the National and Michael Boyd at the RSC, revived their flagships' commitments to new writing. Hytner's predecessor, Trevor Nunn, had begun the process when his 2002 valedictory season, Transformations, involved the staging of eight new plays – by playwrights such as Roy Williams, Tanika Gupta and Richard Bean – in a temporary studio space called The Loft. When Hytner arrived, he stated that 'as a nation we think we know who we were, but we need to find out what we're becoming [. . .] I want the National to find out what national means'.[43] Because the National is a high-profile institution, its new plays are always highly visible. And because even its smallest space, the Cottesloe, is almost as large as the Royal Court, it rarely hosts first-time playwrights, who – according to current wisdom – should be allowed to make their early mistakes away from the intense scrutiny that this venue attracts. In general, the sheer volume of new writing staged by the National is impressive, and its chief characteristic is its populism. Under Hytner, the National has become a palace of varieties, and his secret weapon is the National Theatre Studio, based in a separate building next to the Old Vic. By offering dramaturgical feedback, regular workshops, public readings, desk space and meeting opportunities for playwrights, the Studio helps scores of writers and plays a vital part in the country's new writing ecology. Things are less stable at the RSC. Because it no longer has a regular London home, and because many of its commissions ask playwrights to engage with the bard (with often difficult and sometimes intractable results), its contribution to new writing has – with only a handful of exceptions such as David Greig, Martin McDonagh and Roy Williams – so far added to various tributaries rather than to the mainstream.

The new writing system in Britain is complex because there are dozens of theatres which occasionally stage new plays, especially in the past decade. Significantly, these theatres don't have literary managers, although some do have writers' groups. In London, the most important are two exceptional community theatres: Theatre Royal Stratford East, led by Kerry Michael (who took over from Philip Hedley in 2004), and the Tricycle, led by Nicolas Kent. Significantly, neither is in the centre of town and both stage work of relevance to their local ethnically mixed audiences. By contrast, in the commercial West End, new writing is notable by its absence (most new plays in Theatreland are transfers from state-subsidised venues). But there are a couple of exceptions: the first is the New Ambassadors Theatre, which producer Sonia Friedman dedicated, in the late 1990s, to new work by visiting companies. Playwrights who benefited included Michael Wynne, Mark Ravenhill and Ayub-Khan Din. In 2006, this venue staged Kate Betts's *On the Third Day*, which had been developed through a reality TV show, Channel 4's *The Play's the Thing*, a nationwide search for a new play by a first-time playwright. A year earlier, the Ambassador Theatre Group launched the Trafalgar Studios.

Housed in the former Whitehall Theatre, this venue has two spaces, Studio 1 and Studio 2, the smaller usually staging new plays which have been developed on the fringe. Other London theatres that occasionally contribute to new writing include classy Off-West End boutique theatres, such as the Donmar and the Almeida, although they rarely stage cutting-edge work. Finally, the studio theatres attached to some London venues are important, for example the Young Vic and the Lyric, Hammersmith, and the various spaces of the Riverside Studios and the Pleasance Theatre all host touring companies.

London fringe theatres are important in the new writing system because they are small venues whose low profile allows many young playwrights to start their careers in relative obscurity, making initial mistakes far from the public gaze. Staffed by unpaid volunteers and theatre eccentrics, the fringe is one of the glories of London's can-do culture: in good years, such as the mid-1990s, it buzzes with creativity and innovation. But there is a downside: in bad years, it stagnates. Although the fringe originated as a radical alternative in the 1960s, commercial pressures since the 1980s have assimilated it into the mainstream. Today, the fringe can no longer be defined in political terms as an oppositional arena, but rather should be seen in economic terms as a poor relation. By 2000, a new 'two-tier class system' saw a division between a subsidised Off-West End and an unsubsidised fringe.[44] Fringe theatres are an exception to the rule that new writing theatres must have government funding – most of them have no regular funding whatsoever. In 2004, critic Jane Edwardes noted that the fringe was 'more commercial' and that its best theatres survive on 'talent, energy, dedication and non-existent wages'.[45] So while it is a sign of rude health that the ecology of London theatre can find room for anyone who can afford to work for free, and find the funds to stage a professional show, it is also true that most people working on the fringe soon move towards the money. So, with the exception of venues such as Theatre 503 and the Finborough, the forty or so fringe venues often have poor production values and tiny audiences. During the bad years of the 2000s, the costs of mounting professional productions rocketed, and the overwhelming impression of fringe offerings is of writers who briefly surface and then disappear, and of shows that are barely noticed and never revived. Tellingly, many of these plays were directed by their authors. Most of them were instantly forgettable, and are already forgotten.

Yet a handful of fringe venues did make an important contribution. In 2000, the main ones which included new writing in their repertoire were two old pub theatres: the Finborough and the Old Red Lion. The tiny Finborough in Earls Court, led by Neil McPherson, established a bold programme of thought-provoking new drama and well-chosen revivals of neglected works from the past, especially the recent past. His vision of new writing encompasses the USA, Canada and Australia, and he sums up the characteristic themes of his programming: 'Somebody once claimed that the Finborough only does plays about genocide, war and disease – which I take as a compliment.'[46] The Old Red Lion's polymath artistic director Ken McClymont programmed a mix of plays characterised, in the words of Dominic Dromgoole, by 'an eye for talent, a relaxation with big risks and an openness to innovation'.[47] But, following his departure in 2002, the venue lost its way.

In 2002, another fringe pub theatre, the Latchmere (formerly Grace) in Battersea, was relaunched as a home for new writing. Under Paul Higgins, and following another name change – to Theatre 503 – it demonstrated its specialist new writing cred by rapidly premiered more than fifty younger playwrights, including Dennis Kelly, Phil Porter, Duncan Macmillan and Rachael Wagstaff. Fuelled by a potent blend of excitement, risk-taking and good connections with other new writing venues, Higgins's Theatre 503 became, despite its poverty, central to London's new writing ecology. In his words, 'The big boys are doing good work, but they can't do all of it.'[48] In 2006, he was succeeded by two new directors, Paul Robinson and Tim Roseman, supported by programming manager Gene David Kirk. Recently, the hallmark of Theatre 503 has been high-quality productions, often with innovative stagings which reflect both a respect for the text and a determination for it to be theatrically thrilling.

Other fringe venues with an interest in new writing include the short-lived Chelsea Theatre (2001–5), housed in an ugly former community education centre just off the King's Road. Much more successful, though scarcely more beautiful, has been the Arcola Theatre, set up in 2000 in Dalston by director Mehmet Ergen and producer Leyla Nazli, who converted a former textile factory into one of London's largest and most adaptable fringe venues. As well as staging revivals of classics and plays with an international reach, especially work which resonates with the area's Turkish population, it has also pioneered experiments in verbatim theatre and contemporary adaptations. New writing has been only part of its output. Other notable unsubsidised venues included the Warehouse in Croydon, King's Head in Islington, Union Theatre in Southwark and White Bear in Kennington, which could sometimes, if rarely, punch above their weight. Occasionally, other venues such as BAC (Battersea Arts Centre), Menier Chocolate Factory, Southwark Theatre and the Orange Tree (Richmond) have also staged new plays, although these have usually been just a small part of their overall programming and artistic vision. In addition, the Drill Hall was an Off-West End arts centre specialising in gay and lesbian drama. Numerous other tiny fringe theatres regularly staged new writing, but this was usually work which had already been rejected by other higher-quality theatres – and their productions have generally been poor.

In 2000, theatre outside London was in the doldrums, following years of funding cuts. Specialist activity, such as nurturing new writing, suffered particular neglect. The venues were too big, the plays too difficult. All this changed following the Boyden Report and the injection of cash into theatres nationwide. The result was a lot more new writing, which peaked in the middle of the decade, and which often spoke with a distinctly regional voice. Here, beyond the London coteries, the challenge has been to redefine new writing. 'In terms of sensibility,' says Ben Payne of Birmingham Repertory Theatre, 'there are several writers who don't really fit into the London scene', such as Bryony Lavery, Paul Lucas and Sarah Woods.[49] Some commentators also argue that Scottish playwrights have a 'very different agenda to the fashion-victim, nihilistic "shopping and fucking" introspection of London'.[50]

There are about forty ACE-funded producing theatres outside London, and although most occasionally stage new plays, only a handful have a deeper commitment to new writing. Since 2000, the main centres in England have been Birmingham, Leeds, Manchester, Plymouth and Sheffield. In 2004, Liverpool's Everyman Theatre, on

Hope Street, was relaunched as a producing theatre, and the cornerstone of its programme is new writing. Combined into one organisation with the Liverpool Playhouse, one of the oldest reps in Britain, it is led by artistic director Gemma Bodinetz. However, most new writing theatres outside London produce a variety of new work, including straight plays, verbatim dramas, devised work, adaptations and musicals. For example, Birmingham Rep's recent successes include *These Four Streets* (2005), a collaborative piece written by Naylah Ahmed, Sonali Bhattacharyya, Cheryl Akila Payne, Jennifer Farmer, Lorna French and Amber Lone, and *8sixteen32* (2008) by the Decypher Collective, fusing grime music with the spoken word. Big hits from Liverpool include the verbatim piece *Unprotected* (2006) by Esther Wilson, John Fay, Tony Green and Lizzie Nunnery, as well as new work, such as Nunnery's *Intemperance* (2007) and Wilson's *Ten Tiny Toes* (2008). Some cities also hold new writing festivals, such as Liverpool's Everyword, and some award new-writing prizes, such as Manchester's generous Bruntwood Prize. Other examples of theatres with some interest in new writing include the Palace Theatre (Watford), Northern Stage (Newcastle), New Wolsey (Ipswich), Nuffield (Southampton), and the Bolton Octagon, which have been active in co-productions, where two or more theatres share production costs and each stage the resulting play. In fact, the co-production is a vital part of the nation's new writing system. For example, the Plymouth Drum's co-productions include work with venues such as the Royal Court, Traverse, Bush, Hampstead and the Tron (Glasgow), as well as with touring companies such as Paines Plough, Frantic Assembly and Actors Touring Company (ATC). Numerous other cities stage new plays either through co-productions or by themselves. As well as these, there have been significant contributions from the venerable, and long-lasting, Chichester Festival, plus the brand new, if rather shorter, HighTide Festival. Finally, two notable theatres were run not by directors but by playwrights, Alan Ayckbourn and John Godber. From 1972 to 2008, Ayckbourn was artistic director of Stephen Joseph Theatre in Scarborough, which produced his new plays (and continues to do so), as well as other new work. In Hull, Hull Truck stages, among others, the new plays of its head, John

Godber. In 2009, the company moved out of its tin shed and into a spanking new building.

New writing beyond England offers a similarly varied picture, with each devolved corner of the UK asserting its own identity. In Scotland, new plays have been presented by Glasgow theatres such as the Tron, the Tramway and the Citizens – as well as at Edinburgh's Traverse, one of the big six. Of course, the annual Edinburgh International Festival, plus its amazing Fringe, have traditionally provided miraculous opportunities for the staging of new writing at every level. But the most exciting new kid on the block is the National Theatre of Scotland (NTS). Set up in 2004, and headed by artistic director Vicky Featherstone and associate John Tiffany (both formerly Paines Plough), the NTS does not have a theatre building, but takes the form of an independent commissioning body which produces shows in theatres and other venues all around the country. In 2006, the NTS hit the ground running with its debut, a series of site-specific events called *Home*. As Trish Reid points out, 'As a statement of artistic intent *Home* demonstrated the existence of a confident, exciting, ambitious and forward-looking Scottish performance culture that was ready to seize its day.'[51] Within a couple of years, the NTS felt like one of the most innovative and thrilling theatre companies in the UK, promoting Scottish new writing as well as other work. Finally, in Scotland, there have been numerous co-productions with theatres such as the Dundee Rep and Perth, as well as with companies such as 7.84, Suspect Culture, Borderline and Tag.

In Wales, 2001 saw the setting up of Sgript Cymru, a Cardiff-based company that specialises in new writing in Welsh or English by Welsh playwrights. Despite the presence of writers such as Ed Thomas, Gareth Miles, Michael Povey, Marc Jenkins, Sion Eirian and Sera Moore Williams, and a distinct tradition of both experiment and populism (by companies such as Brith Gof and Bara Caws), there was no specialist venue dedicated to new writing until 2007, when Sgript Cymru joined forces with the Sherman Theatre in Cardiff, under director Chris Ricketts. Elsewhere in Wales, Theatre Clwyd in Mold was renamed Clwyd Theatr Cymru in 1998 to reflect its new national identity, and stages some new writing, while Theatr

Genedlaethol Cymru, a non-building based organisation touring Welsh-language theatre (including new plays) has been active since 2003. The most important recent development is the arrival in 2009 of a National Theatre of Wales on the Scottish model, led by John E. McGrath. Across the Irish Sea, in Northern Ireland, the new writing scene is small. Based in Belfast, the well-established Tinderbox Theatre Company, led by Michael Duk, is dedicated to new writing, while DubbelJoint produces new work, mainly by Marie Jones and strongly coloured by its West Belfast roots. But local playwrights such as Gary Mitchell and Owen McCafferty have made their careers in London.

On mainland Britain, a handful of touring companies, which have no theatre building for a base, have also made an essential contribution by performing new writing at various venues nationwide, usually a circuit of places which habitually host new work. The most important are Out of Joint, led by Max Stafford-Clark, and Paines Plough, headed successively by Vicky Featherstone and Roxana Silbert, whose co-productions have included the best new writers. Out of Joint has premiered plays by David Hare, Caryl Churchill, April De Angelis and Timberlake Wertenbaker, as well as launching first-timers such as Mark Ravenhill and Stella Feehily. Likewise, Paines Plough produces shows, plus workshops and public readings. In 2005, its thirtieth-anniversary *This Other England* season asked Enda Walsh, Philip Ridley, David Greig and Douglas Maxwell to 'think about English as a language and how it shapes our identity'.[52] Four other touring companies have also been important. Oxford Stage Company – led by Dominic Dromgoole until 2005 and then re-named Headlong by its new artistic director Rupert Goold – used to produce a mix of twentieth-century classics and new work. Since Goold arrived, and with Ben Power as literary associate, the concentration has been on new writing. As Goold says, 'If there was only one play produced in the whole country every year you would rather it be a new play than a revival. Because new plays speak to the society they are in.'[53] Another company, Frantic Assembly, led by Scott Graham and Steven Hoggett, focuses on the fusion of movement, music and dance and has had a mixed experience of working with writers such as Nicola McCartney,

Abi Morgan, Mark Ravenhill, Gary Owen and Bryony Lavery. Suspect Culture, which specialises in experimental work, is a Scottish-based company with Graham Eatough as artistic director. Finally, an oddity: the Wrestling School, established in 1988 under Kenny Ireland, is a company dedicated exclusively to developing and producing the work of maverick playwright Howard Barker, who has been its artistic director since 1996. In 2007, the Wrestling School lost its Arts Council grant, but refused to go down quietly. 'We are describing censorship, not by the police, nor even the critical police, but by a process of selective de-funding,' wrote Barker.[54]

In addition, there are other touring companies that produce new work while also specialising in other areas. For example, Tamasha, led by director Kristine Landon-Smith and playwright Sudha Bhuchar, is a British-Asian theatre company best known for its adaptations, musicals and dance pieces. Likewise, Jatinder Verma's Tara Arts produced little new writing in the 2000s, although its epic historical trilogy *Journey to the West* (2002) used Verma's trademark Binglish – a spoken mix of English and Gujarati, Hindi, Punjabi and Urdu – to suggest an evolving new hybrid identity. Of similar vintage is Talawa, a black theatre company led by Patricia Cumper, which stages classics, musicals and revivals, its new work including Kofi Agyemang and Patricia Elcock's *Urban Afro Saxons* (Stratford/Talawa, 2003) and Michael Bhim's *Pure Gold* (Soho/Talawa, 2007). Tiata Fahodzi is a small company, led by Femi Elufowoju Jr, which explores the experiences of Africans in Britain, while Kali, led by Janet Steel, promotes new writing by Asian women. Other companies with different agendas include Clean Break, Sphinx, Graeae, ETT and ATC. Good work has also come from Pilot Theatre (especially its cracking 2006 revival of Roy Williams's *Sing Yer Heart Out for the Lads*), Theatre Absolute, Banner Theatre and Eastern Angles. But while most touring companies produce good quality shows, their relative influence has been smaller than that of building-based organisations because they are only funded to stage one or two productions a year.

All over the country, as well as big theatres, there are dozens of small companies or self-help bodies dedicated to developing new writing. These include New Writing North, North West Playwrights (Manchester), Script (Birmingham and West Midlands), Menagerie (Cambridge), The Playwrights' Studio (Glasgow), New Writing South and Pier Playwrights (Brighton). For them, this was an optimistic decade: in the West Midlands, Stagecoach developed its relationship with Birmingham Rep, and, in Coventry, the Writing House worked with the Belgrade Theatre and Theatre Absolute. Even areas which were previously moribund, such as the East Midlands, experienced a revival of interest in new writing. On the London fringe, informal groupings such as the Apathists, Minimalists, DryWrite and Antelopes, plus small companies such as Nabokov, have promoted new writing.[55]

One of the most significant material factors in staging new plays is the size of the venue. Traditionally, these have been small. The iconic Royal Court is a modest Victorian theatre with a 400–seat main auditorium and a 90–seat studio. Even smaller are the Hampstead (325), Traverse 1 (250 seats) and Traverse 2 (100 seats), Soho (200), Live (200) and the tiny Bush (80). What this means is that new writing often plays to a small audience. While typical studio theatres seat about 100, most fringe venues are below this size. But because of the recent boom in new writing, many larger theatres have also staged new plays. These range from the National's huge Olivier auditorium (1,200) to the Theatre Royal Stratford East (460). A big theatre could be defined as having 500-plus seats. Outside London, the West Yorkshire Playhouse in Leeds has two spaces, Quarry (750) and the smaller Courtyard (350). Equally large are Birmingham Rep (800), Manchester's Royal Exchange (750), while Sheffield Theatres comprise the Crucible (980) and a large studio (400). Liverpool's Everyman (400) and Plymouth's Drum (175) exemplify the range of sizes.

The outstanding feature of the new writing system in Britain is its emphasis on staging new work. In other countries, there are play readings and workshops, but far fewer new plays are given a full production. In Britain, the advantages of giving scores of new voices a theatrical staging are obvious: new writers learn from seeing their work performed before an audience; talent can be honed and lessons learned. But there are also disadvantages to this cult of the new. Whereas in other countries a successful play might be taken up by several theatres, and thus enjoy several different productions, here things are different. Second productions of new plays are very rare. Although the 2000s saw more second productions than previous decades, this remains a problem. 'One of the remarkable things about the recent boom in new writing,' says playwright David Eldridge, 'is that there has been all this wonderful work, which is great for playwrights, but what's missing is the pleasure of seeing your work revived.'[56] Each theatre in Britain is so busy chasing new writers and brand new plays that they rarely pause to stage a previously produced play, however successful. Competitive feeling between venues scorns the revival of another's play. However, a new play can be staged in different venues if it is produced by a touring company or is the result of a co-production between two or more theatres.

Power is always a material force, and the power in new writing theatres resides with artistic directors. They are the ones with the mission. After discussion with their literary managers (who are usually unsung heroes, given to hard work but shy of publicity), they choose or commission new plays. It's their decisions that result in a season's programming. But it's very rare that they will honestly say why they have decided to stage one play and not another. Power needs its little secrets. Sometimes, however, you get a glimpse of what writers think about commissioning. When playwright Fin Kennedy wrote an article about the risks writers take in writing big, bold plays, he canvassed other writers:

> The response was overwhelming. Today's playwrights are a motivated, opinionated, highly intelligent, politically aware group of angry young men and women. It's not that we don't want to write big, demanding plays. It's that we're so often frustrated in our ambitions. And why? One reason comes up time and again: money.[57]

Most commissions from theatres are worth between about £6,000 and £10,000 for a full-length play regardless of whether the work is the result of a year's research or just a slice of life about 'me and my mates'. Likewise, few writers are lucky enough to have more than a couple of their plays staged in one year. This means that, unless they are veterans living off royalties or fees from the translation of their plays into foreign languages, times can be very tough. From the point of view of the writer, there are two new writing systems: the visible and the invisible. The visible, promoted by artistic directors and literary managers, claims that theatres commission the best writers, help them make their plays better and then put them on. But there is also a parallel reality, an invisible system which you only hear about when writers talk frankly about their experiences. In this reality, theatres tend to over-commission and so reject many new plays. Writers complain that they are now expected to pitch ideas, as if writing for TV. Sometimes, scene-by-scene breakdowns are asked for. With poor pay for new commissions, many playwrights have day jobs, in education (if they're lucky), in the service industries (if they are not) – or write for film and TV, which pay better. As in other areas of British life, the market has had its effect: what was once fixed and stable is now fluid and changeable. Once directors acted in partnership with writers; now the writer is just a commodity, and the play a product. A system of liberal corporatism, in which theatres invested in writers and allowed them to make mistakes, has become a free-market. And, in such a competitive environment, failure is punished: a show that bombs can make its author's future work unwelcome. In general, for the writer, all these changes can be a bracing experience: not all new writing theatres embrace you, not all schemes are open to you – and not all commissions result in productions. The cult of the new means more writers' programmes, more teaching, more schemes, but this doesn't lead to better plays. Just more average ones. Still, every writer retains one powerful weapon: the right to say no.

Finally, if this country is a world leader in playwriting, what does its new writing system say about the state of the nation? It might not be too fanciful to see this system as typically British, in terms of both our national strengths and, yes, our weaknesses. It is pragmatic, not ideological: no one planned the national distribution of new writing theatres – it just happened. It is tolerant, not autocratic: writers, an unreliable bunch, are at the centre of the creative process, not directors. It is fair-minded, not political: plays are tested out in public performance, rather than being promoted for nepotistic reasons. It is metropolitan, not regional: new writing, in common with so much of the nation's culture, has had, until recently, a very strong London bias. It is literary, not performance-based: most new writing is part of a text-based tradition that ignores more imaginative types of theatricality. It is also quintessentially British in that new writing theatres were often created by eccentrics, from George Devine at the Royal Court to James Roose-Evans at the Hampstead, and the whole system evolved through improvisation rather than edict. Of course, in the 2000s, not only has the concept of a single British nation become increasingly problematic, but the distinctive play-making traditions of different parts of the UK have been accentuated in the era of devolution. At its simplest, English playwriting specialises in naturalistic social realism; Scottish playwriting in hard-headed realism with a populist vaude-villian flair; Welsh in devised performance presented outside traditional theatre spaces; Irish in tragi-comic, word-drunk poetic tales. But not all is rosy in the garden: if the characteristic tone of much English playwriting is irony and self-deprecation, that might well be due to the typically English 'sense of superiority and smugness'.[58]

People create culture, but only in pre-existing cultural conditions. If culture is powered by everyday myths, what are the often unspoken assumptions underlying the new writing scene? Clearly, the idea that the new is good has created a culture of novelty that is destructive to long-term investment in writers. The current system is also much more of a free-market economy than ever before: and this rests heavily on the unspoken assumption that the market knows best, a myth that the credit crunch of the late 2000s has done little to destroy. Despite all the successes of the past decade, theatre's obsession with the new remains a problem. In 2009, Mark Ravenhill voiced a common complaint by pointing out that while the British theatre industry is geared to finding and helping first-time playwrights, it fails to offer them sustained support over the course of their careers. He argued that, 'We are so excited by the brand new that we push [more experienced] writers aside and rush towards the first-time writers.'[59]

There is also something very British about this cult of the new, and obsession with youth, as if we are determined to distance ourselves from an old country we know but do not love. But if the new writing system in Britain is a mongrel rather than pedigree, a result of improvisation rather than planning, what exactly is new writing?

2 WHAT IS NEW WRITING?

Katurian   Well . . . I kind of hate any writing that's even vaguely autobiographical. I think people who only write about what they know only write about what they know because they're too fucking stupid to make anything up.

(Martin McDonagh, *The Pillowman*, 76)

So strong is British culture's cult of the new that the idea of new writing is almost always associated with youth. New writers are young writers, and new writing is work by writers at the start of their careers. Usually, these new writers are in their twenties, and indeed British theatre has often been seduced by the aura of youth. But some voices have criticised this notion. In 2009, one blogger asked, 'When is a new writer not a new writer?', and questioned whether the label, and thus the idea of new writing, should be restricted to playwrights at the very start of their careers.[1] Another common criticism of new writing is that it emphasises novelty. After all, isn't the label 'new writing' a classic bit of marketing? The 'new' sells the product as good, modern and up-to-date. But, as theatre-maker Chris Goode points out, 'Most young playwrights produce desperately old writing: poor, tired language, barely fit to describe what we already know, let alone take us somewhere new.'[2] And doesn't the focus on youth lead to the ticklish question of when does a new writer become an old hand? After three plays, or thirty? After age thirty, or sixty? In practice, however, the age of playwrights is less important than the character of their work. At the 1999 London New Play Festival, for example, ten out of the twelve writers were over forty years of age. And that didn't matter – they were all new. Age is less significant that the distinctive and original voice of the work. For while it is true that some playwrights do not keep up, and their writing style becomes increasingly old-fashioned, there are plenty that remain as contemporary as any youngster. Think of Caryl

Churchill, Martin Crimp or Mark Ravenhill. The best way to avoid this difficulty is to look at the writing rather than the writer. So what exactly is new writing?

New writing is plays that are written in the great tradition of British text-based theatre, which re-established itself in the brave new state-funded postwar world. Just as, from the 1950s onwards, adverts for every kind of consumer product constantly stressed newness, so too the arts began to put a premium on novelty. Gradually, in British theatre, the notion of new writing – as opposed to the simple fact of a play being new – expanded its meaning until it embraced the sense of being contemporary, original and somehow virtuous. In the words of Colin Chambers, '"New" came to stand for a significant, meaningful text that had "relevance" and new plays became the central platform in the emerging theatre.'[3] So, during the 1960s, the term new writing gradually came to mean an individually authored text that has immediacy and relevance. One that is contemporary.

New writing is not only contemporary, but it's a form of fiction. And although fiction – especially in British culture – looks very much like real life, it is simply not the same. Fiction is stories that are invented, made up. As one character says in Ali Taylor's award-winning *Cotton Wool* (503, 2008), 'Of course it's a story. That's what stories are, made up' (46). Playwrights have long realised that invention is plucked out of the imagination. As someone says in Shelagh Stephenson's *Ancient Lights* (Hampstead, 2000), 'All writing's based on thin air' (311). But, sometimes, good stories have an afterlife. 'Stories never die,' says the Romany teenager in Natasha Langridge's *Shraddha* (Soho, 2009). Making things up is the essence of fiction. And fiction has some real advantages over reality. If real life is messy, fiction is usually clear. Real life doesn't usually follow a pattern; fiction does. Real life is often meaningless; fiction abounds in meanings. Fiction appeals to us because it can do things that real life cannot. For example, in the fictional world of the stage, conflicts that are very hard to resolve in reality can be brought to a neat resolution. Deep contradictions can be overcome. Justice can be seen to be done. Love can overcome all odds. Fiction can be so moving precisely because it is unlike real life. In the world of fiction, anything is possible: time can be made to flow in reverse. Two locations can be experienced at the same time. Fiction enables us to time-travel and to jump across oceans; it also enables us to see who we really are by showing us people who are both like us and not like us. In playwright David Edgar's words, 'Drama is a zone in which we can experiment with our dreams and our dreads, our ambitions and our impulses – murderous as well as virtuous – in conditions of safety.'[4] Fiction is where the real world and the imaginary world both talk to the wider world. So narrative fiction, concludes Beckett scholar H. Porter Abbott, offers 'the truth of meaning rather than fact'.[5] In the imaginary world of the stage, we might be able to accept truths about our national identity which we are reluctant to acknowledge before the house lights go down.

But if writers are free to create aesthetic fictions, then so are their audiences. In the end, our aesthetic choices, the kinds of plays we love or hate, are also signposts along the way of self-definition. Today, argues director Dominic Dromgoole, the age of ideology is gone, and we 'work out who we are and let the world know, through our aesthetic'.[6] Our aesthetic choices are our identity.

So, on the road to discussing national identity, here are some notes towards a definition of new writing.

Distinctive and original

New writing has a history, and the weight of this historical tradition tends to bear down on the present, influencing writers and other theatre-makers, both by providing various points of comparison and by creating expectations about what new writing is, and should be. First among these expectations is that new writing is written in a style that playwright Tim Fountain characterises as the 'singular original voice', with 'a very particular vision, well expressed'.[7] As American playwright Phyllis Nagy reiterates: 'Plays are *written*. They are usually written by a single person in possession of an idiosyncratic style and [. . .] a single, intelligent, evocative and compelling point of view.'[8] A distinctive and original voice is valued above the plain style often favoured by TV or film. A distinctive and original voice is what differentiates new writing from adaptations and translations. Of course, this can lead to the Ayckbourn paradox: playwright Alan Ayckbourn's work is often thrillingly contemporary in its experimental approach to theatre form, yet his voice usually comes across as plain and unoriginal. This style of writing, found in TV and film, is straightforward but characterless. It's flat and lacks resonance. If not all playwrights have a distinctive linguistic style, what is a distinctive and original voice? One thought experiment, suggested by Graham Whybrow, onetime literary manager of the Royal Court, goes like this: 'Just imagine taking a single page of a writer's work and throwing it on the floor in a mass of other pages, written by other writers. If you can identify that writer from one page then they have a distinctive voice.'[9] Although this experiment puts a premium on the literary quality of a playwright's dialogue, and not on their dramaturgical skills, it remains a good guide to the singularity and personality of their voice.

New writing belongs to the category of text-based theatre, where an individual playwright is at the centre of the theatre-making process. The mission here is for the director, designer and actors to realise the personal vision of a single writer. Clearly, theatre is always a collaborative process, and numerous practical, personal or political constraints, both aesthetic and economic, might limit the success of this project, but this is the intention. New writing is thus distinguished from other forms of theatre, such as physical theatre (where the emphasis is on the visual), devised theatre (where a group collaborates on a text), adaptations of books or films (where the story and dialogue depend on the source) and verbatim theatre (where the words of real people are used). Clearly, each of these processes might use an individual writer, but they don't necessarily give priority to their individual voice. Some academics, such as Jen Harvie, complain that praise of the British tradition of text-based theatre results in a glamorisation of 'textual patriotism'.[10] Although it is true that the study of text-based drama can be a purely literary activity that ignores the realities of live performance, it is even truer that text-based theatre is one of the art forms at which the British excel. While Continental

Europeans can boast of several powerful theatre movements, the British tradition is different. Abroad has theatre theories, the British have pragmatism; abroad has postdramatic theatre practices, the British have dialogue-based text. In short, here the writer is king (or queen). Indeed, Michael Billington concludes his book on postwar theatre thus: 'The health of British theatre over the past sixty years has depended heavily on its dramatists and their ability to reflect the state of the nation [. . .] the future of the theatre rests with its playwrights.'[11]

In the best new writing, the flavour of the language can be both highly individual and immediately contemporary. But stage characters never speak in real dialogue, of the kind you might record in the world outside the theatre, but rather in an artificial approximation of it, a fiction designed to convey a feeling of real emotion, real communication. Kate Dorney calls this stage dialogue 'lifelike-ese', and a common contemporary form is street slang, with occasional additions of impassioned articulacy or whimsical musings.[12] Rawness, directness and punchy brevity are valued more than rhetorical speechifying or literary extravagance. Contemporary British playwriting is neither literary nor intellectual, but theatrical and practical. As Graham Whybrow says, 'The writers who come forward now very often have had particular strengths with character, language, social world and so on which they can observe or imagine or write about but it's very specific, not an intellectual matter.'[13] Abstract, generalised writing is scorned; concrete, specific writing admired. But only some of these virtues can be taught. 'There are certain things you can't teach,' says director Roxana Silbert. 'You can't give people good ideas, you can't dish out sensibility or teach them to write dialogue. New writers have got to have these skills already.'[14] If you can't teach a writer to have an individual voice, it's easy enough to recognize it when you hear it. Take the following exchange from Scottish-Asian playwright Shan Khan's *Office* (Soho/EIF, 2001):

Showtime   It's like that Fight Club shit, right?
Sharky   What Club?
Showtime   You know, with Brad Pitt and shit. First rule of Fight Club an' all . . .

> **Sharky** You been hittin' the pipe?
> **Showtime** No guy . . . (27)[15]

The taste of the writing is unmistakable, unmistakably contemporary and unmistakably British. It is both distinctive and original. As Tim Fountain says, 'Many of the greatest writers' voices are instantly recognisable in play after play. One only has to hear a line of their dialogue to identify the work of Alan Bennett, Caryl Churchill or Harold Pinter.'[16] You can savour this distinctive originality in a variety of writers. The icy satire of Martin Crimp and the cool irony of Mark Ravenhill; the Fife demotic of Gregory Burke and the Yorkshire accents of Richard Bean; the delightful quirkiness of Charlotte Jones and the insistent repetitiveness of debbie tucker green; the gutsy hilarity of Liz Lochhead and the visceral punky spirit of Polly Stenham; the poetic concision of Howard Barker and the fractured sentences of Dennis Kelly. New Writing Pure has a distinctive taste. Often, writers are the best guides to other pensmiths. Here is Terry Johnson talking about Joe Penhall:

> Good dialogue has a rhythm. If Pinter works at a strict four beats to the bar, and Mamet instinctively pushed it to a more contemporary sixteen beats, then Penhall matches Mamet, and very often outstretches him. [. . .] He's one of the few writers who can accurately time dialogue to the pace and vicissitudes of the thoughts behind it.[17]

Writers are also drawn to distinctive relationships: some, such as Joe Penhall, write about two brothers; some, such as Martin Crimp, prefer parents and daughters to fathers and sons; others, such as Mark Ravenhill, return again and again to absent or surrogate fathers; some, such as Anthony Neilson, avoid writing about family life; others, such as Ayub Khan-Din or Charlotte Jones, can't leave it alone. Matriarchs, brothers and lost kids feature strongly in Philip Ridley's plays. Some writers (such as David Hare) love sensitive women characters, others (Terry Johnson, Georgia Fitch) field funky ones. Richard Bean and Jez Butterworth put eccentrics centre stage; other writers find hope in the image of a mixed-race woman.

Plays written in a contemporary style have a language that is instantly recognisable as the voice of today. In the 1990s, new writers transformed the language of British theatre, making it more direct, raw and explicit. In terms of dialogue, they introduced a new contemporary vocabulary, and a new sense of verbal life. As director Dominic Dromgoole comments, 'Each year could turn up twenty or thirty plays that would give you a sense of life lived.'[18] And it's language that conveys that sense of vitality. In play after play, neologisms barged into the theatre, some common ones being 'bling', 'minger', 'stud muffin' and 'totally gay', plus lashings of other street slang. But writing in a contemporary style is not just a matter of sprinkling the text with 'wicked', 'whatever' or 'innit?'. In fact, plays that ring with these tags often feel dated. Slang like this might still be used on the streets, but on stage it rapidly becomes a linguistic mannerism. Tellingly, in Kwame Kwei-Armah's *Seize the Day* (Tricycle, 2009), a thirtysomething black man says to a teenager: 'May I ask that we ban the word "innit" from all of our conversations?' (129).

Other verbal expressions have a complex and often contradictory history. For example, in Joe Penhall's *Landscape with Weapon* (National, 2007), a central character says: 'I don't understand what you mean. Does not compute' (17). It's a phrase that also crops up in Khan's *Office* (33), Roy Williams's *Fallout* (Royal Court, 2003) (11) and Steve Waters's *The Contingency Plan* (Bush, 2009) (59). The phrase 'does not compute' sounds contemporary, but is it really? Well, at first sight not: it was originally used in sci-fi writing in the 1960s. However, like many 1960s tags, it gained renewed life in the late 1990s. Then, in 1999, it went global when it was used in the film *Star Wars Episode I: The Phantom Menace*. That made it contemporary again in the 2000s.[19]

For sheer verbal energy, black playwrights are outstanding. Take three examples from the Tricycle Theatre's *Not Black and White* season (2009). In Roy Williams's *Category B*, someone says, 'I am going to take my time wid you, cos no one, especially some fucked-up druggie-killing batty bwoi prisoner, is going to make a mug out of me' (58); in Kwame Kwei-Armah's *Seize the Day*, 'He's always like that, moody git, but he's a good man. Love him like cook food' (138); in

Bola Agbaje's *Detaining Justice*, 'You suffer more mood swings than a woman on her reds' (215). This is ordinary chat, but polished and honed. In *Fallout*, Williams's language sounds realistic, but is actually highly elaborate, full of tags such as 'You deaf?', 'Yer soff' and 'Shame'. The verb 'to sex' replaces the more common 'to fuck'. Hearing dialogue as direct, rhythmic and alive as this suggests that black writers were not just reporting language, they were new minting it. This was linguistic diversity – on a skateboard.

Relevant and resonant

New writing embodies national identity because it shows us the world we experience every day. Same language, same subjects. Less the shock of the new, more a recognition of the now. At the start of *Days of Significance* (RSC, 2007), for example, Roy Williams paints an instantly recognisable picture of an English market-town invaded by binge drinkers, what *Time Out* magazine called 'the local slags and pricks' out on a Saturday night 'lash'.[20] It is a familiar scenario that has so many echoes in the wider culture – from TV to pop music – that it defines our contemporary national character. Other plays have a different kind of immediacy. For example, it was hard not to be moved by the ending of Tanika Gupta's *White Boy* (Soho, 2007), which put on stage a shrine to a teenage victim of knife crime. Every week, during the play's first run, and again during its revival in January 2008, the news was full of similar stories, and of similar tributes. Sometimes the characters in a drama are themselves illustrative of contemporary preoccupations: a good example is Kwame Kwei-Armah's *Let There Be Love* (Tricycle, 2008) with its West Indian man, Alfred, and Polish woman, Maria. The playwright comments: 'Just as every West Indian was Jamaican when I was growing up, every Eastern European person was Polish [in the 2000s]. I found myself becoming almost like a teacher of Britishness for them.'[21]

In this play, Alfred, as his name suggests, is a Caribbean Alf Garnett, full of noisy prejudice, and this device offers a cultural commentary on the changing face of Englishness. On their first meeting, he accuses

Poles of 'thieving work from we young people' (270) but when he tells Maria that he's been in England for more than forty-five years, her reply, 'So you English then!', instantly offends him (277). Attitudes to national identity are invariably complex.

Many fictions are clearly inspired by current events. Take just three examples from 2007: Dan Rebellato's *Mile End* (EFF) was based on the case of Stephen Soans-Wade, who pushed Christophe Duclos under a Tube train in 2002; David Dandridge's *Twisted* (Oval House) was partly inspired by the discovery of Stuart Lubbock's body in Michael Barrymore's swimming pool in 2001; Raman Mundair's *The Algebra of Freedom* (7:84) bore similarities to the shooting of Jean Charles de Menezes at Stockwell Tube station in 2005. Sometimes, changing a play's context changes its meaning. A good example is Simon Stephens's *Punk Rock* (Lyric Hammersmith/Manchester, 2009). When the play opened in September 2009, critics saw its evocation of the Columbine school massacre as mirroring the trial of Matthew Swift and Ross McKnight, who were then accused of planning a similar atrocity in Manchester. When they were acquitted, however, the play seemed to be less a mirror of reality than a vividly written fantasy about schoolboy fantasists. On the other hand, when two or more plays explore the same social issue, it's a clear signal of national concerns. For instance, conflicts within the black community between West Indians and Africans are the subject of Roy Williams's *Joe Guy* (Ipswich/Soho, 2007), Kwame Kwei-Armah's *Statement of Regret* (National, 2007), Bola Agbaje's *Gone Too Far!* (Royal Court, 2007) and Femi Oguns's *Torn* (Arcola, 2007). In 2009, there were three verbatim plays about the Stockwell Tube shooting. But there are dangers in being too contemporary. You could call it the curse of the now. The title of Richard Davidson's *Badnuff* (Soho, 2004) sounds of the moment, but for how long? And the easiest way of making sure that your play will date quickly is to fill it with contemporary references. Already a mention of a mobile phone aerial dates a 1990s play; portable CD-players seem passé; how long before talk of an iPod or Facebook does the same to work written in the late 2000s?[22]

When new writing reflects reality, it's easy enough to appreciate its timeliness. Sometimes, another reality unexpectedly intrudes on the stage. When Steven Hevey's *In My Name* (Old Red Lion, 2008), a play about London life on the day of the 7/7 London bombings, transferred to the West End, the opening night performance was followed by a heartfelt speech by actor Ray Panthaki, boyfriend of Brooke Kinsella, dedicating the evening to her brother Ben, who had recently been murdered in a well-publicised knife crime. Apart from such horrible coincidences, new writing often allows audiences the space to think about current news stories. At its best, it also offers a vision of the future. For instance, the image of sixteen-year-old Luka threatening his mother with a knife in Judy Upton's *Sliding with Suzanne* (Out of Joint/Royal Court, 2001) or a teacher's re-enactment of a knife attack in David Eldridge's *Under the Blue Sky* (Royal Court, 2000) seemed both to reflect teen anger and to anticipate its barely controllable explosion in the later part of the decade. On a different subject, publicity for the 2008 revival of Fin Kennedy's *How To Disappear Completely and Never Be Found* (Sheffield, 2007) emphasised the way the play seemed to anticipate the case of John Darwin, the 'canoe man' who faked his own death, and then turned up alive five years later in December 2007.

What makes the best new writing? RSC literary manager Jeanie O'Hare says, 'There are three ingredients in a good writer: instinctive rawness, linguistic invention and concern with ideas. If you have all three of those, you have something very exciting.'[23] Young writers often have the rawness and linguistic invention but not the ideas. And its ideas that onetime National literary manager Jack Bradley emphasises when he uses the slogan: 'Make 'em laugh, make 'em cry, make 'em think!'[24] New writing often sizzles with ideas, and you can see why American playwright Neil LaBute praises British writers for being 'not afraid to ask the big questions'.[25] David Greig, for example, in *San Diego*, tackles huge themes such as globalisation and migration with a beautifully light touch; at one point, even his stage directions have a satirical charm: '*They are dressed casually, with an impeccable grasp of the contemporary*' (68). New themes that emerged in this decade include the surveillance society, people trafficking and the credit crunch. Although Lucy Prebble's *Enron* (Headlong/Royal Court, 2009) was about the collapse of an American energy company in 2000, its audiences appreciated its relevance to British economic conditions at the end of the decade. Likewise, David Hare's verbatim *The Power of Yes* (National, 2009) examined the causes of the banking collapse. What these two plays have in common is that both are stories without a satisfying ending, but perhaps that in itself is the perfect summary of the year 2009. Ideas fill the plays of veteran Shavians such as David Edgar and innovators such as Caryl Churchill; they animate the action in the work of Mark Ravenhill, Richard Bean and Simon Stephens; and they give sparkle to writers such as Matt Charman, Fin Kennedy and Ryan Craig.

But while it's obvious that contemporary playwrights tackle national issues, do such plays change anything? Although writers can provoke audiences to think, they can't – in the words of Peter Billingham – 'stop tanks or prevent the bricks thrown through a Pakistani corner shop window in Oldham or Whitechapel'.[26] That's true, but sometimes theatre can be an effective campaigning tool. 'In certain conditions,' says critic Mark Fisher, new plays 'can not only reflect cultural changes but actually bring them about.'[27] His example is *Deep Cut* (Sherman Cymru, 2008), Welsh-resident Philip Ralph's verbatim drama about the death in 2005 of Private Cheryl James, from Llangollen, one of four soldiers who died at Deepcut barracks. Although only about 2,500 people saw the show at the EFF, it had major political repercussions, and stimulated James's parents to mount a formal campaign for a public enquiry. In the same year, Fiona Evans's *Geoff Dead: Disco for Sale* (Live, 2008), about the death of Private Geoff Gray at the same barracks in 2001, added its voice to the debate.

Theatre's role as a public forum is further demonstrated by Tanika Gupta's *Gladiator Games* (Sheffield/Stratford, 2005), about the murder of young Zahid Mubarek by Robert Stewart, a racist psychopath in Feltham Young Offenders Institution in 2000. The aim of this play was, in the words of Imtiaz Amin (Mubarek's uncle), 'to expose the catalogue of failures that led to Zahid's brutal murder'.[28] The play, incidentally, also had other resonances. I saw it at the Theatre Royal Stratford East and, at the very end, the onstage Zahid says that he loves his mum (107). It was an emotional moment, and somebody from the balcony shouted, 'Tell her again mate.' For them, the issue was also family.

Plays such these are often examples of verbatim drama. Pioneered by the Tricycle's tribunal plays of the 1990s, which staged edited versions of public inquiries, verbatim theatre is the latest incarnation of a long tradition of fact-based drama. In the 2000s, it was a market leader in the decade's revival of political theatre. Its popularity might be due to a hunger in audiences for factual truth, theatre's answer to reality TV, when what you see is not fiction at all. But because it uses the recorded words of actual people it doesn't, strictly speaking, qualify as new writing: there is no distinctive and original authorial voice. Verbatim theatre is less about writing than about researching and editing. In the published playtext of *Deep Cut*, for example, the eighty-page play is followed by sixty pages of factual notes and appendices. Another playwright, Steve Waters, sums up the case against verbatim drama:

> The theatre of fact offers a necessary challenge to writers to embrace contemporary life, and proves the stage is one of the few public places where complex stories may be told. However, the playwright's imagination should be chastened, but not defeated, by actuality; in a world flooded with information, its task remains to reveal the facts behind the facts.[29]

Some plays, such as *Gladiator Games* and David Hare's *Stuff Happens* (National, 2004), mix verbatim material with imagined dialogue. As Peter Billingham notes, in Gupta's play 'one of the most powerful scenes dramatically was the [fictionalised] interchanges between Stewart and Zaheed [sic]'.[30] Thus factual theatre moves closer to the individually imagined worlds that new writing is so good at showing.

Some individually imagined worlds depart from the familiar shores of realism. Indeed, occasionally writers dip into the dimension of the imagination, drawing on older, more Continental, traditions of surrealism and absurdism. Good examples of this new magic realism from 2002 include Royal Court plays such as Jez Butterworth's *Night Heron* and Nick Grosso's *Kosher Harry*, as well as Caryl Churchill's *A*

Number. Unusually, innovative plays such as hers also did good box office. Often a barometer of trends, the Royal Court's Young Writers Season featured, in 2004, two plays – Clare Pollard's *The Weather* and Robin French's *Bear Hug* – which used boldly theatrical devices such as an onstage poltergeist and a teenager turned into a bear. Both plays argued that hell is not just other people, it's Mum and Dad. Even in the West End, there was room for a more poetic sensibility, with the transfer to the Wyndham's Theatre of Moira Buffini's *Dinner* (National, 2002) in 2003. Yet, however imaginative, these plays dealt with recognisable situations involving recognisable Britons.

If contemporary writing shows us a recognisable world, and has such a long history, little wonder that its preferred aesthetic is realistic or naturalistic. British playwrights are the most naturalistic in the world, at least according to British notions of how people behave naturally: 'natural' often means dirty realism, with lots of swearing and argumentation. In this national culture, brutal frankness and raw directness is a mark of authenticity and truth. But despite the hegemony of linear, realistic dramas, new writing can sometimes also question theatrical form.

Form and content

If a realistic and naturalistic style embodies the Britishness of British theatre, then plays that challenge that style represent a rewriting of this national tradition. Work that goes beyond traditional forms, such as the well-made three-act drama, expresses its nowness through an experimental attitude to structure. This emphasises the theatricality of theatre, and at the same time positions the play in relation to theatre history, to other plays that have come before it. For example, Sarah Kane's innovative *4.48 Psychosis* (Royal Court, 2000) has no named characters, no stage directions, no plot: instead it is a series of discourses, some thoughts, some conversations, some quotations, mainly about the subjects of psychotic breakdown and love. The play's form reflects its subject matter. It also attempts to redefine what contemporary British theatre should be. And it's a pivotal work: on the one hand, it was part of Kane's ongoing conversation with the work of Martin Crimp, and especially his enormously influential *Attempts on Her Life*;[31] on the other, it in turn influenced, to take just one example, Anthony Neilson's *The Wonderful World of Dissocia*, which also looked at psychotic breakdown, with a form that mirrored the experience: at first subjectively (Act One) and then objectively (Act Two).

As David Edgar says, 'Play structures fall into two categories: those using linear time and those which disrupt it.'[32] But disrupting linear time does not necessarily mean telling the story backwards. For example, Crimp's innovative trilogy of short plays *Fewer Emergencies* (Royal Court, 2005) uses a radical form to tell three familiar stories – an unhappy marriage, a school massacre and a street riot. In each case, a small group of unnamed speakers narrate the stories, all of which collapse under the weight of their own emotional content. For example, the school massacre story veers off into a surreal direction when its narrator, who appears to be an actor performing a scripted version of the story, finds he can't remember the words because of the horror of the subject matter. As he struggles with his memory, and tries to hold off an ever-helpful prompter, the story gradually morphs into another, that of an incidental figure: the psycho-killer's postman. As if infected by the homicidal subject matter of the main narrative, this simple story of a postman who finds it hard to wake up in the morning is equally violent, and Crimp tells it in the form of a twelve-bar blues song. It's not only surreal, but grimly enjoyable too. And it is suffused with a postmodern sense of being both a fractured narrative and resisting narrative closure. Linear time evaporates. The complexity of the piece highlights the fact that all stories are artificial constructs and also suggests that the contemporary world is too complex to grasp.[33] In Crimp's coolly ironic, acidly self-aware and occasionally surreal *The City* (Royal Court, 2008), Chris and Clair are a suburban couple who, when they try and communicate, tell stories which seem to implode, and are always left incomplete. But as well as being a satire on British marital life, and an expression of anxiety about children, the play is also a meditation on playwriting itself. The subverted narratives and increasingly bizarre events are, to a certain extent, explained when, in the last scene, Chris reads Clair's diary, which gives an account of how she 'invented characters' (62): what we have been watching is Clair's attempts, to use a very Crimpian word, to be a writer. To describe the inner space of her imagination, she uses the metaphor of the city: 'a city inside of me', 'an inexhaustible source of characters and stories for my writing' (61). But her characters don't come alive: 'They lived a little – but only the way a sick bird tortured by a cat lives in a shoebox' (62). The writer is a cannibal or vampire, sucking the vitality out of life. And the city is a super-metaphor which, in the words of Professor John Stokes, 'is both inner and outer, where we live and how we live, continually terrifying us with thoughts of its demise even as it makes our lives intolerable'.[34] Such experiments represent a radical rewriting of traditional theatre form. As Kane once said, 'All good art is subversive, either in form or content. And the best art is subversive in form *and* content.'[35]

One of the most adventurous British playwrights is Caryl Churchill. In play after play, she has reinvented theatrical form, choosing metaphor over literalism, and imagination over realism. For example, in *Drunk Enough To Say I Love You*, the familiar theme of the Anglo-American Special Relationship is imagined afresh by having the two countries represented by a gay couple, (Uncle) Sam and Jack. Here, gender politics mingle with global criticism. But all writers are fallible and Churchill only realised that Jack would be seen as referring to Britain (Union Jack) after the play opened. Because her intention was that the character should 'be an individual, a man who falls in love with America' she changed his name to Guy for the American premiere (269–70). Here one character is a country and the other is an individual man, the intention being to illustrate American global influence in a metaphorical way. As Elaine Aston says, 'Churchill's formal experimentation is also inextricably bound up with the political.'[36] Such formal daring is not only a cogent criticism of American power, it also points up the timidity of bog-standard British realism. And it's surely an example of what Dan Rebellato means when he says, 'Now aesthetic experiment may be the right means to achieve an effective political response to the challenges of a consumer culture and a marketized world.'[37]

Following in the footsteps of Crimp and Kane, the playtext of Simon Stephens's similarly adventurous *Pornography* (Traverse/Birmingham, 2008) has no specified speakers. Set in London in July 2005, the play comprises dialogues and monologues against the background of the Live 8 concerts, the G8 Summit, winning the 2012 Olympics and the 7/7 bombings. The author's intention is clear: 'This play can be performed by any number of actors. It can be performed in any order' (2). The seven scenes are numbered in descending order, beginning with scene seven and ending with scene one, like a countdown to 7/7. Each scene alludes to Shakespeare's idea of the Seven Ages of Man. Each also involves a transgression: betraying your boss; having incestuous sex; suicide bombing. The final scene is a list of fifty-two mini-biographies, each of which represents one of the real victims of 7/7 (number 43, which is blank, and thus denotes an unidentified victim, is arguably the saddest). In the first British production, directed by Sean Holmes, this list was projected onto the back wall of the stage after the curtain call. Apart from this scene, the rest of the play is purely fictional: significantly, the suicide bomber in scene four travels from Manchester not Leeds. One of the play's implicit arguments is that the defining thing about the 7/7 bombers was that they were so English. In this way, the form and content of Stephens's play not only rewrite contemporary history but also recast our naturalistic tradition.[38]

Sometimes theatre form causes controversy. In 2005, Michael Billington denounced the 'fashionable tyranny' of the typical ninety-minute play as 'crippling ambition, ironing out contradiction, and effectively de-politicising drama', while director Ian Rickson and playwright David Eldridge defended short plays, the latter by arguing that 'it's not length that matters but what you do with it'.[39] As well as Eldridge and Stephens, other writers who constantly recast the structure of their plays include Anthony Neilson, Mark Ravenhill, Richard Bean and Dennis Kelly. And good examples of experiments in form by women include Kerry Hood's *Meeting Myself Coming Back* (Soho, 2002), Helen Cooper's *Three Women and a Piano Tuner* (Chichester, 2004), Laura Wade's *Breathing Corpses* (Royal Court, 2005) and Winsome Pinnock's *One Under* (Tricycle, 2005). Sometimes, plays departed radically from realism, as for example in the case of Joanna Laurens's sensually poetic *Five Gold Rings* (Almedia, 2003) or Lucy Kirkwood's vigorously surreal *Tinderbox* (Bush, 2008). Plays such as these suggest that the dead hand of British naturalism can be shaken off, if only occasionally.

New writing, not

If new writing is plays written in a distinctive and original voice which deal with contemporary issues, and sometimes experiment in form, are there any types of new play that are not New Writing Pure? The answer is yes, and a good example is Alan Bennett's award-winning *The History Boys* (National, 2004), directed by Nicholas Hytner and one of the most popular plays of the decade. This was certainly a new play, but it didn't feel like a piece of new writing. Why? First, because it was a history play, set in a northern secondary school in the 1980s. Yet this school bore little resemblance to any real school: it was Bennett's fantasy, a nostalgic evocation of his experience of the 1950s. Second, the linguistic register never felt contemporary, despite some good-natured swearing, as when Mrs Lintott – played by Frances de la Tour, the only woman in the cast – called one of the boys 'cunt-struck' (22), a line which regularly raised a laugh. Critic Lloyd Evans, who went to a state school in the 1980s, skewers Bennett's wishful thinking with deadly accuracy: all the play's 'sublimely gifted' boys 'recite poetry, dispute metaphysics, play duets at the piano, sing four-part harmonies and improvise comic playlets in fluent French. Ah yes, I remember it well.' When one boy talks about his sexual progress, 'he relates the experience [. . .] using metaphors drawn from the first world war. Spot-on, Alan. That's just how we talked about losing our virginity in the 1980s. Ypres, Mons and the drive for Berlin, those were our first points of reference.'[40] Or, as Keith Miller put it, the problem with the play is 'that you cannot quite work out when and where it is supposed to be set'.[41] Bennett's play is a fairy tale about gay teachers and gay pupils that bears no relation to the real world. And its popularity is an example of British audiences' love of escapism. Bennett's play is not bad; it's simply not contemporary. It is a good example of old writing, entertaining but complacent, untruthful and unchallenging.

As such, it paints a deeply traditional picture of all things English. Similarly, many of the most popular, award-winning plays of the 2000s were history plays. From Nicholas Wright's *Vincent in Brixton* (National, 2002) to Michael Frayn's *Democracy* (National, 2003), from Peter Gill's *The York Realist* (ETT, 2001) to Richard Cameron's *The Glee Club* (Bush, 2002), and from Brian Friel's *The Home Place* (Gate, 2005) to Tom Stoppard's *Rock 'N' Roll*, these plays explored the lives of painter Vincent Van Gogh and Chancellor Willy Brandt, gay men in 1960s York and macho men in 1960s Yorkshire, the Anglo-Irish conflict of the 1870s and the Cold War in Prague and Cambridge. All very interesting, but hardly the raw gristle of the contemporary. This looking back says a lot not only about some of Britain's most senior playwrights, but also about audience tastes. In British culture, nostalgia sells. In fact, these highly successful plays – which all transferred to the West End – are not just history plays: they represent a flight from the contemporary, a refusal to look reality in the eye.

Of course, the present can see itself in the past. And history plays can certainly have a contemporary resonance: the classic example is J. B. Priestley's *An Inspector Calls* (New Theatre, 1946), which – although set in 1912 – felt like an implicit argument in favour of the 1945 Labour government's welfare policies. This is clear when, near the end, Inspector Goole says, 'We are members of one body. We are responsible for each other' (207). History plays can also act, in the words of director Ramin Gray, 'as a corrective to our myopic and self-regarding times'.[42] True, but more often they are costume dramas with little relevance to today. The past is still, in L. P. Hartley's phrase, a foreign country – they do things differently there. They also speak a different language. And most history plays are written without a distinctive and original voice.

There are exceptions: some history plays have moments of relevance, and revelation, when they connect directly with today. At one point in Stoppard's *Rock 'N' Roll*, Lenka describes the state of the nation: 'This place has lost its nerve [. . .] It's a democracy of obedience. They're frightened to use their minds in case their minds tell them heresy. They apologise for history. They apologise for good manners. They apologise for difference. It's a contest of apology' (113). While Eastern Europe has a hunger for freedom, we let ours dribble away. But the play's ending, as the characters dance to the music of rock pensioners The Rolling Stones in post-Communist Prague, suggests a flight from politics. Its final words are: '*I* don't care. I don't care. I don't *care*' (119).

In the final analysis, new writing is not about history plays, adaptations of novels or films, or old-fashioned genre pieces (like courtroom dramas), or devised work produced by a group of writers, or verbatim theatre, or musicals. It is not Lite. No, what makes new writing special is that it is written in a distinctive and original voice that speaks of the here and now. And that it does hold a mirror up to the nation.

Stimulating and provocative

Since the 1950s, the mission of new writing has been, in George Devine's words, to produce 'hard-hitting, uncompromising writers [whose] works are stimulating, provocative and exciting'.[43] If new writing is plays that challenge their audiences, one of the ways that they rewrite our images of the nation is through provocation. Some plays are a scandal even on the page. For example, Philip Ridley's *Mercury Fur* (Paines/Plymouth, 2005) – about a youthful gang arranging for a child to be sacrificed to a rich pervert in a dystopic London – was so outspoken as a playtext that his publisher, Faber, refused to publish it. On stage, another Ridley play, *Piranha Heights* (Soho, 2008), played an equally provocative game with audience expectations: Lilly, its niqab-wearing Muslim, whose rudimentary English veers from 'Yo alla!' to 'Soldier with tick-tick vein and marble teeth stick cock in' (9, 26), seemed at first to be a victim of war crimes, but her stories turn out to be cock-and-bull. And, in the end, Middle Eastern Lilly is revealed to be an ordinary East End Lil'. Both plays are confrontational, and both suggest that behind the contemporary Britain that we know there lurks a far darker landscape of horrors.

The most provocative thing that a playwright could do in the 2000s was to criticise segregated communities, especially those with a distinct religious identity. For example, in December 2004, the Birmingham Rep's production of Gurpreet Kaur Bhatti's *Behzti* (*Dishonour*) was cancelled after militant Sikh demonstrators rioted outside the theatre. They were outraged because they thought the play insulted their religion by depicting sexual abuse inside a Sikh temple. The controversy had many levels. As its director, Janet Steel, remembers, 'Most of the men we offered the [acting] work to turned it down because of the nature of the piece.'[44] Just before the play opened, Bhatti wrote: 'I believe that drama should be provocative and relevant. I wrote *Behzti* because I passionately oppose injustice and hypocrisy' (18). In this case, the play not only provoked thought, but unthinking censorious violence too. As Ash Kotak, author of a similarly provocative *Hijra* (Plymouth/Bush, 2000), wrote: 'The truth hurts, is rarely simple and some people aren't going to like it.'[45] The *Behzti* incident both reflected the tensions in Britain between faith and secularity, and added greatly to a perception that it was necessary to take sides in a struggle between religion and non-belief. In the mindset of British theatre, it also created an atmosphere of self-censorship. To give but one example: Richard Bean's *Up on Roof* (Hull, 2006), about a prison riot in Hull, featured a character pretending to be a Muslim in order to wear his hair long (the play is set in the hippy 1970s). Originally, in the playtext, the character referred in passing to Mohammed. In the staged version, these innocuous references were removed by the theatre for fear of provoking another *Behzti* incident. In Bean's words, 'The cuts in *Up on Roof* were very minor, but they do illustrate the climate of fear and self-censorship that is beginning to pervade the arts in Britain.'[46] Sometimes in theatre, which is after all a live art, the provoked bite back. Ryan Craig's *The Glass Room* (Hampstead, 2006) put a Holocaust denier on stage at a venue whose core audience is Jewish. Although Craig identifies himself with that community, he was surprised at the 'wave of hostility [. . .] an incredible, visceral, palpable feeling' that greeted his character.[47] Similarly, Caryl Churchill's *Seven Jewish Children* (Royal Court, 2009), which was written in response to Israeli attacks on Gaza, provoked huge hostility, often in a demented and exaggerated language, from defenders of the state of Israel.

As ever, sex and nationalism were problematic. Here, the offence given can be trivial as well as serious. Some plays have titles which are too in-yer-face to appear on posters: Tim Fountain's *Deep Rimming in Poplar* played with this title in Scotland, but was renamed *H-O-T-B-O-I* for London (Soho, 2004). In other cases, offended nationalists would sometimes fight back. Dic Edwards's *Franco's Bastard* (Sgript Cymru, 2002) was seen as an attack on the absurdities of Welsh nationalism – and greeted with stink bombs during one performance in Cardiff.[48] Sometimes, the backlash was devastating: in 2005, Northern Irish playwright Gary Mitchell, whose plays describe the grim reality of loyalist life after the Peace Agreement, was forced out of his home on the Rathcoole estate in north Belfast by loyalist paramilitaries, who found his views unacceptable. By doing so, they proved the truth of his work, although this might be small consolation to the writer, or his family.

As well as the obvious provocations of insistent strong language, or taboo-itching content, some plays are also provocative in the way they are staged. The work of two of the decade's most outstanding writers, Dennis Kelly and debbie tucker green, is a case in point. Green's debut, *Dirty Butterfly* (Soho, 2003), is about Jo, a white victim of abuse, whose black neighbours, Amelia and Jason, hear her pain but do nothing. Disturbingly, Jason gets off on her cries. Written in a fractured but poetic prose, the first part of the play takes place inside the characters' heads, with overlapping monologues emphasising the alienation of these urban loners. In Rufus Norris's production, the actors were pinned to a heavily raked stage at the start, then released for the more naturalistic ending in which Jo arrives, with blood running down her legs, in one of the most harrowing scenes of the decade. By contrast, Kelly's *Taking Care of Baby* (Birmingham/Hampstead, 2007) was all about challenging theatrical fashions. As directed by Anthony Clark, the audience at first thought that it was watching a verbatim drama about a woman who'd murdered her child. Then, gradually, it became clear that this was fiction, a parody of the conventions of docudrama. Not everyone grasped this, however, so the audience was divided between those who realised it was fiction and those who believed it to be literally true. Those that understood the play were further divided between those who thought that this fictionality made it more interesting and those who disagreed. Either way, the contemporary quality of the play was enhanced by its subversion of expectations. A final example of provocative staging is *My Child* (Royal Court, 2007), by Mike Bartlett, one of the most talented writers to emerge in the late 2000s, and one who has encouraged experimental productions of his plays, challenging naturalism at every point. Directed by Sacha Wares and designed by Miriam Buether, *My Child* saw the theatre's main house turned into a tunnel-shaped stage which was a cross between a Tube train and an anonymous urban location: before the show began, the cast mingled with the audience. The discomfort of the staging and proximity of the audience to the actors made the play's climactic act of violence almost unbearable to watch.

Truly contemporary plays are ones in which the audience recognises itself. Or ones which split audiences down the middle. Perhaps the best new writing always divides opinion, thus giving off the unmistakable scent of controversy. Obviously, the holy grail of the genre is a play which is contemporary in language, content and form, and provocative with it. The best make us reconsider who we are, rewriting our idea of ourselves, and of the nation. Most new plays, however, fulfil only a couple of these criteria, usually language and content. But when all these boxes are ticked, you can almost hear the champagne corks pop, and an echo of squeals of delight from artistic directors and literary managers, the people whose mission, well defined by Graham Whybrow, is 'to discover the defining plays of our time. If they don't, then they're failing to do their job.'[49] So what are the defining plays of our time, and, if nations really are imagined communities, how do British writers imagine their nation?

II. THEMES

3 GLOBAL ROAMING

Bush   It's about risk.
Rumsfeld   That's what it's about. In this new world, in this
new post-9/11 world.

(David Hare, Stuff Happens, 102)

The world of the 2000s was a world of fear. Everywhere, there were
reasons to be fearful: millennium bug, Frankenstein foods, Ebola
virus, genocidal war, bird flu and global warming. Nearer home,
there was stranger danger, cyber-bullying, toxic loans, credit melt-
down and epidemics of anxiety about mobile phones, knife crime and
childhood obesity. Food fads made eating a problem; swine flu
turned a sneeze into a chill. Broken Britain's feral hoodies, ASBO
yobs and binge-drinkers forced us to stay inside. After 9/11, terrorism
became a symbol of all the bad stuff in a world full of bad stuff. The
inflation of worry corrupted our enjoyment of life, while irrational
anxiety marched through the media – fear sells newspapers. In
Britain, we might be safer than ever in history, but we felt more
vulnerable than before. Despite the fact that we lived in the CCTV
capital of the world, fear of crime was more common than crime
itself, fear of terror more paralysing than terrorist attacks. Fear was
the new world order. The idea of extreme risk grew into a new
bogeyman, stalking through our lives and casting horrific shadows
across our imaginations. Fear was the whip that compels conformity.
Everywhere, this was reflected in paranoid, apocalyptic culture:
Spooks, Survivors, State of Play. Adam Curtis's influential 2004
documentary was aptly called *The Power of Nightmares*. Most
significantly, fear drove out hope. A couple of days after 9/11, veteran
socialist Tony Benn noted that: 'It's a completely different world.
Everything's changed. Fears have increased, hope has diminished.'[1] As
Professor Frank Furedi argues, 'It is not hope but fear that excites and

shapes the cultural imagination of the early twenty-first century.'[2] But how does this state of mind affect ideas about Britishness?

War, of course, is an example of an emergency which tests our ideas of who we are as a nation. Unsurprisingly, the War on Terror provoked a theatrical response – new writing embraced politics, and political theatre became fashionable again. Audiences craved plays that reflected their concerns. In the 2000s, the Tricycle continued its tradition of staging verbatim tribunal plays with Richard Norton-Taylor's *Justifying War* (2003), about the Hutton Inquiry into the death of weapons expert David Kelly, and Victoria Brittain and Gillian Slovo's self-explanatory *Guantanamo: 'Honor Bound To Defend Freedom'* (2004). The trouble with *Justifying War* was that it was staged before the inquiry issued its final report and, because it reached opposite conclusions to those of Hutton, it seemed like fantasy politics. In another moment of wishful thinking, the Tricycle also staged Norton-Taylor's *Called to Account* (2007), an imaginary trial indicting Prime Minister Tony Blair for aggression against Iraq, a show which attracted the highest amount of pre-opening bookings in that theatre's history. The Brits, it seems, longed for trial and retribution. Other theatres also explored verbatim drama. A big success was *My Name Is Rachel Corrie* (Royal Court, 2005), edited by actor Alan Rickman and Katherine Viner. This piece told the story of the twenty-three-year-old American activist (played by Megan Dodds) in her own words, offering a highly sentimental view of the Israeli–Palestinian conflict. Meanwhile, Robin Soans's *Talking to Terrorists* (Out of Joint/Royal Court, 2005) was certainly timely, arriving at the Court, after a nationwide tour, in the same week as the 7/7 London bombings. But although it was topical, the play suffered from the way it had been put together, being based on interviews with penitent or former terrorists from all over the world. While yielding some interesting material, and staged with theatrical verve by Max Stafford-Clark, the play missed the point: it is precisely the terrorists that won't talk to us that are the problem. They are the ones to be afraid of.

Prophesying war

By far the most high-profile account of the war in Iraq was David Hare's *Stuff Happens*. Although often scorned by academics, Hare is clearly a major playwright who has, in the words of Richard Boon, consistently 'succeeded in capturing the zeitgeist' while identifying 'his political battlefield as essentially a moral arena'.[3] Taking its title from the offhand response of Donald Rumsfeld, US Secretary of Defense, to news of the looting of Baghdad in April 2003, *Stuff Happens* charts the run-up to the invasion of Iraq. Partly, it is a verbatim piece which quotes world leaders, especially President George Bush and Prime Minister Tony Blair. But it is also a work of impassioned fiction: as Hare says, 'When the doors close on the world's leaders and on their entourages, then I have used my imagination.'[4] Theatrically, Hare's punctuation of the narrative with a series of Viewpoints – direct address to the audience by characters ranging from a pro-war journalist to a Brit in New York – helped to create a sense of fair play, a very British quality.

The play shows how the Bush administration – led by Rumsfeld, Dick Cheney and Condoleezza Rice – decided on a grand strategy to attack the so-called Axis of Evil. In this 'defining drama of the new century' (9), Bush used an idea of the War on Terror that was deliberately vague. Dismissing Blair's wish to hunt down Osama Bin Laden with the words, 'focusing on one person indicates to me that people don't understand the scope of the mission. Terror is bigger than one man' (30), Bush saw the war against Saddam Hussein as part of a vast God-given mission. Ironically, the more the Bush administration sought to eradicate terror, the more it spread: 'America has taken a country that was not a terrorist threat and turned it into one' (116). As dramatised by Hare, the conflict pits the Bush administration's hard-liners against Secretary of State Colin Powell, the one man who truly wants a solution that is backed by international law. When he finally capitulates, there is a tragic sense of him betraying his own better self. By contrast, Blair comes across as desperate both to support Bush and to appease the anti-war critics in the Labour Party.

The play shows a world in which there is only one superpower, yet the US is not confident of its supremacy. In the minds of the Bush administration, a sense of fear is ever present. But as well as articulating the idea of terror without end, Hare also suggests that, in the new world order, there is a tension between the US (strong but morally wrong) and the UK (morally right but weak). The major disappointment, he argues, is that Blair is unable to maintain the moral high ground: the desire to be an actor on the world stage corrupts his integrity. In Hare's words, the 'thesis of the play' is to show how Bush, cunning rather than intelligent, always got what he wanted, while Blair, despite his intelligence, 'got nothing'.[5] This neatly encapsulates the view that the UK is a second-rate nation trying to piggyback on US shoulders, and that the War on Terror is just another chapter in the tale of Britain's national decline: poor Blair doesn't even make it onto the poster advertising the play.

As directed by artistic director Nicholas Hytner on the National's huge Olivier stage, *Stuff Happens* attracted an enormous amount of media attention. Everywhere, opinion pieces jostled with previews, and newspapers sent political commentators to see the show ahead of their theatre critics. There was a real buzz in the air. The debate concerned both form and content. Voices on both left and right argued that the content was 'déjà vu', a dull documentary about stuff that had already happened, and Hare was accused of telling audiences 'nothing they did not know already'.[6] But while *The Times* attacked his 'tendentious mixing of fact and opinion', the *Guardian* praised the way he 'avoids the trap of agitprop by cannily subverting the play's anti-war bias' and 'questions our complacency by reminding us of the pro-war arguments'.[7] Most critics agreed that it was a play about power in which Bush comes across as a man of few words but great determination. As Peter Ansorge points out, Hare's Bush is a listener, not a talker, yet at the same time, in one critic's words, he exudes 'surprising vulnerability and a gentle manner – frequently reaching out to touch the arm of an advisor'.[8] This engrossing performance by Alex Jennings contrasted with Nicholas Farrell's more comical Blair, suggesting a second-class leader of a second-league nation.

Hytner's *Stuff Happens* was a three-hour epic in which more than forty characters, mostly men in suits, dominated the stage. Dark suits on dark carpets against a dark background. Visually it has a good claim to being one of the decade's dullest, if also one of its worthiest, theatre experiences. The play was more satisfying as an event than as a drama, although it still reads well. On the other hand, the mere fact that the prestigious National Theatre staged a play about what critic Michael Billington calls 'the most divisive war in British society since Suez' was surely a cause for self-congratulation.[9] In the words of another critic, Michael Coveney, the play's 'extraordinary "aliveness" as a dramatic document of what people were talking about in their homes was something relatively new in recent British theatre'.[10] If *Stuff Happens* was a reminder that we could be a fearful nation, it also demonstrated that the spirit of protest hadn't entirely deserted us.

Other responses to war were more indirect and more imaginative. For example, Caryl Churchill's prescient *Far Away* (Royal Court, 2000) has been hailed by playwright Simon Stephens as 'the strongest theatrical response to 9/11', even though it was written before the event happened.[11] When Stephens first read the play in 2000 it felt absurdist; after 9/11, it seemed like social realism. This visionary play premiered in November 2000 in Stephen Daldry's production, which transferred soon after to the West End. A state-of-the-nation play, as evidenced by its curtain, which was painted with an idyllic picture of the olde English countryside, this was a fifty-minute account of a young woman who grows up witnessing the brutalisation of asylum-seekers, the genocide of nameless victims and finally the war of every element of nature against every other. The opening is full of fear, as the child Joan witnesses the beating of prisoners. Her aunt tells her that she has seen 'something secret' (139), and warns her not to tell anyone. Next, there is a procession of prisoners, wearing elaborate hats made by an older Joan, on their way to death (149): in the original production, scores of volunteers were enlisted by the Royal Court to suggest the mass of victims. In the last scene, Joan arrives home after experiencing a world at war with itself: 'It wasn't so much the birds I was frightened of, it was the weather,' she says (158). There are bodies everywhere, killed by pins – or by coffee. Others were massacred 'by heroin, petrol, chainsaws, hairspray, bleach, foxgloves' (159). The alliances are equally bizarre: 'The cats have come in on the side of the French' (153); Mallards ally with elephants and Koreans (155). In a surreal fantasy of immense imaginative power, the final scene of *Far Away* is one of the best pieces of new writing to have come out of Britain in the past decade. Its mix of the mundane (attacking wasps), the phobic (dangerous butterflies) and the extraordinary (deer charging shop windows) is breathtaking in its confidence and precision. But it's not just the exhilarating wildness of Churchill's imagination that appeals. Her use of language is thrillingly nimble, jumping in mid-sentence from the prosaic to the surreal, and from the absurd to the familiar. And the structure is exciting too: a naturalistic scene followed by a slightly bizarre scene followed by a completely visionary scene. These unsettling jumps are part of the play's meaning. Although the content is often bizarre, the way the characters talk is recognisably British. The *Sunday Telegraph* wrote: 'Churchill moves into new territory by inventing new speech habits; in this case, a prosaic acceptance of extreme horror coupled with the old language of middle-class values.'[12] Perhaps the most chilling aspect of the play is that everyone reacts to genocidal war as if it was an everyday fact of life. The nation is reimagined as unheroic, complacent and finally paralysed by fear. Instead of the traditional idea that the death camps couldn't happen here, we watch ordinary Brits accept horror. You can see why director Dominic Dromgoole calls Churchill's work 'always bold, always new, always ahead of the game', although Billington criticises her for being 'alarmist' and 'despairing' in her 'vision of a whole world at war'.[13] Certainly, she doesn't offer the consolations of hope. Further, as Professor Elaine Aston acutely points out, in *Far Away* 'children can no longer save the world, but are forced to live its dangerous realities'.[14] As in the work of Martin Crimp, such as *Fewer Emergencies* or *The City*, kids suffer the brunt of their parents' paranoia and brutality. The world of *Far Away* is dominated by the culture of fear. Not so far away after all.

A different, if equally powerful, sense of an oppressive world order is conveyed by Mark Ravenhill's *The Cut* (Donmar, 2006). Since his emergence in 1996 with *Shopping and Fucking*, Ravenhill has become a leading figure in the British new writing scene, acting as an advocate of young writers and a cultural commentator. But as well as writing 'me and my mates' plays, Ravenhill has also penned resonant fantasies, and *The Cut* is one of those. Set in an unspecified time and place, the ninety-minute play opens with a striking scene in which Paul, a torturer, and John, his victim, discuss the impending administration of 'the cut', an unspecified procedure which the playwright says is meant to evoke 'a hidden fear'.[15] In a satirical reversal of the usual relationship between master and slave, John demands to be tortured while Paul tries to avoid the moment of agony. In this highly symbolic scene, with Paul finally begging John to shoot him, you feel the influence of French playwright Bernard-Marie Koltès and philosopher Michel Foucault. The relationship between Paul and John is that of, in Peter Billingham's words, a 'sado-masochistic, psycho-economic transaction', 'the complex territory of desire-as-torment or the torment of desire'.[16] It is also a good example of what Professor Dan Rebellato calls Ravenhill's 'complex and difficult relationship with fathers', a staging of the dialectic between the good father (saviour) and the bad father (abuser).[17] At the same time, the play's world is essentially British. Take, for example, Paul's comments on universities and the army, his 'new guidelines for talking' (190), 'inclusion' policy (192), and the 'off the record' comment about a 'working party' looking at the cut (189).

Scenes two and three show Paul's home life with his wife Susan, and then what happens to Paul when regime change puts his son in power and himself in prison. Paul is, in Ravenhill's words, 'racked by the liberal guilt about his role in the regime and it's destroying his relationship with his wife and by the end of the play he can't accept the new regime's offer of a form of forgiveness – he wants to be punished.'[18] In *The Cut* punishment is a fetish, and this idea plays a game with ideas about right and wrong in Western society, deliberately preferring a perverse solution to a standard sense of Christian forgiveness. The piece articulates the way a pervasive sense of fear circulates through society – from torturer to victim and from victim to torturer, from husband to wife and from wife to husband, and from father to son and from son to father. Glowering over the fiction is the sense that Britain is a nation capable of slipping into a very British form of fascism.

Michael Grandage's production had a superb cast – Ian McKellen (Paul), Jimmy Akingbola (John) and Deborah Findlay (Susan) – but critical reaction was negative, with the *Evening Standard* attacking the play for 'trailing clouds of murky symbolism, dripping with grave pretension and oozing vapid absurdities', and the *Guardian* calling Ravenhill's use of the cut 'a vague symbol that could apply to any regime'.[19] Other critics, however, acknowledged that the play's subject was liberal guilt and a divided Britain. In part, the critical reaction was a response to the hyped expectations raised by three theatre-makers at the top of their game – Ravenhill, Grandage and McKellen – but something else was also happening. It was the tenor of the play, its deliberate mix of psychological realism and fantasy, that antagonised the critics. Having been given a metaphor, they just didn't get it. Still, the play worked. While its opening articulated a vivid sense of a world of terror, and showed two different individuals reacting to the system of power which underlies the cut, its ending felt like a moment of exhausted resignation. Fear, suggests that last image of a lonely old Englishman rejecting forgiveness, is exhausting, futile and nihilistic. Hopeless.

Ravenhill was also responsible for one of the decade's most ambitious, if also most problematic, theatre epics. *Shoot/Get Treasure/Repeat* was first staged as *Ravenhill for Breakfast*, a series of readings at the Traverse, part of the 2007 Edinburgh Festival. In April 2008, all sixteen twenty-minute plays were put on at various locations around London. The project was described on the playtext's back cover as 'an epic cycle of plays exploring the personal and political effect of war on modern life', and Ravenhill says that he aimed to 'suggest a big picture through little fragments'.[20] The plays, as one journalist put it, 'link the anxieties of affluent Westerners with the shock and awe violence of their governments abroad', and the cumulative effect of them is powerful and disturbing: they create an impression of fear that is livid and loud.[21] On reflection, however, this effect palls, and soon it is the narrowness of Ravenhill's imagination that is most apparent. Moreover, here, as in much of his most recent work, he owes a heavy stylistic debt to Martin Crimp. When staged, the main problem was that most of these plays – the result of a complex co-production – had such short runs that very few spectators could have seen more than a handful. Perhaps this epic is fated to be more often read than seen in performance. Much more successful was Ravenhill's *Product*, in which he himself played James, a movie producer who – in a brilliant piece of satirical writing – pitches an outrageous film script to a Hollywood actress, a story in which she meets Mohammed, an attractive Muslim terrorist. The play was based, in Ravenhill's words, on 'the way we were redefining ourselves as Westerners even as we created a new "other", the Muslim'.[22] At one wicked moment, the couple get a visit from Bin Laden himself, and she is 'kissed, a warm breathy kiss on the forehead from Osama' (163). Here fear is beautifully subverted by the uncanny hilarity of the ridiculous.

But Ravenhill and Churchill were not the only playwrights to have visionary premonitions of the future. The start of the decade saw the opening of newcomer Leo Butler's *Redundant* (Royal Court, 2001). Set in Sheffield, this council-estate drama shows a year in the life of seventeen-year-old Lucy, who makes one bad decision after another. Late in the play, Jo, her exasperated gran, says:

> Someone should bomb this bloody country. That'd wake us up a bit. Saddam Hussein or someone. IRA, bleedin' whatsisface? Bin Laden. Yeah. He could do it. Drop a few tons of anthrax. Teach us what it really means to suffer. (164)

On the press night, the reference to Bin Laden was cut. And you can see why – it was 12 September 2001, the day after 9/11. Even with the cut, as Butler himself points out, the speech was enough 'to send a collective gasp over the theatre'.[23] But such sentiments were not uncommon: Fin Kennedy's *How To Disappear Completely and Never Be Found* includes the lines: 'Stinking rotten heap. Blow it up. Blow it all up' (12). At moments such as this, British self-deprecation turns into a yearning for self-destruction.

Home front

A number of plays brought the War on Terror into British living rooms. Scottish playwright Henry Adam's *The People Next Door*

(Traverse, 2003) used farce to examine the post-9/11 domestic world. In it, Nigel – a mixed-race grungy druggy played by the wonderfully gormless Fraser Ayres – has renamed himself Salif, and spends most of his time hanging out with his black mate, the teenage Marco, or the mouthy Scottish widow Mrs Mac (who gives a down-to-earth view of the War on Terror). When a psychopathic cop, Phil, tries to get him to contact his estranged brother, Karim, a suspected terrorist, the deadbeat Nigel is drawn into danger. Slickly directed by Roxana Silbert, who pointed out that 'it's one of the first Scottish plays that tackles cultural diversity', this hilarious comedy explored the conflict between, in *The Scotsman*'s words, 'Phil's rampant *Daily Mail* world-view' and 'a dose of practical common sense, oddly boosted by the emergent liberal folk-wisdom of Britain's soap-and-chat-show daytime television culture'.[24] Opening with a blast of Afroman's 'Because I Got High', the play, which was set in a scuzzy housing association flat, voiced more than one contemporary anxiety. When Phil says, 'I don't want some Mullah shoving his stone-age monkey religion down my fucking throat' (64), it's a good illustration, in a comic key, of Samuel P. Huntington's idea of a clash of civilisations. In the farcical figure of Nigel, Adam also imagines a character who symbolises a mutating national and cultural identity: mixed race, he calls himself by an Asian name but talks like a black gangsta; a lonely dopehead, he is drawn to Islam. The play loses momentum in its second half, but its use of comedy to explore ideas about terrorism is provocative, especially because those ideas are so sharply contested. Not everyone, for example, will agree with Nigel's assertion that terrorism is created by the state's repressive machinery: 'It's cause you and people like you treat people like that that kids decide they want to put [sic] off bombs' (64). As *The List* pointedly asked, 'Is our brutalised culture responsible for the recent spate of acts of terror?'[25]

To this question, newcomer Dennis Kelly's provocatively titled *Osama the Hero* (Hampstead, 2005) provided an answer: in the affirmative. This in-yer-face play by one of the most distinctive new voices to emerge in the 2000s is a perceptive study of the effects of the climate of fear encouraged by the War on Terror. Teenage Gary, says the play's opening line, is 'not stupid' (51). But he is different. After all, he once did a school project in which he playfully praised Osama Bin Laden as a hero. So when someone starts blowing up garages on Gary's estate, the finger of suspicion points at him. Meanwhile, the chavish Louise and Francis watch fiftysomething Mark luring teenage Mandy into his garage. When that also gets torched, the blame falls on innocent Gary. Louise and Francis decide to make an example of him, and beat him to a pulp in an excruciating torture scene which echoes American military misbehaviour in Abu Ghraib. As they torture Gary, Francis and Louise demand his confession, despite the fact that, in her words, 'You don't need evidence for terrorists' (100). Kelly has an uncanny ability to grasp contentious issues, and to blow apart theatrical form in his search for the most provocative way of addressing a subject. With *Osama the Hero*, the thrilling mix of narrative monologues, dialogues and realistic scenes enables you to get right inside the heads of the characters, alternating between despair and horror. The play roars out of its garage like a car packed with screaming joy-riders. Fuelled by a torrent of language, it skids through issues like an ASBO-kid on speed. The style might be called council-estate magic realism, but its politics are clear: governments and the media can encourage a climate of fear but cannot control its wider social consequences. As Gary observes, 'People laugh a lot nowadays. I think that's fear' (59). Similarly, in a later play, *Orphans* (Birmingham/Traverse, 2009), Kelly evokes the fear of crime: 'You don't go out after dark anymore. You cross the street when you see a group of lads' (86). *Osama the Hero*, powerfully directed by Anthony Clark, was a ninety-minute account of mass anxiety, with a strong cast headed by Tom Brooke as the nerdish Gary. The final sight of the yobbish characters – confused by media images of terrorism, and glumly thinking, 'That's why everything's so shit' (119) – was bleak and devoid of hope. By contrast, Kelly's *After the End* (Paines/Bush, 2005) features Mark, a loser who kidnaps Louise and holds her in an old nuclear shelter. He then tries to convince her that terrorists have exploded a 'suitcase nuke' (132), although she retains a healthy scepticism, arguing that, even in a world of fear, 'The only way people can destroy you is if you let them make you become something else' (160).

In *Artefacts* (Bush, 2008), Mike Bartlett, another emerging talent who was quickly promoted by the main new writing theatres, also articulated the connection between the Iraq War and daily life in Britain, this time by creating a character who is half-English and half-Iraqi. So here is sixteen-year-old Kelly, who is gobsmacked to learn that her absent father is from Iraq. She describes how she looks at herself naked in a mirror, especially at her 'little pot belly', 'where my genes got confused. This belly is not Iraqi or English. It's Engraqi. Iringlish' (9). Like Adam's Nigel, Kelly's mixed-race origins reflect a tension at the heart of the nation. Not so much a hybrid, more an uneasy mix. But the state of the world impacts on more than her sense of identity. When her father, Ibrahim, who runs the recently looted Baghdad Museum, meets her for the first time, he gives her a priceless Mesopotamian vase. When she smashes it into three parts, it's a powerful stage image that suggests the political strains between the north, centre and south of Iraq. Then she glues the parts together with superglue, leading to her despairing father's comment: 'The British make good glue, don't they? [. . .] Because they are always breaking things' (38). This eighty-minute play is written with impressive economy and offers a critical snapshot of the disaster of the Iraq War. When Kelly travels to Baghdad, she is confronted by what the Iraqis think of the imperialist English: 'When you are a child in England you are still taught underneath that you should rule the world' (42). The failure of her attempts to help her Iraqi family leads Kelly into realising just how English she is. In the end, without irony, she prefers shopping to politics, saying, 'Yeah. I'm lucky. I'm British. I don't need to fight' (64). One result of embracing the wider world is to fall back on a sense of self that puts being a full-time consumer before being a part-time Iraqi.

Many plays explored the idea of an oppressive culture of fear. One particularly fearsome example was Ali Taylor's *Overspill* (Bromley/Soho, 2008), a sixty-five-minute white-knuckle ride through Bromley High Street on a binge-drunk Friday night. When an explosion rocks the town centre, the three lads who are taking turns in narrating the story each try and pull events in a different direction. But everywhere they turn they find fear. Anxieties about random bombings, hidden terrorists and vigilante justice collide with worries about knife crime, drink, drugs and despair. Behind everything lurks 'the Nameless', a shadowy figure who exemplifies paranoia: 'There he is in front, behind and beside us / Everyone is him and following us' (36). At one point, one of the lads glimpses a 'St George's flag hanging limp / All its reds turned to dirty pink' (33) – an apt symbol of national fatigue.

Trips abroad

Other plays made difficult trips to the Middle East. In *Mappa Mundi* (National, 2002) by 1990s veteran Shelagh Stephenson, the elderly Jack is haunted by the memory of having knocked down and killed a black kid while drunk-driving in Aden in his youth. And Ryan Craig's *What We Did to Weinstein* (Menier, 2005) is a psychological thriller which follows Josh, an idealistic young Jew from Hendon, who goes to Israel, joins the army and kills a terrorist suspect. In work such as this, Britons go abroad but they fail to make the world a better place. Scottish playwright David Greig, who has worked with theatre-makers in the Middle East since 2000, articulates some of the deepest anxieties of the West.[26] In his *Damascus* (Traverse, 2007), the Scottish Paul travels to Syria and finds a world that attracts him, even if he cannot quite comprehend it. The local intellectual Wasim's verdict (translated from Arabic) is devastating: 'You know nothing about the country I live in [. . .] You know nothing of its complexities and conflicts. You come here with all the shine of your English education, so certain of your values, and you lecture me about truth' (66). Wasim adds: 'Nothing has brought more blood to this region than Anglo-Saxon idealism' (66). In another play, Greig's *The American Pilot* (RSC, 2005), an American military flyer crashes his plane into the side of a mountain in some far-off country, which might be Afghanistan or northern Iraq, and then experiences the reactions of the locals. The injured pilot instantly becomes both an object of attraction and an intractable problem. To the Farmer and the Trader, he appears as an unnecessary complication. To the Farmer's stoical wife, and their teenage daughter, he is a fascinating, exotic creature, someone who's literally fallen out of the sky. With the swift arrival of local fighters, led by the Captain and his sidekick, the Translator, the geopolitics of power take centre stage. As the Translator says, 'We are all terrorists now' (33). Greig shows how the Pilot – merely by existing – irrevocably affects everyone concerned, upending the established order as profoundly as any revolution. Yes, it's a real clash of cultures. Or is it? After all, the locals now live in a global village, and, like any Western teen, recognise American cartoons and the music on the Pilot's iPod. And their political understanding of propaganda is perfectly media-savvy. Plus, they also understand a central contemporary truth: Americans tend to think that being American equates with being human. But the Captain also understands the brute facts of power: 'If you cause pain. / You have power. If you have power. You cause pain' (36). The strength of Greig's play is that it focuses less on the known, the Pilot, and more on the unknown, the villagers. As directed by Ramin Gray, the play had a highly charged climax as American Special Forces invaded the theatre, liberating the Pilot and slaughtering the locals. Our government's complicity in the Iraq War made it hard to shrug this off as a just another act of cowboy imperialism.

Cowboy culture also features in veteran playwright Kay Adshead's *Bites* (Bush, 2005), set in a diner on the edge of a land ripped apart by conflict, a world divided between gluttonous Texans and starving Afghans. In Texas, God is an American, and excessive eating symbolises a culture of plenty, where strutting diners abuse and humiliate Hispanic waitresses. By contrast, Afghanistan is shown as a place of hardship and scarcity – even ice cream is forbidden. On a post-apocalyptic set, director Lisa Goldman brought out the piece's wicked humour and her cast's strong performances proved that you can be feminist without being dull. Adshead shows how men oppress women, whether they are dressed in burkhas or miniskirts. But an anti-abortion homily by a female Texan preacher is a reminder of how some women are equally repressive. In another scene, a terror suspect's ironic confessions are taken seriously: chillingly, he claims, 'We have targeted the London underground for a gas attack [. . .] with or without me it's unstoppable' (98). With its mix of surrealism and satire, *Bites* is a freewheeling fantasy: its effect was like watching a suppurating wound, vivid in its agony, fascinating in its horror.

Most ambitious of all the projects designed to enlighten us about the reality of distant conflicts was *The Great Game: Afghanistan* season (Tricycle, 2009), which included exhibitions and films, as well as a dozen short plays, presented over three evenings. These covered the history of British–Afghan relations from the nineteenth-century imperial politics of the strategic Great Game against the Russian Empire to more contemporary pieces, such as Abi Morgan's *The Night Is Darkest Before Dawn*, Richard Bean's *On the Side of the Angels* and Simon Stephens's *Canopy of Stars*.[27] But although British theatre often grappled with the War on Terror, what was missing was voices from the Middle East. So *Baghdad Wedding* (Soho, 2007), an award-winning debut by Hassan Abdulrazzak, a new writer whose family once fled Iraq, offers the refreshingly frank perspective of exile, and the result is suffused with a heady mixture of delicate melancholy, fierce indignation and a fine perception of the workings of the human heart. Drawing on his Iraqi heritage, Adulrazzak creates a hybrid sensibility, mixing poetic Arabic elements with a good-natured British naturalism. Jumping between London and Baghdad in the years 1998 to 2005, the play is about a love triangle involving Salim, a doctor, Marwan, his best friend, and Luma, a London-educated good-time girl. After the fall of Saddam, all three return to Baghdad, where a US missile destroys Salim's wedding. As he's captured in turn by Fallujah-bound insurgents and the US army, the story becomes a metaphor for his country's woes. On a versatile set, which alllowed us into the insurgents' hideout and a US military prison, as well as visiting the flats and cafés of Baghdad and London, director Lisa Goldman's fluid production staged a satisfyingly blend of laughter and horror. But as well as being a state-of-Iraq play, *Baghdad Wedding* is also a joyous hymn to lechery. When Salim writes a novel it is not about politics but about sex, the provocatively titled *Masturbating Angels*. Indeed, his view of England uses a variety of sexual images: the tower of Imperial College, a relic of Empire, is 'like a beautiful, long phallus' (42), and Salim's line, 'You know sometimes it takes an outsider to show the native what he keeps missing' (64), could be Abdulrazzak's manifesto.

Comparing the two countries, Marwan says, 'A wedding is not a wedding in Iraq unless shots are fired. It's like in England where a wedding is not a wedding unless someone pukes or tries to fuck one of the bridesmaids' (23). As in *Artefacts*, England is a nation characterised by tawdry excess. In the fictional world of the play, Salim and Luma prefer to stay in dangerous Baghdad rather than safe London. England, after all, is not their country.

Soldier boys

The state of the world could also be explored by looking at the way British troops behave abroad. The army remains a potent symbol of Britishness. As Richard Bean's Keith puts it in *The God Botherers* (Bush, 2003), 'I'm a pacifist, naturally, but you've got to admit, the British army is the best in the world. [. . .] If it had been us at Srebrenica instead of a bunch of Dutch transvestites there would be six thousand Muslim men still alive today' (188).

Joking apart, there were several notable army plays. Colin Teevan's timely *How Many Miles to Basra?* (WYP, 2006) tells the story of a four-man British patrol, joined by a female BBC journalist and an Iraqi guide, on an unauthorised trip through the desert in April 2003. Originally broadcast as a radio play,[28] it's mainly about different definitions of truth, but the central plot device, in which the decent commanding officer, Stewart, decides to make amends for killing three civilians at a checkpoint, offers a generous view of the British army abroad. At one point, when the Northern Irish journalist does a deal with the guide, the latter says, 'Let us keep the relationship colonial.' To which she replies, 'I come from a colony too, remember' (46). The joke is that she's as British as Stewart. Directed by Ian Brown, the show certainly had an impact on its audiences, but the play is mild compared to the sheer verbal drive of other testosterone-soaked outings.

Among the best was Roy Williams's *Days of Significance*, a thrillingly contemporary account of masculinity and war. After starting out in the 1990s with explorations of his West Indian heritage,

Williams made his name with punchy accounts of the relationship between black and white youth, in plays such as the award-winning *Clubland* (Royal Court, 2001), and *Days of Significance* has his trademark ferocity of dialogue. Although billed as a response to *Much Ado About Nothing*, little remains of Shakespeare's play apart from the names of Ben (Benedick) and Trish (Beatrice), and one line about 'Fight Jamie [. . .] Beat the shit out of him', which echoes the bard's 'Kill Claudio' (205). Instead, this story of men signing up to fight in Iraq starts off with a familiar portrait of an English market town swamped by binge-drinkers: gutters flow with beer and vomit, men strut and fight, women give as good as they get. When I saw the play at the Tricycle in March 2008, in Maria Aberg's vivid and raucous production, the atmosphere was heightened not only by signs warning of bad language and scenes of an 'adult nature', but also by two actors who, as part of the show, began fighting in the bar just before the audience had taken their seats. But although Ben and his mate Jamie are shown to be needy as well as arrogant, their experience of Iraq turns sour: Ben is killed and Jamie arrested for mistreating Iraqi prisoners in Basra. On his return, Jamie has to face military justice and public disgust. Williams shows how the impoverished moral codes of these young men and women destroy the West's moral authority. The drink-fuelled fear that paralyses the streets of Britain is exported to terrorise Iraq; and the link between ignorant male posturing and military malpractice is clearly outlined. When Hannah tries to better herself by going to college, her mates deride her ambition. Likewise, in the conflict over Dan going on an anti-war march, we see Britain as a divided nation. Equally divided were the reviews. The original promenade production at the Swan Theatre in Stratford-upon-Avon in January 2007 was denounced by the *Daily Mail* as having the 'bitter taste of treason', while the *Daily Telegraph* defended it as 'an appalled meditation on dumbed-down, boozed-up modern Britain'.[29] Williams implies that noisy working-class patriotism is based on masculine insecurity, fear of the feminine, and hatred of the Other. White working-class Englishness is a form of social pathology. Which is incurable.

War sometimes looked like a branch of big business. Adam Brace's meticulously researched *Stovepipe* (National/Bush, 2009) was also a promenade production, this time staged deep inside a West London shopping centre. Set mainly in Amman, and telling the compelling story of three mercenary soldiers working for a private security firm in Iraq, it was a thrilling theatrical experience that, in Michael Longhurst's excellent production, often felt dangerous and occasionally fraught. From the Arabic graffiti on the subterranean walls to the hymn sheets given to the audience during the final scene, a memorial service, this powerfully evoked a different world. And, like most stories about soldiers, the play was as much about the men's camaraderie as about the wider political issues. But a sense of national identity was also inescapable: here, Brits abroad are the objects of derision, as well as of fear.

Soldiers were also the subject of one of the most phenomenally successful plays of the decade: *Black Watch* (NTS, 2006) by Gregory Burke, the most thrilling new Scottish playwright of the decade. After opening at the Edinburgh Festival, the play, in the words of journalist Ian Jack, came to London 'after a two-year campaign that has conquered hundreds of audiences and won over almost every critic who has seen it'.[30] And it wowed not just the critics. Alex Salmond, leader of the Scottish National Party, in power in Edinburgh since 2007, also loved it.

During its world tour, *Black Watch* became an ambassador for the new National Theatre of Scotland (NTS). Something of its importance to the NTS can be gauged by the fact that, on the cover of the playtext, the name of the theatre is the same size as the playwright's. Everywhere, the location of the performance was an important factor in the play's meaning: an Edinburgh drill hall, the Highland Football Academy in Dingwall or an old hydraulics lab in Pitlochry. Ordinary theatre spaces were avoided. And, with this play, process was as significant as the final result. As director John Tiffany says: 'At the end of 2004, as one of the first things she did as Artistic Director of NTS, Vicky Featherstone asked Greg [Burke] to keep an eye on the story of the Black Watch, who had just returned to Scotland from Camp Dogwood [in Iraq].' Instead of asking Burke to write a war drama, Tiffany got him to tell the soldiers' stories 'in their own words'.[31] The result is that *Black Watch* is not so much a play about soldiers as a play about a writer who interviews a group of Scottish soldiers in a pub, interspersed with scenes about their experiences in Iraq, plus additional material about the regiment's history. Instead of dramatising war, the NTS dramatised the process of creating the play. And although it aimed to tell the men's story in their own words, the style of the language is – in both cadence and orthography, in its wry humour and insistent filthiness – recognisably Burke's own. On stage, the NTS used the talents of Frantic Assembly's Steven Hoggett to create dance-like movement, which contrasted with the brutality of soldiering. Its staging was also a response to the official representation of Scottish militarism, the Edinburgh Tattoo.

Watching the show, what you remember is the exuberant theatricality of the production: the way the narrated history of the regiment was told through the dressing and undressing of one of the uniformed men (30–3); the precision of the drill; the evocative music and songs; the use of a pool table as an armoured car; the gentle sign-language of the soldiers which illustrated their letters home (39); the harmony of singing which indicated the bonds between the boys; the flash and crash of mortar fire; the slow-motion movement of the fight sequence; the excruciating threat to break the arm of the playwright; the slow fall of dead soldiers through the air; the audible breathing of the actors at the end of the hectic final quick-march sequence, in which the actors supported each other just as soldiers support each other during battle. Both exhilarating and moving, the play ends on a note of disillusion: 'This is pish. Sitting about daying camp security. Getting mortared all the time. Getting fucking ambushed. Getting killed by suicide bombers. And for what?' (70). The punchline is the truism that soldiers fight for their 'mates', and not for 'our government' (72).

The politics of *Black Watch* are simple. The British government uses the Scots to do their dirty work in building empire. Then it betrays them. For despite its long history (since 1739) and distinctive uniform (especially the hat feather, the red hackle), the Black Watch was amalgamated with five other Scottish regiments in 2006. Bureaucratic neatness trumps military tradition. So the play was both an account of soldiering and a requiem for a regiment. As the Officer concludes, 'It takes three hundred years to build an army that's admired and respected around the world. But it only takes three years pissing about in the desert in the biggest western foreign policy disaster ever to fuck it up completely' (71). But, according to the *Observer*, *Black Watch* is not 'an anti-war play, by which I mean an anti-Iraq war play. What it is is pro-soldier.'[32] As such, it is a slap in the face of the theatrical convention of liberal anti-war plays.

It was also a play about identity. By excluding Iraqi characters, Burke underlines the distance between occupiers and civilians; all the scenes show the men's assertion of their masculine identity; at the same time, the production was a triumphant statement of Scottish identity, both in its rejection of what David Greig calls English naturalism, and in its confident demonstration of Scottish traditions of theatre-making, with its use of direct address to the audience, movement, songs and storytelling. In John Tiffany's words, Scottish theatre is about 'a form of theatre and a connection with the audience, about urgency, populism, accessibility, about music and about movement'.[33] In this case, the ghosts of vaudeville communed with the spirit of Scottish alternative theatre. Its strength came from the deliberate contrast between the brutality of soldiering and the exquisite delicacy of some of the staging. As an example of Scottish theatre-making, the play threw down the gauntlet to the rest of British theatre.

Like *Stuff Happens*, *Black Watch* seemed to be a definitive Iraq War play. It did what all contemporary theatre aspires to do: in Greig's words, 'It caught the mood of the nation in a way I have not seen before.'[34] But although the show felt emotionally true, with braveheart performances, some aspects of the play were unsettling. For a start, it gave soldiering a battered glamour which did nothing to question the equation of national identity with military might. By excluding the families of the men, especially their wives, it also presented war as a delirious festival of masculinity. And because it felt like a triumph for Scottish manhood, Scottish theatre and Scottish national pride, few were brave enough to raise an eyebrow about its implicit militarist ideology. While the English working class appeared on stage as symbols of an anguished, bewildered nation, Scottish lads seemed confident and pugnaciously proud. This play underlined the fact that, since devolution, Britain is deeply divided.

Special relations

Plays about the Special Relationship between Britain and America were among the most problematic – perhaps it was the hardest thing to get right. Still, it was a subject close to the hearts of audiences. For example, in Roy Smiles's *Kurt and Sid* (Trafalgar, 2009), a comic fantasy about music icons Kurt Cobain and Sid Vicious, the biggest laugh was the joke about how Americans have Bob Hope, Johnny Cash, and Stevie Wonder, while the Brits have no hope, no cash, and no bloody wonder! Self-deprecation remains a national mindset. Although underrated by most critics, Tamsin Oglesby's *US and Them* is an appealingly clear account of tensions between Brits and Yanks. When the British Martin and Charlotte meet the American Ed and Lori in a Manhattan restaurant, their mutual attraction is mediated by misunderstandings. At first, this transatlantic comedy of manners gives the down-to-earth Brits all the best lines; the Americans – brash, insensitive to irony and addicted to positive thinking – immediately grate on the nerves. But Oglesby inverts these stereotypes by introducing the couples' kids: American Jay (repressed and introverted) and British Izzie (extroverted and noisy). Another twist comes as the couples begin to argue among themselves about their new friends. The play's background is a culture of fear: 'Fear is inimical to friendship,' says Ed during a discussion of global politics (60). Then, during the climactic showdown, the characters fall back on cultural prejudices. Ed attacks Britain: 'Your collapsing infrastructure and your rude, incompetent, ugly people and your arse-licking prime minister' (135), while Charlotte accuses Americans of 'dropping bombs on everyone who isn't like you' (134). In the end, a genuine friendship between these couples is out of the question – but their kids hold the possibility of change. The play ends with Jay and Izzie expecting a baby, an optimistic conclusion that implies a hybrid solution.

Another underrated play, Shelagh Stephenson's *Ancient Lights*, focuses on Tom, a fortysomething American actor who comes to Northumberland for a Christmas reunion with some English friends from college days. To his Californian eyes, 'The Brits are a very ugly race [. . .] stumpy little pig folk' (32). But he also idealises this old island, mistakenly thinking that the sign 'Ancient Lights' means something 'English and historical and mysterious [. . .] about place and rootedness, and belonging', so mythic, so poetic. In fact, it means 'You can't build another house within fifty yards because you'll block the light to the windows' – it's a kind of 'building regulation' (83–4). But although his idea of Englishness is deflated, Tom is not the only one to be disillusioned. His old friend Bea is gobsmacked when it turns out that her boyfriend, Tad, an Irish novelist, is actually called Michael, born and bred in Hull. Like most of the other characters, he has invented his own identity: 'I feel Irish,' he says, and then: 'Maybe I'm the cultural equivalent of a transsexual. An Irishman trapped in an Englishman's body' (59–60). Here national identity is a garb you can put on, or perhaps a lie.

As so often, it was David Hare who put his finger most surely on the pulse of Anglo-American relationships. His *The Vertical Hour* (Royal Court, 2008) shows what happens when Philip, a British physiotherapist, brings his American girlfriend, Nadia, a war reporter turned academic, to meet his father, Oliver, a doctor living in Shropshire. As well as making points about the climate of fear – 'There was far more terrorism in the 1980s,' says Nadia, 'when nobody thought about it than there is today when nobody thinks about anything else' (47) – the play also outlines the differences between Oliver's ironic scepticism and Nadia's wilful idealism. As Professor John Stokes points out, in his ideas about war, Oliver also embodies 'the patronizing implication that Britain knows what America has yet to learn'.[35] Similarly, Ella Hickson's *Precious Little Talent* (EFF, 2009) is about New York carer Sam and English law-graduate Joey, and plays delightful games with their different attitudes to sex. But despite some cruel moments, the play ends on an optimistic note, and argues that the young might be able to transform national stereotypes.

Other plays tackled the theme of transatlantic relations by

experimenting with theatre form. Caryl Churchill's nimble *Drunk Enough To Say I Love You?* reimagined the Special Relationship as a troubled gay love affair between Jack and Sam. Sam is the dominant partner; despite doubts, Jack submits. In a dialogue that is uncompromisingly fractured and fragmentary, they review the entire history of the postwar era, taking in the Korean War, Cuban Crisis, Vietnam War and the current War on Terror. Written in Churchill's most elliptical style, with short sentences cut off as soon as they are uttered, and ideas left hanging tantilisingly in the air, this economy with words makes the point that lovers know what each other is thinking (and that audiences know what Churchill means). It also enables her to cover a lot of ground very rapidly.[36] Finally, the play reminds us that the Special Relationship never really makes Britain look good.

References to the special relationship can be found peppered across the decade. In Emma Frost's *Airsick* (Bush, 2003), British Lucy has an American boyfriend, Joe, who quits New York because he can't keep up with the aggressively competitive culture. This gives him a sour attitude to New Yorkers: 'I was even pleased about nine eleven. Because at least it took some of them out of the running. At least it opened up a chance for me' (64). Similarly, in *The Dysfunckshonalz!* (Bush 2007), irrepressible penman Mike Packer's high-octane comedy about the reunion of a 1970s punk band thirty years after their chaotic career smash-up, there is a scene in which Billy, the leader of this bunch of losers, does a sensational rant against American consumer culture. Spewing bile over McDonald's and Disney, Billy raves, 'Have a nice day? I'll tell you a fuckin' nice day. I'll tell you when I had a nice day. September the eleventh. What a lovely fuckin' day that was. 11/9, not 9/11, 11/9' (25). For the whole play, there's a tension between the profound attraction of American culture and an equally deep resentment of the American Way. His losers constantly define themselves by what they reject, which is 'being consumed by consumerism' (14). To be British, Packer's characters imply, you have to define yourself against the world's only superpower. What such plays suggest is that, despite the common elements of our culture, for many Brits it is Americans that sometimes seem like aliens.

World news

Although the War on Terror dominated the way playwrights viewed the state of the world, there was plenty of room for other subjects. Oddly enough, Britain's uneasy relationship with Europe was rarely examined. Only two plays took the Chunnel to Euroland: Tim Luscombe's *The Schuman Plan* (Hampstead, 2006) and Richard Bean's *In the Club* (Hampstead, 2007), the first as tragedy, the second as farce. Luscombe took a grand historical view which told the story of Bill, a Suffolk boy who grows up in a fishing family in the 1930s and then becomes a Eurocrat in the postwar era. The quintessential Englishman, he starts off idealistic and ends up disillusioned: 'Now all I see is details. Fiscal, merchantile, boring details.' 'Don't worry,' advises his colleague. 'It's a very English response to being in Europe' (81). By contrast, Bean created a political sex farce by looking at the misfortunes of a hapless Euro MP, Philip Wardrobe, who is venial, shifty and selfish. 'I've only ever been any good at two things. Fucking up and apologising,' he admits (119). Other playwrights looked further East. In scene two of David Edgar's *The Prisoner's Dilemma* (RSC, 2001), set in a former Soviet Republic, the fear of the new world order was summed up by the stage image of a tortured naked man tied to an office chair, an airport Duty Free bag on his head. Equally vivid was April De Angelis's *Wild East* (Royal Court, 2004), in which Frank, a nerdish anthropology graduate who wants to work for a British marketing firm in Russia, finally goes native. On the set was a large metallic sphere squatting in the middle of a coffee table: the way its surface distorted reality was an apt metaphor for rampant capitalism: bright, shiny and yet completely inhuman.

While precious few playwrights travelled to China, India or Brazil, a couple did look at do-gooding women abroad: in the provocatively titled *Mother Teresa Is Dead* (Royal Court, 2002), Helen Edmundson – better known as an adaptor of classic novels for Shared Experience – focuses on Jane, an unhappy middle-class woman who abandons home and travels to Madras to look after children in India. When her husband Mark comes to fetch her, he comes into conflict with Srinivas, a local charity worker. Working-class Mark is appalled that Srinivas smiled when he heard about 9/11. For his part, Srinivas sounds like

Cassandra: 'Your country will become sick, hopelessly, terminally sick, until it finally implodes under its own obese, corrupted weight!' (34). Similarly fraught is the intervention of Fiona Russell, an idealistic international election observer in Matt Charman's *The Observer* (National, 2009), which is set in Africa and which ends with a local man telling her: 'WE DON'T NEED YOU TO SAVE US' (124). In Edgar's *The Prisoner's Dilemma*, one of the minor characters, Floss Weatherby, a British aid worker, fails to prevent murder when she visits a conflict zone in the former Soviet Union. But Edgar livens up the grim subject matter with some jokes, the best of which is 'the three great lies': 'The check [sic] is in the mail, my wife doesn't understand me, I'm from the UN and I'm here to help you' (13). The 'porno version' of the third lie is 'I'm not going to come in your mouth' (22). Jokes such as these are a reminder that humour is part of British national identity, and images of troubled but helpless British women abroad suggest a nation whose global influence has declined.

Several excellent plays looked at Africa. These included Richard Bean's provocative comedy *The God Botherers*, in which Keith, a middle-aged aid worker who has seen it all, tries to help Laura, a naive young do-gooder, avoid any clashes with complex religious sensibilities. With the character of the local man, Monday, Bean gives us a comic example of cultural hybridity:

> I was born a Muslim, but in the orphanage Jesus Christ came to me one night when I was playing Scrabble and made me his lifelong friend [. . .] I am also technically Jewish, but that was a clerical error. I am circumcised, and a very poor job they did too. I could have done better myself. (141)

Conflicts between blacks and whites were more seriously explored in Fraser Grace's thought-provoking *Breakfast with Mugabe* (RSC, 2005), in which the Zimbabwean dictator, haunted by his demons, employs a white psychiatrist, and in Kay Adshead's redemptive *Bones* (Bush, 2006), set in post-Apartheid South Africa, where Jennifer, the fiftysomething wife of a policeman, is confronted by Beauty, her black maid, about the atrocities he once committed.

One of the best plays about Africa and Europe was playwright and academic Steve Waters's *World Music* (Sheffield, 2003). Loosely based on the fallout from the Rwandan genocide, the play focuses on Geoff Fallon, a socialist MEP who, as a young man, taught in Africa and made friends with Kiyabe, a local politician helping to rebuild his country after its colonial past. Deftly jumping between the present and scenes set in 1980, Waters convincingly shows the machinations of the European parliament, the painful private life of Fallon (who ignores his son while picking up Florence, a black woman working illegally in a Brussels cafe) and the contrast between an idealistic view of Africa and the reality. Past and present co-exist on stage, just as they do in Fallon's head. At the climax of the play, Fallon is crushed by the revelation that Kiyabe is a war criminal – and that Florence is not an innocent victim but a guilty perpetrator of violence. Although some critics pointed out that Fallon seems a bit too blinded by his loyalty to Kiyabe to acknowledge the latter's guilt, this never spoils what is a beautifully constructed story. The play tactfully evokes the horror of genocide and mercilessly exposes the falsity behind liberal good intentions. It also comments on national identity. At one point, Kiyabe asks Paulette, a black colleague of Fallon's: 'Tell me who you are.' To which she answers, 'I'm, well, I'm British. Well with the usual hyphens' (26). Against the tentative identity of Paulette and Fallon is juxtaposed the murderous intensity of Kiyabe and Florence. Kiyabe's reiterative words, 'All killed all in fear in fear. It was war' (30), contrast with the penitent Florence's appeal to Fallon, 'Aides moi Geoffrey j'ai peur, j'ai peur' (74). Of Josie Rourke's dynamic production, *The Times* wrote that it 'recalls events in Rwanda and Burundi as well as sweeping a moral searchlight over Britain's asylum debate'.[37] Just as the music of Africa can seem strange and 'takes some getting used to' (79) so Waters exposes how little we know about the wider world. And asks the question, guaranteed to unsettle traditional notions of decency and fair play: how can you make moral judgements about countries you know so little about?

Like Dennis Kelly, debbie tucker green was one of the decade's most distinctive new voices. Director Jenny Topper summed up her qualities: 'She has the three essential elements of a new voice: she is concerned with ideas, she is concerned with form, and she has the courage to stay true to her intuition and let her own linguistic invention come through.'[38] Green's *Stoning Mary* vividly imagines three scenarios: 'The AIDS Genocide', 'The Child Soldier' and 'Stoning Mary' (3, 10, 41). It sounds like Africa, or an Islamic republic. But the playwright's challenge, as specified in the playtext, is simple: 'All characters are white' (2). Using a white cast to play these stories destroys the safe distance that audiences usually put between us and them. Here, a recognisably British Wife and Husband argue over an antiviral prescription to save one of their lives, while their Egos (inner thoughts) are played by another two actors. Meanwhile, the Child Soldier's parents, Mum and Dad, talk about his absence, while Mary waits for her execution and the last visit from her Older Sister. The three stories effortlessly fuse together, and the text sings off the page. As a gritty vernacular slams against a poet's sensibility, the words fly around the theatre piercing the dark like shards of glass. The dialogue suggests a meeting between Sarah Kane, Ntozake Shange, Louise Bennett and Beverley Knight, powered by the cadences of street chat and rap music. Its insistent repetitions and reiterations, its contemporary immediacy and its rhythms, are highly distinctive. Take, for example, the long speech in which the condemned Mary excoriates other women:

> so what happened to the womanist bitches?
> . . . The feminist bitches?
> . . . The professional bitches.
> What happened to them?
> What about the burn their bra bitches?
> The black bitches
> the rootsical bitches
> the white the brown bitches
> the right-on bitches
> what about them? (61–2)

And so on for a whole dizzying page. From the deceptively domestic opening to its ghastly ending, *Stoning Mary* was a sixty-minute howl of fury. Director Marianne Elliott and designer Ultz's production thrillingly mixed refinement with intensity. By taking out the stalls from the Court's main house, and replacing them with a blue bearpit stage, it felt as if the audience, who had to look down on the action, were voyeurs of Mary's brutal end, as a British bobby cuts off her hair just before she is executed. Green's uncomfortable idea of having British white people perform acts we usually associate with foreign black people calls into question the idea that our identities are fixed by birth or by skin colour. It also sharply questions our notion of the UK as a liberal safe haven.

Another play by green, *Generations* (Young Vic, 2007), revisits Africa. A story about the AIDS crisis in which AIDS is never mentioned, it puts three generations of a bickering South African family onstage at mealtime: gradually, family members melt away. As the youngsters die off first, we see the ravaging effects of disease. For this thirty-minute show, director Sacha Wares and designer Miriam Buether turned a studio space into a South African landscape, complete with red earth underfoot and the glare of bright light above. The walls were painted in hot colours with shadowy snapshots of happy families, while the audience sat on petrol drums and plastic crates. As a choir of fourteen sang, played and danced around the space, in and out of the makeshift seating, some audience members joined in, but some were nervous about this breakdown of the usual distance between performers and spectators. Yet this abolition of the usual comfort zone gave the play an immediate intensity. It felt thrillingly contemporary.

In the past decade, British theatre has boldly engaged with global politics in general, and the War on Terror in particular. Written under the influence of verbatim theatre, they were usually well researched and sympathetic to the men and women on the ground, whether they were politicians or soldiers. In the great majority of these plays, the self-image of the nation has been instantly recognisable. In their dealings with the outside world, the typical Briton is an Englishman and appears as a repressed individual, both smug about Britain and ignorant of foreign cultures. Socially incompetent, politically naïve or economically troubled, they are perfect stereotypes of English nationhood. Whether this is the Prime Minister or a white-working-class squaddie, the general message is the same: Britain is great at giving good advice, but bad at sorting out its own problems. In these plays, the Brits stubbornly remain British through and through. Occasionally, there are glimpses of cultural hybridity, but mainly from Scottish writers, black Britons or foreigners. In the culture of fear, playwrights have succeeded better at articulating this sense of anxiety than at providing an image of any way out of it. If the only thing to fear was fear itself, repeated reminders of our worries may have only succeeded in making the audience feel more powerless than it already was. Yet if playwrights have had mixed success at representing the world's woes, how have they fared closer to home?

4 MARKET FORCES

Bruce OK. In a perfect world, forgetting about 'resources', forgetting about 'budgetary constraints' – say we've got unlimited beds – what would you do?

(Joe Penhall, *Blue/Orange*, 31)

Britain in the 2000s lay under the long shadow of Thatcherism. Although the country was governed by New Labour, the essence of Thatcherite Toryism – the privatisation of services, the deregulation of markets and the making-of-life-easy for big business – was the dominant political ethos. Financial deregulation, introduced in the 1980s, remained in place and contributed to the credit crunch of 2008. So the story of the past decade was the onward march of the market. Old social democracy, killed off in the 1980s, was not revived in the 2000s. Despite all the rhetoric of modernisation, New Labour ministers were Thatcher's Grandchildren, and the results of this embrace of Thatcherism included greater division between rich and poor, intense social fragmentation and the glorification of the individual self. Although Margaret Thatcher's oft-quoted remark about there being no such thing as society was regularly wheeled out, what was less often understood is that most of the social problems of the 2000s had their origins in the policies of her governments. Or in the legacy of her successor in the 1990s, John Major. It's hard to deny the proud boast of the Margaret Thatcher Foundation: 'The Labour Party leadership was transformed by her period of office and the "New Labour" politics of Tony Blair would not have existed without her.'[1] As Professor Stuart Hall concludes, 'Marketisation is now installed in every sphere of government. This silent revolution in "governance" seamlessly connects Thatcherism to New Labour.'[2]

When new writing in the new millennium took up the old tradition of engaging with a social issue, it often tackled the long legacy of Thatcherism. For example, David Hare's verbatim play *The Permanent Way* (Out of Joint/National, 2003), examined the privatisation of the railways, which was pushed through by Major in 1993. The beauty of this play is that although it's about one specific subject, the way that privatisation led to a series of train crashes, it also paints a general picture of Britain as a country where 'nothing works' and 'nobody believes that by being angry, by expressing anger, anything changes, anything *can* change' (4, 9). This sense of an unchanging society was emphasised whenever the Iron Lady herself made a stage appearance: the best example is David Eldridge's *Market Boy* (National, 2006), where she descended from above like a vampire bat. Directed by Rufus Norris, this epic play was a cheery evocation of the 1980s, and featured a scene when the stage was decked with Union Jacks, which evoked a proud and boastful patriotism. As Eldridge says, 'At one matinee, there were two couples who were behaving as though they were at the last night of the Proms, and there were two couples in front of them who were turning around in horror.'[3] Liberals, squirm in your seats. Talking of Thatcher, a more surreal staging was James Graham's *Little Madam* (Finborough, 2007), which imagined the Iron Lady's childhood, complete with talking teddies. Other examples couldn't keep their feet still: Jill Dowse's *Thatcher the Musical* (Foursight, 2006) closes with no fewer than eight Maggies in purple feather boas prancing in front of Number Ten, while Tom Green's *The Death of Margaret Thatcher* (Courtyard, 2008) ended with a drunk newsreader dancing on her coffin. But the final word comes from Kristin, the 1968er in Alexi Kaye Campbell's *Apologia* (Bush, 2009): 'Thatcher wasn't a woman. She was a man with a vagina' (109). This kind of irreverence seems to be very British: we don't do anger very well, but humour, yes.

Thatcher's legacy

One of the decade's first plays to tackle the legacy of Thatcherism was Joe Penhall's award-winning and much-revived *Blue/Orange*. Although he emerged in the 1990s, Penhall differed from many

Trainspotting-generation playwrights by avoiding hip subjects such as drugs, and preferring to focus instead on mental illness, 'which affects many more people' but remains 'unfashionable, troublesome, taboo'.[4] In the words of one of the characters in *Blue/Orange*: 'Schizophrenia is the worst pariah' (54). But it's an issue near to Penhall's heart after a friend of his suffered from mental illness, and his early play *Some Voices* (Royal Court, 1994) was about the same subject. The background was the Conservative government policy of closing mental hospitals and leaving patients to Care in Community, a move acidly described in Mike Packer's *The Dysfunckshonalz!* as 'Don't Care in the Community' (21). *Blue/Orange* dramatises this social problem as a power struggle between two doctors, Robert and Bruce, over the treatment of Christopher, a troubled Afro-Caribbean youth. As Christopher reaches the end of his bureaucratically allocated twenty-eight days in care, Robert wants to discharge him and free up bed space for other patients while Bruce argues that he is still seriously ill. At first the patient's fantasies of being fathered by Ugandan dictator Idi Ami sound plausible, but when he describes an orange as bright blue, his condition suddenly seems much more serious. By this time, Robert has lost patience with Bruce, his prodigy, and persuades Christopher to lodge a complaint against him for racism.

Robert and Bruce have different diagnoses for Christopher. The senior Robert argues that he has borderline personality disorder while the junior Bruce sees him as on the verge of acute schizophrenia. Penhall contrasts the two conditions in this way:

> Schizophrenia is like cancer: you never get rid of it, it's terminal, it has a terrible stigma attached to it. It scares people and doctors are very loathe to diagnose it. It's really quite a wild illness. A borderline personality disorder is something that's reasonably manageable.[5]

The cleverness of *Blue/Orange* comes from the ambiguity with which Penhall invests his characters. Because the way we see Christopher is affected by what his doctors say about him, we are never sure just how disturbed he is. Robert, who is researching the cultural determinants of human behaviour, is both an appealingly freewheeling R. D. Laing figure, all 1960s hippie humanism, and a government functionary who needs to obey market principles, by processing patients. The younger, more idealistic Bruce is both certain that he knows what's wrong with Christopher and gauche about making his point. Robert is charming – like recent politicians, a spinner of truth – and Bruce always puts his foot in his mouth when he tells it as it is. In this battle of wills, the political football is Christopher, who is so busy reacting to every move his doctors make that he struggles to find his own voice. When he does, the effect is explosive.

The drama is also about a clash of cultures. Robert wants to prove his thesis that although 'there is more mental illness amongst the Afro-Caribbean population in London than any other ethnic grouping', the reason for this might be mainly cultural. He's looking for 'a "cure" for "black psychosis"' (48–9). As Bill Nighy, who played Robert in the original production, says, 'The play raises questions about the role of the medical profession itself in creating a "Black Psychosis".'[6] It's a contentious issue, so while one critic pointed out that 'Apparently there is more mental illness in the Afro-Caribbean population in London than in any other community', another countered that 'the National Schizophrenia Fellowship doesn't accept that any individual ethnic group has "greater inherent susceptibility to severe mental illness"'.[7] Clearly, *Blue/Orange* also picked up on widespread anxieties about psychotic individuals roaming the streets of Britain's cities, and a fear of violent black men. And it also articulated other urban fears: at one point, Christopher is paranoid about racist skinheads: 'a race apart. Zombies! The undead. Monsters!' (65).

The play's wider political resonance is summed up by the back-cover blurb of the original playtext as a Darwinian power struggle at the heart of a dying NHS. What Penhall seemed to be saying is that while the Tories were to blame for running down the NHS, it was not as safe as we thought in New Labour hands. But one of the play's chief delights is that it is so much more than a piece about the politics of mental health. At one point, it includes a stimulating discussion about French surrealist Paul Eluard's poem 'The World Is as Blue as an Orange' and the Tin-Tin adventure where he foils a 'mad professor' who invents a bright blue orange that tastes salty (45–6). Eloquent without being ornate, Penhall's characters speak with the precision and aggression of duelists. But the cut and thrust of debate always moves the situation forwards, pausing only for set-piece speeches that deliver repeated body blows. This is a play of ideas which is both exciting intellectually and thrilling emotionally. In the original production, directed by Roger Michell, the minimalist set – dominated by a bowl of oranges so bright they almost glowed – was surrounded by seating and, in its bare simplicity, resembled a boxing ring. Watching Bill Nighy's silky Robert struggle with Andrew Lincoln's awkward Bruce over Chiwetel Ejiofor's increasingly aggravated Christopher was like seeing two vultures circling a wounded animal. One message was clear: this is a nation where basic values are contested. What Amelia Howe Kritzer calls 'the mercantile structures of central concern to Thatcher' clash with community needs.[8] But if *Blue/Orange* paints a picture of the Brits as passionately argumentative, as well as institutionally racist, other plays had different views of Thatcher's legacy.

David Eldridge's *Under the Blue Sky* is about a nation whose educational system is torn between the state sector and private provision. It is also a beautiful play about the love lives of three teacher couples. Eldridge who, like Penhall, emerged in the 1990s, sees the play as being both about the nature of unrequited love and 'the nature of public service in teaching'.[9] What's most impressive is the sheer elegance of its structure. The play has three apparently unrelated Acts, each of which involves a different pair of teachers. Cleverly, the story of the first couple is then continued in the dialogues of the other two, and the disconnection of the scenes mirrors the emotional disconnection of two of the couples. So Act One shows the awkward relationship between Leytonstone comprehensive teachers Nick and Helen: although she loves him, he is less enamoured and tells her that he intends to move to a public school in Essex. In Act Two, two teachers from that school, Graham and Michele, tumble into view, '*snogging furiously*' (214), although the evening quickly turns from lust to humiliation. By contrast, Act Three shows the mature relationship between Robert and Anne, and ends on a hopeful note. Each couple symbolises a generation, the first being in their twenties, the second in their thirties and the third in their forties and fifties. Each act has a different style: tragedy, comedy and love duet. According to Eldridge, each act also shows a stage of drunkenness: first drink, being drunk and then hangover.[10] Linking the three scenes is the story of Nick and Helen. In Act Two, Michele tells Graham that she's in love with Nick, who has rejected her for Helen. In Act Three, it emerges that Helen was killed in a car crash, and that Robert met Nick and confronted him about his selfishness.

Unlike the fiercely argumentative doctors of *Blue/Orange*, the teachers of *Under the Blue Sky* come across as quiet heroes, spending their lives in unrewarding attempts to make the lives of others better. As Rufus Norris, who directed the original production, says, it's 'a big brave play about personal responsibility, how to love and how to live'.[11] At the same time, these teachers scorn the popular image of 'being a noble profession' (189). Eldridge shows how teachers, who deal with children all day long, are themselves susceptible to adolescent emotions, childish whims and immature evasions. This might be true of everyone but the irony is stronger because you instinctively feel that teachers should know better. He also suggests that they are hard-working types whose pleasures are often undercut by the knowledge that they have to face a class of teens first thing in the morning. In fact, his dialogue is a masterclass in undercutting. Few writers use bathos to such critical effect: whenever a character gets too pretentious, another brings them down. Despite the comedy of their personal repressions and mutual antagonisms, these teachers – especially Helen, Robert and Anne – are clearly committed to their work. But they also live in a country where teaching in a private fee-paying school is more rewarding than working in the state sector. As Nick argues, 'I want to be challenged. Intellectually', and 'I want a career. Not a slog' (195). Still, the play ends on a moment of possibility, symbolised by a cloudless blue sky, and Eldridge's optimism is striking – for a moment, at the turn of the millennium, the British middle classes seemed set to remake their world. But, by the time of its West End revival in 2008, the play had a different resonance: now the bugle playing the last post (a reference to the play's military theme), says Eldridge, evoked a sense of 'Union Jack draped coffins' being shipped backed to Britain from the Middle East.[12] Optimistic Britain had turned fearful.

New Labour emphasised education, and the pursuit of youth audiences meant that there was a crop of plays about schoolkids. The best of these, and Simon Stephens's *Punk Rock* is a good example, didn't just reflect social reality, they reimagined it. At one point, one of Stephens's kids offered a view of the teaching profession: 'I'm not surprised teachers have heart attacks. They wander round like trauma victims. You look into their eyes. They're terrified' (61). If teachers, however worried and undervalued, were good people, then so were social workers. Fin Kennedy's well-researched and award-winning *Protection* (Soho, 2003), which was inspired by David Hare's work, is a rare example of a sensible portrait of a profession usually demonised by the media. In it, one social worker answers the bemused question 'How do you cope?' with a direct 'Because no other fucker gives a shit' (22). With its over-stretched social workers and cynical executives, *Protection* is clearly sceptical of government targets, which result in social workers being under pressure to open fewer cases and close them sooner. But the strength of the play lies in its awareness of human frailty. If social workers are failing to protect their vulnerable clients, then who will protect the protectors?

In contrast to social workers, some of the other victims of Thatcherism were delightfully offbeat. For example, Michael Wilcox's *Mrs Steinberg and the Byker Boy* (Bush, 2000) looks wryly at what happens when market forces invade a Newcastle charity shop. Occasionally, writers would also cast themselves as heroes. Simon Block's *A Place at the Table* (Bush, 2000) is an acerbic comedy about how a female TV executive chews up a young writer, using the Thatcherite jargon of a public-service broadcaster which has been taken over by market imperatives. At one point, the executive sums up contemporary TV: 'Smart, decent individuals making stupid, vulgar programmes because somewhere along the line they lost the will to battle a bureaucracy that values numbers before people' (35). But an awareness of Thatcher turned up in the most unexpected places: even a surreal play such as Anthony Neilson's *Realism* (EIF, 2006) has an imagined rant that concludes: 'We've got a society – a post-Thatcherite society – that is so fractured and dysfunctional that the only way a semblance of unity can be preserved is to feed it a constant stream of state-approved scapegoats for us to mutually fear or disdain' (111). Thatcher's ideology of market forces seems to linger, more than a decade after her fall, like a bad odour. And Britain was a nation still absorbing her impact.

Money problems

Plays about unsung heroes were matched by plays about victims of the global market. However, for a society which has the highest levels of indebtedness in the world (one result of Thatcher's vision of a home-owning democracy), there were remarkably few plays about debt. The best was Dennis Kelly's *Love and Money*, an exciting experiment in form that also both captured the spirit of our debt-ridden times and seemed to anticipate the credit crunch. In what the cover blurb of the original playtext calls a world of easy credit, David and Jess are a young married couple whose relationship is soured by her compulsive shopping and his need to control. Kelly tells their story by using a fractured form which not only jumps back and forth in time, but also obliquely mirrors the emotional confusion of the relationship and the mental upset caused by indebtedness. The first scene, told through an email exchange between David and a French woman he's met through work, reveals that Jess committed suicide after running up debts of £70,000 and that David helped her die. Next, we see her Mother and Father vandalise a vulgar graveyard monument that stands next to, and eclipses, their daughter's grave. Scene Three flips back in time to show how David asks an old girlfriend for work, as he quits his teaching job for the more lucrative activity of selling, followed by a scene that explores Jess's mindset, while also introducing us to the way banks profit by encouraging debt. In Scene Five, the sleazy Duncan is persuading young Debby to work in porn, and he shows her a photograph of David performing fellatio, a reference to a previous scene when this was suggested as a way of making easy money (262,

239). The final two scenes also travel back in time to show David catching Jess out in a lie, as she continues to spend money even though they have agreed to pay back their debts, and, finally, casting an ironic light on the story, Jess shares a moment of bliss as we see her in love's first bloom. As well as this fractured form, the scenes are constructed in a variety of ways, some played straight, some narrated, some performed as a chorus. Most daring of all, Scene Five introduces two characters who have nothing to do with the main story, but which show how wide the net of neediness is flung when debt spreads throughout society. Instead of telling the story in a linear way, Kelly shatters it into dislocated scenes, shuffles its chronology, and then adds tangential material which throws a lurid light on the whole dead-end job and credit-card lifestyle.

If money can't buy love, *Love and Money* is saying, debt can certainly put relationships through the mincer. Influenced by Caryl Churchill, Martin Crimp and Mark Ravenhill, Kelly's picture of a Middle England stricken by anxiety over debt, bad faith between couples and thwarted ambition at work is satisfyingly contemporary: 'This life here where everything is measured in pay grades and pension schemes and sales targets' (213). In an echo of Leo Butler's *Redundant*, at one point Duncan says, 'They should napalm this lot. Makes me sick. Get Bin Laden round here' (255). Then there's Jess's speech in which she is riveted to the spot by the sight of an expensive bag in a shop window, and meditates that 'the bag was designed not to hold things, but to hold me' (245). In this world of compulsive consumerism, not only does David and Jess's marriage come under strain, but Jess's Dad is able to overcome his sense of loss for long enough to calculate the VAT on his daughter's gravestone. And when Val, David's ex, loses her faith in God, she transfers her belief to money-making.

Directed by Matthew Dunster, *Love and Money* was a gut-wrenching but exhilarating drama and the perfect show to open the Maria, the Young Vic's new studio theatre. Anna Fleischle's set was a cold businesslike nowheresville of filing cabinets, a curving bank of compartments which could instantly produce the furniture needed for any location. To underline its relevance, the programme fielded an essay, by a BBC economics editor, about our debt-ridden society. Apart from a couple of exceptions, most reviewers recognised the play as true. So although the *Daily Mail* denounced it as 'gibberish', *The Times* said that 'Kelly points up the way in which material good can be used to fill an emotional void, as well as satisfying aspirations fed by advertising, easy credit and competitiveness' and the *Daily Telegraph* concluded: 'I have rarely seen a work that more accurately captures the discontented spirit of our materialistic age.'[13] And, as a portrait of today's Britain illuminated by the fluorescent glare of bad debt, bad faith and soullessness, the play was not alone.

In Leo Butler's *Faces in the Crowd* (Royal Court, 2008), Sheffield-born husband Dave meets his wife Joanne again ten years after doing a runner, leaving her with a mountain of debt. Here debt is both literal and metaphoric: he owes her. But that doesn't stop his recriminations: remembering how he's grown up in 'the fuckin' shadow of Margaret Thatcher', Dave blames Joanna for her consumerism: 'You spend and you spend and you spend', all 'for a life built on credit cards and debit schemes, this towering fuckin' inventory of plastic, of borrowed goods and lowered interest rates' (74). By setting the origin of the couple's marriage problems in the 1990s, Butler is making the political point that the origins of the credit crunch lie in the easy credit of the Conservative era. Moving on from ordinary people, an overtly satirical view of today's investment bankers was Steve Thompson's *Roaring Trade* (Paines/Soho, 2009), which had a lovely scene in which a City bond trader explained the A, B, C of his work to his ten-year-old son by using food leftovers on a McDonald's restaurant tabletop. By contrast, in Stella Feehily's *Dreams of Violence* (Out of Joint/Soho, 2009), the direct action that office cleaners take against their banker employer involves making him clean the office. Poetic justice. When Mike Bartlett's absurdist workplace nightmare *Contractions* (Royal Court, 2008) was staged in an office space rather than an auditorium, this move underlined the managerial nature of its bureaucratically inspired dialogues, as in, for example, 'Have a look at page three will you? Paragraph five' (7). Market principles, the play demonstrates, have successfully corrupted our language.

Sometimes, it felt as if the market was everywhere. In Richard

Bean's Ortonesque black comedy *Smack Family Robinson* (Live, 2003), the Whitley Bay Robinsons are a family of drug dealers. Sean, one of their sons, sells off the debts that their customers owe them to the Russian mafia. It's called factoring. As Sean explains, 'Some bastard owes you four grand, you sell the debt to a factoring consultant for three grand – cash. He makes a grand when he collects the four grand off the piss taking cunt' (161). It's a joke that is now sadly prophetic: by the end of the decade, a play such as Natasha Langridge's *Shraddha* could include a character almost driven mad by 'credit credit credit' (54). And, appropriately enough, one of the decade's greatest commercial successes was Lucy Prebble's award-winning *Enron*, a play whose phantasmagoric staging was both theatrically exciting and symbolic of the shallowness of this company's schemes for the creation of a virtual market which could only be sustained by fraud. Rupert Goold's spectacular production, which starred Samuel West, featured visual metaphors such as baby dinosaurs, light sabres and the Lehman Brothers memorably portrayed by two actors in one suit. Although the play was about a Texan energy company's decline into scandal, it had a wide resonance as well as a tragic undertow in its portrait of company president Jeffrey Skilling, who came up against the hubris of trying to create a virtual economy (abandoning making energy for inventing a market to sell it) and the nemesis of fraudulent accounting (setting up fake companies to hide its losses). A savage comedy as well as an extended lecture about economics, the play ended on a parody of St Paul's Letter to the Corinthians (13:13): Skilling says, 'All our creations are here. There's Greed, there's Fear, Joy, Faith . . . Hope . . . / And the greatest of these . . . is Money' (124).

Celebrity cheats

In this cultural atmosphere, where market values are all that matter, there were plenty of plays about celebrity, usually involving media cheats. One of the very best was Mark Ravenhill's *pool (no water)*, which was written in collaboration with, and given an exemplary staging by, Frantic Assembly. Ravenhill's text has distinct lines of dialogue but does not specify who says what, or how many actors are needed. It's about a group of artist friends who share experiences, but only one of them becomes a success. Now rich and famous, she invites her old friends (four in the original production) to join her at her luxury mansion and use its pool. When she dives into it, unaware that it has been drained, this horrific accident – described in eye-watering detail – lands her in a coma. As she lies in the hospital, her friends visit and think the unthinkable: let's turn her ruined body into a work of art. They take pictures of their comatose friend: 'An image a record a frame' (307). Day after day, the pictures show her recovery, fascinated by 'the way the bruises and the swellings grow and ripen' (308). When she recovers, she takes the pictures and decides to exhibit them herself. But, as she gets ready for the celebrity launch, which involves 'Selling. Packaging. Promoting. Launching' (317), her friends viciously delete all the pictures. Her reaction? She denounces them as jealous 'small people' (322).

Ravenhill foregrounds direct address to the audience, with only brief moments when the characters talk to each other, and this allows him to tell the story with flair and rapidity. His is an acerbic take on contemporary art as a parasitic activity. As, without her knowledge, the group leeches on the celebrity artist's suffering, questions about the ethics of creativity and the relationship between life and art take centre stage. The play also explores the opportunism of friendship with a celebrity, and examines the resentment inspired by another's success: one of Ravenhill's favourite quotes is Gore Vidal's 'Every time a friend of mine succeeds, a part of me dies.'[14] In *pool (no water)*, he throws his unnamed characters into the emotional deep end and watches them splash about. The result is a glimpse of the darker side of life, even if the psychology on view is childish in its playground petulance and narcissistic egotism. Here Ravenhill's writing is characteristically ironic and gloriously dirty.

Frantic Assembly's production raised your pulse rate from the moment you set foot in the theatre. Yes, pumping techno music does wonders for the spirit. Directed by stalwarts Scott Graham and Steven Hoggett, the show's nerve-zapping music mixed with dance moves and simple props to create a compelling piece of theatre. As Peter

Billingham puts it, it was most impressive 'when the two contrasting languages of movement and text spoke either simultaneously, or better still, in atonal counterpoint to each other'.[15] What was so impressive was the discipline of the directing, which ensured that the actors were constantly restrained. Then, just as the audience became impatient, it delivered a short blast of pounding music and a few rapid dance moves. The restraint kept the powerful emotions in check, and produced an evening which mixed excitement and revulsion in equal measure: there's a particularly gross scene in which the group sexually abuse their comatose friend as if she was already dead. As an image of both the attraction and repulsion of celebrity in Britain today it's hard to forget.

Everywhere, the desire for fame attracted attention. In David Farr's *The Danny Crowe Show*, Miles and Magda are two execs scouring the north-west for freaks to put on a reality TV show that aims to expose the agonised underbelly of British society. But two youngsters, Peter and Tiffany, plan to fool them into staging a made-up story that exemplifies 'the holy grail of pain' (42): Peter's murder of his drunken, abusive father. As Miles says, 'The rawest slice of underbelly you have ever tasted' (23). But as well as mocking the national obsession with celebrity, the play also ridicules the positive thinking of popular psychology. In a typical example, Peter says: 'You may be an actress with a peculiarly dramatic haunted quality, Tiffany. But that quality is worth *nothing* unless it is allied with a mental toughness and a finisher's poise. An ability to stay focused' (50). Like most plays about celebs, Farr's showed a satirical awareness of the contemporary marketplace: at one point, Peter explains how he plans to exclude his mother from his autobiography, only including her if 'the market demands it' (43). Equally acerbic is the idea that reality TV could be 'one of the great moral contributions to the twenty-first century' (74). Similar sentiments were common. For example, Terry Johnson's *Piano/Forte* – a play which features an unforgettable scene when two Spanish aerial artists fly on, complete with strap-on dildos – also includes a handful of digs about celebrities, as in: 'Let a couple of celebrities take the piss out of you on BBC2 and some of that celebrity will eventually rub off, like lard on a pig' (27), plus a wedding where *Hello!* magazine has gazumped *OK!* (47). Criticism of such cultural intermediaries was popular. As one character says about an agent in Patrick Marber's *Howard Katz* (National, 2001), 'The *size* of the arse is irrelevant, you're still *kissing* it. You *lie for a living*, mate' (43).

Two plays about newspapers showed media cheats at work. In Joe Penhall's *Dumb Show* (Royal Court, 2004), journalists Greg and Liz organise a sting to trick Barry, a partly washed-up TV comedian, into giving them the story of his life. At one point, Greg denounces celebs as 'fakes', and opines: 'Fame is a cancer. It's a cancer. It's a plague' (163). As one critic wrote, Barry's 'only real crime is celebrity'.[16] Similarly, Steve Thompson's *Damages* (Bush, 2004) argues that, according to its heroine, a lawyer, tabloid newspaper content is 'shit. All the ugliness packed into sixty-eight pages' (64). By contrast, the journalists see the media as a corrective to celebrities who 'surround themselves with Yes-men' (78). In fact, via the play's satisfying plot turns, the celebrity is less of a victim than the journalists themselves. Other plays crossed similar ground. In Toby Whithouse's *Blue Eyes & Heels* (Soho, 2005), Duncan (played with relish by Martin Freeman in Jonathan Lloyd's original production) is a young TV producer who oozes ambition and uses all his manipulative powers to bring wrestling back as a TV spectator sport. The production's staging, which featured a wrestling ring, emphasised the voyeuristic aspects of this combat between celebrity-obsessed journalism and sincere sportsmanship.

David Hare's *My Zinc Bed* (Royal Court, 2000) likewise explored the celebrity-soaked atmosphere of contemporary Britain.[17] With enormous compassion, he shows a love triangle between Victor, a failed communist but successful internet entrepreneur, his wife Elsa, a Danish ex-drunk, and Paul, a young poet struggling with his addiction to drink. As well as being a subtle and accurate account of the mixed emotions of three people, the play also presents, in the larger-than-life Victor, a symbolic figure of our times, the entrepreneur as celebrity (he meets Paul when the latter is sent to interview him for a newspaper article). Using the metaphor of addiction – to drink, to certain types of people, to our illusions about ourselves, to self-destructive behaviour – Hare questions the efficacy of the self-help culture, attacks the hollowness of today's journalism and criticises the unpredictability of the stock market as an index of worth. As Victor says, 'Because we lack any wisdom ourselves, we will all pretend that the market is wise' (100). By 2009, when he wrote *The Power of Yes*, a verbatim play about the global financial crisis, Hare could claim that his scepticism about market values had been consistent. In *The Zinc Bed*, he also has a perceptive take on English society. 'The English love clubs,' says Victor, because clubs are a means of social exclusion: oh, the heady 'delight of keeping people out!' (15). What all these plays have in common is the idea that celebrity seems to be a way not only of behaving, but of being. It is one of the key phenomena of contemporary existence.

Migrant moves

Globalisation has created a world market in human beings, a phenomenon explored through plays about migration, one of the most hotly debated issues of the decade. With newspapers such as the *Daily Mail* leading the charge against refugees, and even the liberal press wavering in its sympathy, it was left to theatre-makers to give an insight into the experiences of asylum-seekers and other migrants. In one of those telling coincidences which capture the spirit of the times, two productions tackled this issue in February 2001: Kay Adshead's *The Bogus Woman* (Bush) and Timberlake Wertenbaker's *Credible Witness* (Royal Court).[18]

Commissioned by the Red Room, *The Bogus Woman* was partly based on the case of the Campsfield Nine, a group of inmates at the Oxfordshire detention camp whose protest against their conditions was savagely put down. 'I could not believe,' Adshead wrote, 'that the violation of human rights of vulnerable people was happening in England in 1997 (outside Oxford no less) and more shocking still in the first year under a Labour government.'[19] Her play is a monologue which tells the story of a nameless Young Black Woman who leaves an African country after writing newspaper articles critical of the regime, an act which results in the massacre of her family, including her newborn baby. She survives, but is brutally raped. The play not only dramatises the horror of the massacre, but also denounces the woman's treatment in Britain. Here, she is treated as a bogus refugee and subjected to one humiliation after another. Despite the kindness of strangers, and some Kafkaesque hilarity, the system fails her and she is sent back to Africa, where she is killed. Adshead not only describes the woman's feelings, she also includes a range of other characters: immigration officials, camp guards, do-gooders and fellow asylum-seekers. But her main achievement is to take the audience into the mind of her refugee, who is a poet as well as a journalist, which enables her to distil her experiences into rapid, rough and ready stanzas: for example, in her cell she sees that 'England is a / rectangle / above my head, / out of the corner / of my eye, / a small grey rectangle/of sky' (18). She also communes with ancestral gods. More important than such devices, however, is the way Adshead reproduces the uncertainties of a traumatic experience – while it is clear that the woman was raped, it is uncertain whether her memory of a miscarried foetus is a real event or a horrific nightmare. Adshead's point is that victims of trauma do not remember every detail of what happened and can thus give conflicting accounts of their experience, without necessarily lying. Her skill in conveying this ambiguity gives the drama its punch.

By contrast, Wertenbaker's *Credible Witness* – the title refers to the interrogation of asylum-seekers, many of whom are deemed to be unreliable witnesses – takes the form of a state-of-the-nation play. This is less a personal drama than a wide-ranging vision of Britain as a global crossroads. Written in the form of a quilt of stories, the play follows Petra, a Macedonian woman, who comes to London on a false passport, trying to find her son, Alexander, who has fled his homeland after being beaten up for teaching a subversive version of his embattled community's history. When she eventually finds him, he is no longer the fierce nationalist he was brought up to be, and she disowns him. At the same time, other refugees appear – a Sri Lankan, a Somalian and an Algerian. In the play's climax, Petra confronts the immigration official, symbolically named Simon Le Britten, with Ameena, a credible witness whose body bears the scars of multiple rape. Petra finally blesses her son, and, speaking on behalf of all the detainees, tells Le Britten: 'History shifts, Simon, we can't hold it. And now, when we turn to you, don't cover your eyes and think of the kings and queens of England. Look at us: we are your history now' (63). Not for the first time, outsiders are rewriting a nation's identity. In *The Bogus Woman*, Noma Dumezweni played the asylum-seeker as well as all the other sharply observed characters, including Karen the camp guard, the lawyer with a bumpy personal life and the African lad who becomes one of the Campsfield Nine. In *Credible Witness*, Olympia Dukakis's outstanding Petra brought a powerful sense of dignity to the piece. Although both plays deal with similar themes – atrocity, migration and identity – the forms they adopt are quite different, and so is their view of the world. While Adshead's portraits of immigration officials and camp guards are satirical, critical and realistic, Wertenbaker's version inclines towards a liberal fantasy: Simon Le Britten is a warmhearted individual with a tender conscience, and her security guard is a gentle Asian. This difference in authorial perspective means that while Adshead's play pulses with truth, Wertenbaker's is an essay in wishful thinking. So, as critics watching the original productions were quick to point out, Adshead's characters, however roughly sketched, are recognisable individuals, but Wertenbaker's are ciphers, walking history lessons. So while *The Bogus Woman* is a genuine howl of outrage, *Credible Witness* is less successful.

In British drama, the garden is often the symbol of Englishness, so the set of Tanika Gupta's *Sanctuary* (National, 2002), with its lush but foreign plants, immediately suggests a world that has moved on from the tradition of roses and manicured lawns. This '*small Eden-like*' corner is partly a meeting place, partly an old graveyard (15). Owned by the church, whose female vicar – the liberal Jenny Catchpole – is fighting the threat of eviction, this garden is also a sanctuary for Kabir, a Muslim gardener from Kashmir, Michael, a refugee from Rwanda, and Sebastian, a West Indian photographer. It also offers a refuge for Jenny's grandmother, the ex-colonial Margaret, and Ayesha, a half-Turkish teenager who illustrates the complexity of inheritance when she says: 'Dad wasn't really English. His Dad was Scottish – that's my grandfather and my grandmother's half Irish and a quarter

Norwegian' (58). Gupta, who after starting out in the 1990s with explorations of her Asian heritage then turned to examining issues which grip the wider society, presents the complex tensions of her characters: Margaret is embarrassingly colonial in her attitudes, but has no problem with the idea of having sex with a black man; Kabir is lonely and wants to adopt Ayesha; and Sebastian suspects that there is more to Michael than meets the eye. As Kabir and Michael tell their stories of atrocities in Kashmir and Rwanda, questions of personal responsibility come into focus. What would you do, Gupta asks, if you were caught in a genocidal situation? And, she suggests, it's easy to be brave in the safety of an English garden. This almost magical churchyard is, according to Professor Gabriele Griffin, 'symbolically the site that is the legacy, and in this play contains the remains, both of the colonial empires and of the church as an institution'.[20] It is also the place where Margaret hands Ayesha a blood diamond to finance her ambition to travel. The play ends, therefore, in Howe Kritzer's words, with a mixed-race 'representative of the post-Thatcher generation [who] will have to find her own way in the adult world'.[21] Here, a mixed-race, hybrid individual symbolises hope in a cruel country.

Asylum was a tenacious subject during this decade. One of the richest plays to tackle the subject of migration and assimilation was Charlotte Eilenberg's award-winning *The Lucky Ones* (Hampstead, 2002), which focuses on two Jewish families who fled from Nazi Germany. Whereas in Germany, their identity was defined by the tyrannical power of the state, in Britain they are able to define themselves, often as individuals in the process of becoming something new. Note the tenses in the following line of dialogue: 'Now we are British, but originally we were from Berlin' (23). But as well as showing the mental flexibility of new arrivals – 'none of us are English here, so we can invent our own rules!' (22) – the play underlines the importance of sex to hybrid identity: a Jewish refugee has a passionate but secret affair with the daughter of a Nazi; a Jewish son marries a Lebanese woman. But there were plenty of other shows about asylum, and while some, such as Nicola McCartney's *Cave Dwellers* (7:84, 2002), used an impassioned poetry to describe the effect of long journeys on an ever-shifting personal identity, others, such as Fin Kennedy's *Unstated* (Red Room/Southwark, 2008) turned the theatre building into an immigration experience, complete with brusque security guards and the compulsory fingerprinting of the audience. In a genre which exposed naked wounds, one of the most emotionally painful scenes was that in Bola Agbaje's *Detaining Justice*, when the Zimbabwian refugee is force-fed with dog food (239). The prize for the most claustrophobic experience goes, however, to Clare Bayley's *The Container* (EFF, 2007), which was staged inside a real forty-foot container with only torches for lighting, and told the stories of five illegal migrants, two Afghans, two Somalis and a Turkish Kurd. They dream of their destination: as Somali Fatima says, 'The Queen is really German. Her husband is a Greek. And the government are all Jews or Scottish' (11).

One often ignored aspect of the world market was sex tourism. Tanika Gupta's *Sugar Mummies* explores female sex tourism, showing how white women such as thirty-eight-year-old teacher Kitty and fiftysomething Maggie buy the services of young black men in Jamaica. Gupta also includes Yolanda, an American woman, who was played in Indhu Rubasingham's original production by Adjoa Andoh, a black actor: sex tourism is about class as well as race. In the final confrontation between Kitty and Sly, a 'beach boy', he tells her: 'You tink me a savage, a house slave. You look at me and you is jealous of my skin, but glad you is white. You tink you is superior' (119). As critic Toby Lichtig says, 'A particular Western malaise is under scrutiny, an emptiness that the characters seek to fill with fantasies of dominance and escape.'[22] When the play toured to Bolton, Gupta remembers that the audience was full of white 'sugar mummies'. They loved Maggie, played by Lynda Bellingham, the Oxo mum of the 1990s: 'They would see the show and although it was quite critical of white women, they still loved it.'[23] By contrast, debbie tucker green's *Trade* (RSC, 2005) examined the issue of female sex tourism by having two sex tourists – who are probably white – played by actors who were black, and who also played the parts of local women. As well as dissecting different attitudes to casual sex and paid-for sex, between 'here' and 'there', from both the tourist and the local perspective, green also comments on aspects of British identity, such as the local woman's dry comment that 'Yu h'English like a drink', which is countered by the novice sex tourist, who says she 'aint one a them Faliraki-out-on-the-piss-out-for-days-out-of-me-head-all-night-type-a-traveller' (24). This strongly written play shows not only how sex is part of the global marketplace, but also how national identity can weave itself into our most intimate activities.

Meanwhile, the expansion of the European Union in 2004–7 resulted in a spate of East European migrant dramas. Steve Waters's *Hard Labour* (Hampstead/WYP, 2008), for example, looked at the rise and fall of a Ukrainian gang master, who – in a parody of the Thatcherite free-market – sees little difference between crime and business. Similarly, Tena Stivicic's *Fragile!* (Arcola, 2007) gave a panoramic picture of migrants trying to make a new life for themselves in London, while one of the most powerful accounts of sex trafficking was Lucy Kirkwood's *it felt empty when the heart went at first but it is alright now* (Clean Break/Arcola, 2009), a strong mix of feisty realism, satirical comedy and excruciating heartbreak. With its ironic repeated refrain of 'Welcome to England!' (32, 37), the play looks at the experiences of Dijana, a Croatian woman who is forced to work as a prostitute and ends up in a detention centre, where she meets Gloria, a West African. In Lucy Morrison and Chloe Lamford's beautifully designed and atmospheric production, the audience followed Dijana, moving from room to room as her life spun out of control. Here England appears as an international crossroads of female pain.

The most outrageous, and controversial, play about migration came from the pen of one of the decade's most provocative and hilarious writers. Richard Bean's comic epic *England People Very Nice* covered more than four hundred years of the history of various migrations into London's East End, from yesteryear's French Huguenots to today's Bangladeshis, and including the Irish, the Jews and the Somalis. As each group of new arrivals is met with violence, but assimilated by means of Romeo and Juliet-style love affairs, a picture emerges of a mongrel nation, bonded together by a wild sense of humour, a love of drink and a lusty earthiness. Directed by the National's artistic director Nicholas Hytner on his theatre's huge

Olivier stage, the production was a box-office success, helped by its memorable cartoon projections. Although some scenes made many in the audience uncomfortable because of the play's evident delight in insistent cultural stereotyping, its multicultural cast and high profile all suggested a confidence in dealing with an enormously sensitive issue. When I saw it, the predominantly white audience laughed at all the jokes, even the ones about the white middle-class couple, but people of a different heritage might have felt much more uneasy.[24] If at times the show suggests that behind Bean's breezy humour there lurks an unconscious fury, which is often unsettling, the play is a mine of material about who the English think they are. It also shows how definitions of identity are in flux. As one British National Party character says, 'After 9/11, and today, skin colour is irrelevant. Culture. That's where the battle is. Take Rennie, he's black, but he's as British as hot tea in a flask' (107). The new enemy is militant Islam; the danger is refusal to assimilate. If national identity is created by asserting difference in the face of an alien Other, Bean's uncomfortably sprawling, gloriously offensive and rumbustuous comedy showed how these Others constantly change over time. Although the controversy it provoked was intense and lasted throughout its long run, only rarely did it spill over from blogs and broadsheets onto the streets. On one occasion, Bean recalls, protestors outside Whitechapel Tube station in east London spread the rumour that he had included a dog named Mohammed in a previous play, *The English Game* (Headlong, 2008). This was both untrue, and, unlike the *Behzti* case, failed to mobilise a militant backlash.[25] Summing up, Joshua Abrams says that the play argues that 'England is a nation of immigrants'.[26] It conveyed an acute sense of Britain as a mongrel nation, although perhaps theatre was just reminding us that it has always been like this. As an East End Jewish character in Alexis Zegerman's comedy *Lucky Seven* (Hampstead, 2008) remarks, 'My grandparents were Polish. Arrived here with no English and a sewing machine' (53). Britain has attracted, and assimilated, migrants for centuries.

Hard labour

The New Labour governments of Blair and Brown in the 2000s were heirs to the political and social revolution spearheaded by Thatcher in the 1980s, and they soon attracted a shower of satirical barbs. Satirist-in-chief was Scottish writer Alistair Beaton. As well as having been a speechwriter for Brown, he is also author of books with titles such as *The Little Book of New Labour Bollocks* (2000).

His play *Feelgood* (Hampstead/Out of Joint, 2001) is an enjoyable farce about spin-doctors working on the prime minister's annual party conference speech, while anti-capitalist protestors riot in the streets and a scandal simmers about the release of hormones from an illegal experiment with genetically modified food. As you'd expect from a farce, the main figure of delight is Eddie, a monstrous New Labour press chief who will do anything – well, blackmail usually – to support his government. As he bosses around his entourage of assistants and gag-writers, the only person able to stop him is Liz, an investigative journalist – and his ex-wife. Early on, Beaton underlines the continuity between New Labour and Tories when a speechwriter suggests a line for the PM's speech that is similar to Thatcher's iconic phrase, 'The lady's not for turning'. 'No harm in that,' responds Eddie (2). As well as jokes about New Labour's record in power – 'Nobody can get anywhere on time any more, George. It's called an integrated transport policy' (31) – Beaton also gives Liz some powerful lines which articulate the liberal left's disappointments. 'How about the distribution of wealth? That's not on the agenda, is it? That would upset the rich. You don't believe in doing that. That would mean conflict. That would mean real politics' (74). New Labour is defined as 'Government by headline. Making people feel good. It's the feelgood factor' (74). As directed by Max Stafford-Clark, with Henry Goodman (Eddie), Sian Thomas (Liz) and Nigel Planer (a hapless MP), *Feelgood* summoned up an instantly recognisable picture of manipulative spin doctors representing venal politicians while the only real opposition is a vociferous but unreliable media. To be British means being half asleep, dozing in apathy and indifference. In this climate, satire could seem like a wake-up call.

Equally acerbic was Steve Thompson's snappy *Whipping It Up* (Bush, 2006), although his conceit is that the play is set in the whips' office of a future Conservative government. Although most of the action concerns the Tory whips Chief, Alastair and Tim, Thompson also brings on Delia, the Labour Deputy Chief Whip. She turns out to be as foul-mouthed and as cynically manipulative as any Tory. The play highlights the nitty-gritty of political in-fighting, and shows how the world of Westminster is often little more than an extension of the English public school, where the boys fight it out amongst themselves: what really angers them, in Delia's words, is 'getting shafted by a girl' (57). Despite this, not everything is dishonourable. As one critic points out, Thompson's 'Chief Whip exhibits in extremis the kind of honour which is alien both to the day-to-day running of the office and to contemporary political culture as a whole'.[27] Chief's view is that 'Etched somewhere in marble pillars is the truth about this country: we're a nation of achievers' (50). Not for the first time, England emerges as a land where the values – bad as well as good – of the past persist adamantly in the present.

But the temperature of post-Thatcherite times could rise as well as fall, and the end of the decade saw the arrival of a fine play from one of the best political playwrights. David Hare's *Gethsemane* (National, 2008) was a wonderful evocation of New Labour in power. Its plot, which centres around a Home Office minister who uses a party fundraiser to help cover up her daughter's misdemeanours, includes pen portraits of the prime minister, the fundraiser's acolytes and a seedy journalist. Continuity with the Conservative era is expressed in the phrase, used twice by the minister, that 'This government has always sought to encourage a business-friendly environment' (52, 115). When the play opened, most reviewers were obsessed about whether the figures in the play were true and timely representations of Tony Blair, Lord Levy or Tessa Jowell. Similarly literal-minded was the complaint that the play was out-of-date because Brown had already replaced Blair. As it happens, by the end of its run, another party-funding scandal occurred, and Hare appeared on national TV to argue that his work was suddenly 'topical' again.[28] So although Hare's statement, in the programme, that the play is pure fiction, is clearly ironic, he is not satirising individuals so much as chronicling an era when there is no right way to behave. Despite their innate idealism, every one of his characters fails to do the best thing possible. As Lori, the music teacher with a conscience, says, the most that can be hoped for is 'behaving in a way which does least harm' (78). Several of the characters experience a moment of self-doubt, but the play zooms in on Lori's Gethsemane, her self-regarding notion that she has given up education for a noble reason. Finally, as this is exposed as a fundamental misreading of the original New Testament story, it emerges that, despite her desire to do good, she's been kidding herself. *Gethsemane* examines the state of the nation in a poetic rather than a literal way, and the result is emotionally much more powerful than any docudrama. Howard Davies's production, which included Tamsin Greig (the minister), Stanley Townsend (the fundraiser) and Nicola Walker (Lori), offered a brisk and incisive evening, with a quietly moving finish. At the end, Lori sits down and plays an imaginary piano, a scene which seemed to affirm the value of art as consolation. On the night I went, Neil Kinnock (leader of the Labour Party in the Thatcher era) and his wife Glenys were in the audience – and they didn't look very happy. In general, the spectators tutted, muttered and scoffed at the platitudes of the politicians. When the minister said, 'Sorry, but you have to trust us. You have no choice', people reacted with audible disgust (80). Afterwards, a feeling lingered of a nation beset by self-doubt, disillusioned with New Labour and deeply troubled. Like the best British plays of the 2000s, *Gethsemane* was sceptical of government slogans, averse to market targets and proud of the servants of society, such as teachers and social workers.

In the past decade, British theatre painted a liberal picture of post-Thatcherite politics, showing how many social problems had their origins in the Tory doctrine of market economics. National identity is represented as an unhappy present haunted by an unjust past, a country in thrall to images of the Iron lady, or tormented by the legacy of Empire, in the shape of migrant stories and the challenges of runaway globalisation. Everywhere the influence of the market has undermined old social certainties, and created new cynical character types. Whether they are celebrity cheats, sad migrants or white working-class discontents, the most memorable stage figures tended to be the bad boys, with good people, or do-gooders, coming a very distant second. Everywhere, national pride was asserted in the face of an alien Other, the new arrival whose assimilation could only be a long and painful process. As social problems became mired in fierce conflict there seemed little evidence that a hybrid solution, or any kind of solution, could tackle the malaise of what has increasingly become a nation divided against itself.

5 TWO NATIONS

Lucy Just lookin' through window. For ages like. Livin' room. Books. Plants. Carpet. Big leather sofa n'that. Pictures on walls. (*Pause.*) Must o'been out to a restaurant or somert. Fuckin' theatre. Sort o'thing they'd do innit?

(Leo Butler, *Redundant*, 179)

Britain in the 2000s was a divided nation. As ever, the main dividing line was class: everywhere, class distinctions, whether celebrated or resented, were a defining feature of daily life. Same old story. Despite the project of New Labour to create a more just society, class divisions were worse than ever: the gap between rich and poor had never been wider. If class was about poverty, it was also about fear: underclass chavs and the scary poor haunted the popular imagination. If Britain was a fractured society, another powerful division was racial, with different ethnic and religious groups more segregated from one another than in the past. Ghettos were as much about culture as skin colour, but questions of race and racism remained a persistent source of anxiety. So the social landscape was not just fragmented, it rang with cries of injustice. Journalist Polly Toynbee sums up: 'This is what "exclusion" means, if you ever wondered at this modern wider definition of poverty. It is a large No Entry sign on every ordinary pleasure. No Entry to the consumer society where the rest of us live. It is a harsh apartheid.'[1] If, as Professor David Cannadine argues, 'Britons are always thinking about who they are, what kind of society they belong to, and where they themselves belong in it', it is clear that what we think about class or race helps to define what we think about ourselves.[2]

Chavs and have-nots

In the 2000s, class communities were increasingly segregated. On British stages, the respectable working class was far less in evidence than the underclass, or chavs, the latest incarnation of the Victorian idea of the fearsome undeserving poor. Traditionally, the most common way of representing the underclass was the council-estate, dirty-realist play. A superbly written example is Leo Butler's award-winning *Redundant*, which illustrates this writer's ability to thoughtfully present a group of people whose individuality is evident in every line of his forensic analysis. Set in a squalid, sparely furnished council flat in Sheffield, with discoloured walls graced by a Bob Marley poster, the play recounts a year in the life of Lucy, a seventeen-year-old white teen who dreams of having a family, unfazed by the fact that she already has one child in care. While her boyfriend, Dave, a thirty-two-year-old black guy, is away, the lonely Lucy asks young Darren to stay the night. When Dave returns, along with the crack-smoking dopehead Gonzo, it gradually emerges that she is pregnant and, when Dave finds out that the child is white, he moves out. Although Lucy's real family is made up of mixed-race sixteen-year-old Nikki plus Jo, their sixty-year-old Gran, she prefers the family life of her own imagination: she tells Darren, 'All makes sense in the end. You n'me. Our own little home. Do it up a bit, like. Lick o' paint' (137). In the end, she alienates her nearest and dearest, and becomes increasingly dependent on drugs. For the underclass, being redundant doesn't mean losing your job – it means being surplus DNA.

Still, Lucy is, in Butler's words, 'never a victim in her own home',[3] and his portrait of her is defiantly at odds with the simple images of dole scroungers peddled by publicity-seeking politicians and angry newspaper columnists. She is brimming with energy, emotionally volatile and desperate for affection, an heir to the sixteen-year-old Carol in Butler's *Made of Stone* (Royal Court, 2000), with her 'Fuckin' hate this place. Look in the mirror and I wanna puke' (32). Self-hatred and hatred of place are closely connected, and in both plays the absence of parents represents not freedom, but bondage. To avoid facing the truth, Lucy wields empty bravado, brutal stupidities and selfish fantasies. She prefers fantasy to reality because she knows that reality offers no hope. Poverty breeds illusion. Written with excruciating psychological realism, the text is full of evasions, projections and concealed aggression, and the play is raw and raucous. Gran's attack on the link between thoughtlessness and teenage pregnancy – 'Never learn, d'yer?' (124) – feels like an indictment of today's Britain. And Lucy's response to the fact that her child is a girl – 'Another fuckin' cunt in the family' (159) – sums up the disappointment of all the women. Yet even the fierce cruelties – Lucy stabs Darren and hospitalises her Gran – are not the result of some tabloid-style Evil, but rather of a more banal mix of selfishness, inexperience and ignorance. Poverty-line Britain is not so much a Hell on Earth as a place that urgently needs attention.

Each scene change in Dominic Cooke's production was punctuated by a popping flash-bulb which left a livid impression on the retina. As Lucy – played by Lyndsey Marshall – goes downhill, her flat gets more and more empty. At the end, she turned on Bob Marley's 'Satisfy My Soul' for a few seconds before snapping it off. Then she sat on the edge of the bed, and while outside the winter snow glittered in the night air, the ceiling of her flat drifted upwards into infinity to the music of Gary Yershon. It was a sublime moment of theatre. On this main stage, *Redundant* felt like a state-of-the-nation play, a passionate indictment of poverty. But it didn't touch the critics, most of whom despised the show, although the *Independent* praised the text's 'shockingly casual comic buoyancy' and *Time Out* pointed out that it made a change to put women, instead of lads, centre stage at the Royal Court.[4] Like so many underclass dramas, the play also raises the issue of voyeuristic cultural tourism: as Toynbee says, 'The better-off always relish the titillating sins of the underclasses as another way to justify their own lives.'[5] Or, as *Theatre Record* put it, the play 'achieves the divisive effect of sending us home mighty glad we don't live off crack in a tip in Sheffield'.[6] On the other hand, surely theatre has a duty to tell the truth about Britain's two nations, and isn't an intense experience such as *Redundant* advocacy enough for change?

Similar questions about the tension between cultural tourism and theatre as protest could also be asked of *Motortown* by Simon Stephens, one of the most powerful and lyrical writers of the decade, a comprehensive chronicler of both working- and middle-class life in the new millennium. This play is an account of a day in the life of an Iraq War veteran, Danny, who comes back to Dagenham from Basra, only to find that Marley, his former girlfriend, is afraid of what he's become. The psychotic Danny lives up to her fears by buying a gun, kidnapping a fourteen-year-old black girl, Jade, killing her, and then menacing Justin and Helen, a couple of middle-class swingers. Only with Lee, his autistic brother, can Danny be completely at home, and even then his tenderness turns into sexual manipulation. But Danny's view of England is scarcely that of a patriotic homeland; as critic Lyn Gardner put it:

> To Danny it is not Iraq but England that is the foreign country [. . .] It is an England where the 'war on terror' has become a war waged using the tactics of the terrorists. It is also a place of dubious moralities [. . .] this England has all the stinking attractions of a dog turd.[7]

As a working-class lad, Danny is a study in furious rage: often inarticulate and alienated, he is boiling with resentment at a multi-cultural society that he has fought for, but that doesn't appreciate him. As a squaddie, he is infuriated by the two-million-strong anti-war march of 16 February 2003. When he meets the middle-class Justin and Helen, he asks them if they went on the march: when they say yes, he replies that he wished he'd 'sprayed the lot of yer' with his SA80 assault rifle (65). The play is as much about class war as the Iraq War. As the smalltime firearms-fixer tells Danny:

> You want to know the truth about the poor in this country? [. . .] They're not the salt of the fucking earth. They're thick. They're myopic. They're violent. [. . .] They would be better off staying in their little holes and fucking each other. And killing each other. (36)

With its epigraph by Heiner Müller – 'The first sign of hope is despair / The first sign of the new is terror' (3) – *Motortown* is a mix of Georg Büchner's *Woyzeck*, Martin Scorsese's *Taxi Driver* and any number of road movies. Written because, in Stephens's words, 'I was deeply nervous about that [anti-war] march and that [anti-war] movement' this 'moral chaos of England' play rejects a simplistic division of the world into good guys and bad guys.[8] Likewise, opinions about it were divided between those, such as the *Daily Mail*, who saw it as 'depraved snuff-theatre', and those, such as the *Independent*, who appreciated it as a 'most provocative and gripping piece'.[9] More than one reviewer commented on the fact that Stephens, by revealing that Danny was psychotic at school (71), weakens the central argument that war has brutalised Danny. But Stephens has deliberately not written Danny as a victim of army brutality – if he shows how war brutalises men, he also shows how brutal men discover themselves during war. Danny's deprived background, and his own family, are the cause of his problems. If this seems like a moral cop-out, it is also a powerful image of a morally chaotic nation. When the middle classes have nightmares, they feature characters like Danny.

Ramin Gray's stark production, with its minimal props, visible lighting rigs and plain brick wall, had pounding dance music during the scene changes, with the cast crossing the stage and making choreographed moves with tables and chairs. But the most memorable image was when, after Jade's sickening murder, a wide pool of blood was quietly mopped up by the actors. As well as being a searing moment in the play, this scene gave them trouble: the show report for 25 April 2006 says, 'There was too much blood tonight so we had trouble cleaning the blood', and one of the actor's 'jeans had bloody knees and there was still blood on her shoes from last night'.[10] *Motortown* fielded Danny Mays as Danny, a mix of bruised charm, pent-up energy and battered bewilderment, at best oozing a menacing bonhomie, at worst a walking terror. Disconcerting. Chavdom has rarely been so intense, or so intensely appalling.

On many British stages, the poor have been presented in all their chaotic glory, sometimes with a nod to audience expectations, sometimes not. For example, in Chris O'Connell's confrontational *Street Trilogy*,[11] the young chavs are almost ridiculously aggressive and awful, with one character typically exclaiming how even 'the days are bleeding to death' (60), but the drama refuses to offer any simple answers. Similarly, in Shelagh Stephenson's *The Long Road* (Soho, 2008), the underclass killer acknowledges audience expectations by saying:

> It's ridiculous, it's like a joke my family, you couldn't put us on the telly, no one would believe it, we've got drugs, shootings, being on the game, broken noses, social services, horrible sex stuff and half the time the electric's cut off. We're one of those families you read about in the papers. (40)

Class is also rooted in place: Oladipo Agboluaje's *The Christ of Coldharbour Lane* begins with a thrilling evocation of the buzz of Brixton streetlife and ends up by advocating armed revolution by the London poor, led by a black British woman shouting, 'To the City! To the City!' (91). Similarly, David Edgar's acute picture of cultural conflict *Playing with Fire* is set in West Yorkshire, and climaxes in a full-scale riot with, in the words of one character, 'young [Asian] men defending Broughton Moor from attacks from the Crazy Gang [white football hooligans]' (121). As Michael Attenborough, its director, says, 'Somehow we have translated communities having their own identity into a form of segregation, which breeds a sense of fear, distrust and hostility.'[12] Other social divisions were much less apocalyptic. For example, in Mark Kirkby's *Bus* (WYP, 2006), the split is between incoming media students and Leeds locals who, in the words of the *Guardian* review of this production (set on the top deck of a bus), cook up 'wild conspiracies to rid the town of poncy students'.[13] Despite the humour, the conflict is still about class, and class is central to national identity.

Winning losers

As well as being a nation split between the respectable and the rough, Britain was a country fascinated by crime. Even in David Greig and

Gordon McIntyre's feelgood rom-com *Midsummer*, the main male character is a petty criminal, and one who reads Dostoevsky! Still, few plays about crims had the impact of Gregory Burke's award-winning debut *Gagarin Way* (Traverse, 2001). Taking its evocative title from a street named after Yuri Gagarin in the Fife village of Lumphinnans, 'a municipal reminder of the days when there was a red under practically every bed in industrial Scotland', the play offered a unique mix of criminal thrills with sustained commentary on left-wing history and the effects of globalisation.[14]

The set-up is a classic kidnap drama: one evening in a Scottish factory warehouse, two workers, Eddie and Gary, plan to grab and kill a Japanese company manager. It's meant to be a political statement, but things go wrong when the man they kidnap turns out to be Frank, a Scottish business consultant, while Tom, the student security guard who has been bribed to open the gates, returns and is appalled to discover their plan. Although the plot is a bit static, Burke's riotously irreverent language makes this one of the most thrilling debuts of the decade. By mixing foul-mouthed Fife demotic (the word 'cunt' is used in place of a dozen other nouns) with cultural references, political discourse and economic analysis, Burke created a unique voice with which to deliver his black comedy, with its smattering of politically incorrect jokes, such as when Tom says, 'It's a terrible thing, sexism', and Eddie replies, 'It's a cunt' (18).

Opening with a grimly hilarious and wildly imaginative exchange in which Eddie and Tom swap points of view about French philosopher-dramatists Jean-Paul Sartre and Jean Genet, *Gagarin Way* is a theatrical entertainment rather than a realistic account of Scottish lowlifes. With the arrival of Gary and the hostage, the mood darkens, and the conflict sharpens, for while Eddie is a psycho who has 'always been interested in violence' (41), Gary is a born-again anarchist fascinated by 'the propaganda of the deed' (46). Instead of kidnapping a politician, they kidnap a businessman on the basis that corporations 'hold absolute power in the world' (64). Gradually, it emerges that Frank, and to a lesser extent Tom, share the same working-class roots as Eddie and Gary, coming from the same mining families, with their traditions of class solidarity and communist beliefs.

But the play is also a snapshot of today's Scotland, a land of McJobs and call-centres, described as 'real slavery' (13), where 'dumb fucks' fight over 'ten-pound deals' while the real money is 'tucked up safe and sound in all they little screens in the City' (46). As well as being a picture of post-industrial Britain's divided society, the play is also conscious of the issue of cultural tourism: as Eddie wisely says, 'There's nothing the general public likes better than a vicarious wander through the world ay the full-time criminal' (7).

John Tiffany's ninety-minute production, sporting a spartan set and spot-lit freeze-frame moments, ended with its vision of urban nihilism turning ugly as both Frank and Tom are knifed to death by Eddie. Clearly, this will have no effect on global capitalism, and the piece has a tone of muted despair. The enemy, after all, is distant: as Eddie says, 'But, hey, that's the nature of ay the global economy, you dinnay ken who the fuck's in charge' (39). One of the effects of Thatcher's victory over the miners in 1984–85, alluded to in the play, was a destruction of traditional working-class communities, which results in a choice between becoming a vicious Eddie or a nostalgic Gary. Following the play's worldwide success, Burke participated in discussions about its politics. In the *Guardian* he wrote, 'What it is mostly about is a community' and that 'what really interests me is the ghosts that our governments have always created, and continue to create, in communities here.'[15] Such ghostly presences lend a haunting air to this picture of a nation divided into criminals and slaves. But not everyone agrees with Burke's politics. Criticising plays such as *Gagarin Way* for ending on a 'implied statement of hopelessness', David Greig has suggested that true political drama must in some way expand the imaginative horizons of its audiences, 'resisting the management of the imagination by global capitalism'.[16]

The most popular variant of the criminal play is set among urban youth, often with no adults, showing small segregated communities with their own private language and social codes. In Shan Khan's award-winning *Office*, two petty crims, Sharky and Showtime, work as drug-dealers using a couple of King's Cross phone boxes as their office. Among their friends is Brencher, complete with skate-board and baggy strides, who tells a wild story of a drug-addled trip to

Portugal. The plot is about a doublecross that goes wrong and, like so many debut plays, it was a 'me and my mates' drama, with an absent but all-powerful father figure, Papa, the aptly named gangland boss. When the boys are joined by two young prostitutes, Hazel and Molly, and a bent cop, a darker shadow falls over this criminal 'family'. Hazel, who in Abigail Morris's production had bruises all over her legs, and Molly, a single mother, remind us that the costs of poverty are not carried equally by men and women. In the world of dirty realism, the men misbehave, the women suffer.

Khan says that he didn't stipulate the race of his underclass characters – 'They're not necessarily Black, Asian, White [. . .] They're part of a new culture that's born of Americanisms, hip-hop culture, neither Black nor White' – and that what inspired him was the way 'young people of all colours [. . .] are creating a new culture of fusion'.[17] With its ethnic mix – Asian Muslim Sharky, mixed-race Showtime, white Brencher plus Irish Molly – *Office* offered a snapshot of a hybrid, multiracial street culture that was more alive than many representations of the mainstream. What distinguished the writing was its chatty vigour, street cool and fingerlicking hilarity. You could say that, in Britain today, if poverty has many colours, the identity of young people could be imagined as a vibrant hybrid.

Equally appealing was Mike Packer's *A Carpet, a Pony and a Monkey* (Bush, 2002), an amusing Euro-trot in the company of Baz, a football ticket tout, and his new sidekick, Tosser, peppered with words arcane enough to demand a glossary in the playtext (6). However eccentric, Packer's characters have an edgy relationship, constantly arguing. At one point, Tosser revels in being a hooligan xenophobe – complete with the cross of St George painted on his face – referring to the Germans as 'the fuckin' enemy' (17). Later, he sums up national identity: 'There's something awesome about beating the Krauts [. . .] It's in the genes. Us and them' (32), while 'a good ruck is as British as a Sunday fuckin' roast' (33). As ever, identity is defined against an alien Other. The joke is that when Baz, who knew Tosser's father, tells him he's got Jewish ancestry, he realises he's a 'mongrel', adding 'but I'm a predominantly English fuckin' mongrel' (61). Occasionally, a mythical view of crime could be part of national identity: in Gregory Burke's *On Tour*, the Mancunian H argues that 'We're a country of criminals. Always have been. Outlaws. The highwayman. Pirates. They're the folk heroes of this country' (37). But not all crims were chavs. Dolly Dhingra's underrated *The Fortune Club* (Leicester/Tricycle, 2005) was, according to its programme, 'inspired by a true crime', and featured a white-collar scam perpetrated by a journalist, a maths whiz, a bookstore manager, a office worker, a musician and an actress – as well as by a white-van driver. But the sense of living a life apart from mainstream society cuts them off as surely as any class division.

Like the fraud at the heart of *Enron*, it all ends badly, although not everyone ends up in jail. Other writers focused on people who were much less privileged.

In Simon Stephens's beautifully crafted *Country Music* (Royal Court/ATC, 2004), which spans more than twenty years in a series of duologues, the first scene introduces eighteen-year-old Jamie and fifteen-year-old Lynsey. He's stolen a car and she's absconded from a care home. Yes, it's one of Stephens's 'stories of flight', a motif that recurs in his work.[18] As a result of his wildness, and his violence, Jamie ends up in prison after killing a man. There he learns that Lynsey has moved on and started a new life, but the play's most heart-rending scene is when – after his release – he meets Emma, his daughter from his fling with Lynsey. In a fraught exchange which nevertheless has a redemptive undertow, Jamie, now thirty-nine, is proud that Emma is a receptionist and aspires to be an office manager: 'Office manager. That's incredible to me' (42). He can barely believe that his flesh-and-blood can be upwardly mobile. When she asks him about prison, he says, that, when he was released, he 'just stood there. Couldn't move. Couldn't move my legs' (54). Prison has become so much part of life that freedom doesn't feel free. The final scene is a flashback to the first, and gives us a glimpse of why Jamie was so wild: he caught his mother having sex with a casual lover. The problem of poverty begins with an impoverished family life. Similarly, Chloe Moss's award-winning *This Wide Night* (Clean Break, 2008) examined the desperation of ex-offenders. When fiftysomething Lorraine is released after serving a long sentence, the first thing she does is call on Marie, a younger woman who once shared her cell. But Marie, who has been out of prison for a while, now has serious problems of her own. The play, which is both discreetly delicate and emotionally strong, explores the relationship between the two women in an immensely sympathetic and truthful way. The different shades of feeling, from maternal love to chavvy resentment, build up to a powerful climax.

Clear-headed and unsentimental, Moss shows their struggle against dependence: on routine, on medication, on alcohol, on each other. Occasionally humorous, frequently exasperating, the two are simultaneously highly individual and recognisable social types.

The decade's most moving prison drama was Scottish playwright Rona Munro's *Iron* (Traverse, 2002), which shows what happens when twenty-five-year-old Josie visits her mother Fay for the first time since the latter was convicted for killing her husband fifteen years previously. The iron of the play's title refers not only to the bars separating the women, but also to the hardness of spirit which enables each to survive: the murder has imprisoned both in the past. But while Fay encourages her daughter to enjoy life, Josie becomes convinced that her mother is innocent. Only at the end, when Fay finally confesses her guilt to Josie, is either woman able to move on: the truth, to quote the Bible, shall make you free.[19] But the truth also reveals how humans can act like animals: just before she stabbed her husband, Fay says, 'I bared my teeth like a wolf' (94). Anger is animal. If prison shows us a world of forced segregation, plays such as these also represented Britain as a punitive nation, with a dark love of punishment.

Country matters

When the Countryside Alliance marched in protest against the foxhunting ban on 15 September 2004, it was a reminder to townies that there is a world beyond the tarmac and street lights. Several plays explored the countryside. Foremost was Richard Bean's award-winning *Harvest* (Royal Court, 2005), a comic epic about a farming family in Yorkshire that spanned a century. Bean began his career with hairy-men work plays, such as *Toast* (Royal Court, 1999) and *Under the Whaleback* (Royal Court, 2003), which looked at the Hull working class. With *Harvest*, he listened to the voices of his background: 'My family,' he says, describing his relatives, 'are from East Yorkshire, farming people.'[20] Before the action of play begins, the tenant-farming Harrison family acquire Kilham Wold Farm, some eighty-two acres near Driffield, after winning a bizarre wager with local squire Primrose Agar's grandfather. Bean's comedy follows the fortunes of William Harrison from the age of nineteen in 1914 to 109 in 2005. Over these ninety years, he quarrels with his brother Albert about which of them should volunteer to fight in the First World War – William wins and returns, having lost his legs – and whether the land would be more profitable as a pig farm. The brothers are also rivals for the affections of Maudie, whose niece, Laura, eventually comes to live on the farm, and falls for Stefan, a Second World War German POW. After Albert's death, William converts to pig-farming, and Laura's son, Alan, decides that he doesn't want to be a farmer. So William employs Titch as his replacement. In the final scene, the aged Laura and the ancient William confront and defeat two chavs, who have broken into the farm. The intensity of that final scene, when petty-crims Blue and Danny subject Laura to a horrific ordeal, forces you to reassess the rest of the play.[21]

The wonderful thing about *Harvest* is that Bean is never obvious: he tells the story by imagining quirky episodes which sum up the essence of his tale. In the opening scene, instead of clichés about the First World War, much of the discussion is about the impending visit of the Stallion Man, whose horse is to impregnate the Harrisons' mare. Similarly, the Second World War scene overturns national stereotypes by showing Stefan as a good German, and the local English worthies as bureaucratic busybodies who threaten the family with eviction. In 1958, the weather forecast on the radio is followed by *The Archers* theme, which William instantly turns off. Reality, we are reminded, is no soap. A highpoint is arrival of the mountainous, straight-talking Titch, whose job interview is as hilarious as anything written in this decade. Bean's forte is eccentric but believable Yorkshire characters and, as well as the caustically sarcastic William and the crazily unorthodox Titch, *Harvest* includes

Lord Primrose Agar, the local toff who dresses in Inuit gear and has penned the sensational *Cannibal*. If their voices sound authentic, the humour is antic, strange, appealing. As Maudie lovingly says to William, 'Yer daft in the head you' (54).

A central theme is class conflict, embodied in the uneasy relationship between the Harrisons and Agar. Determined to reverse the loss of the farm by his ancestor, Agar tries every trick to get it back, from not paying rent on the one field he uses to having the land requisitioned during wartime. In a deliciously cranky twist, he falls in love with Laura. Other pressures on the Harrisons include edicts from the central government or the European Community. But the issue of class is always neatly tuned to a comic register. As William says, 'The officers were at Ypres, I was at Wipers' (31). In the final scene, the class antagonism of Danny and Blue is shown in an uglier light: these have-nots misbehave in a vicious way, a sure sign of social decay. But, after the play ends, what you remember most is lines like William's 'No man on this earth can talk with any authority about happiness until he's sold shit to the aristocracy' (52). At its brazen best, Bean's comic brio is a joy. Blessed are the jokers, for they will be called bringers of felicity.

Directed by Wilson Milam, *Harvest* lasted about three hours and had an ace cast, led by Matthew Dunster's acerbic William, and featuring a scene-stealing Adrian Hood as the long-haired Titch. His speech about liking pigs because they're clever – 'Just enough to mek it interesting but not enough to get yer worried' (61) – almost brought the house down, and the scene in which Titch and Laura dance to Dr Hook's 'When You're in Love with a Beautiful Woman' added tenderness to hilarity. Eccentric, comic and celebratory of Yorkshire Englishness, one of the play's messages is that Britain's countryside is neglected and oppressed by foreign powers, whether in Whitehall or in Brussels. And this failure to protect the countryside compromises national identity. If the traditional English breakfast is bacon and eggs, Bean shows how pig farmers have been betrayed by market forces and government indifference. Ours is a land of lost content.

Other visions of rural life were equally vivid. Jez Butterworth, whose *Mojo* (Royal Court, 1995) was one of the most exciting plays of the 1990s, cornered the market by penning three unforgettable rural plays in the 2000s: *The Night Heron* (Royal Court, 2002), *The Winterling* (Royal Court, 2006) and *Jerusalem* (Royal Court, 2009). These are not only characterised by their black hilarity but are also quintessentially rich texts, glowing with symbolism, buzzing with humour and aching with human frailty. Full of bizarre characters and crazy situations, they are shot through with Butterworth's highly individual voice, and, especially the first two, glow with a magic-realist sensibility. *The Night Heron* is set deep in the Cambridgeshire marshes and at its heart is an account of a crazed religious imagination: featuring two unemployed gardeners, one of whom, Wattmore, is a fanatic who recites the biblical story of the Expulsion, and sees devils everywhere, while the other, Griffin, is more down-to-earth, capable of vicious criminality. Among their joyfully odd visitors is Bolla, an female ex-con who has a wonderful way with words and a naked youth who spouts the poetry of Shelley. If Griffin is most at home with comic imagery – 'I'm not stupid Wattmore. Grant me some noodles' (8) or 'he hasn't got the brains of a bucket of frogs' (50) – Wattmore's religious delusions are resonant of Protestantism, of Bunyan and the English imagination: 'Send a Guardian and light braziers . . . and mark the path through Disturbance. Display the dark path to everlasting Peace' (12). Here the myth of Expulsion from the Garden of Eden is reworked for the iPod age, but remains a statement of national identity.

Equally quirky in its sense of the absurd and its picture of the idiocies of bucolic life is *The Winterling*, set this time in an abandoned Dartmoor farmhouse. West, a former gangster in exile from London, lives with Lue, an unusual young woman. When West's old mate, Wally, and his gobby stepson Patsy, arrive, a territorial struggle rapidly develops. If you prod the compost a little, there's a great mythic scenario seething in the ordure: this is a play about archetypal fathers and sons, about rites of passage and about England. Wally is Patsy's surrogate father, and he's brought his 'son' into the wilderness to make him a man. But, as well as the story of the blooding of a youngster, this is also the tale of another, equally primitive, ritual: the proximity of an ancient hillfort, once the scene of human sacrifice, suggests the beating

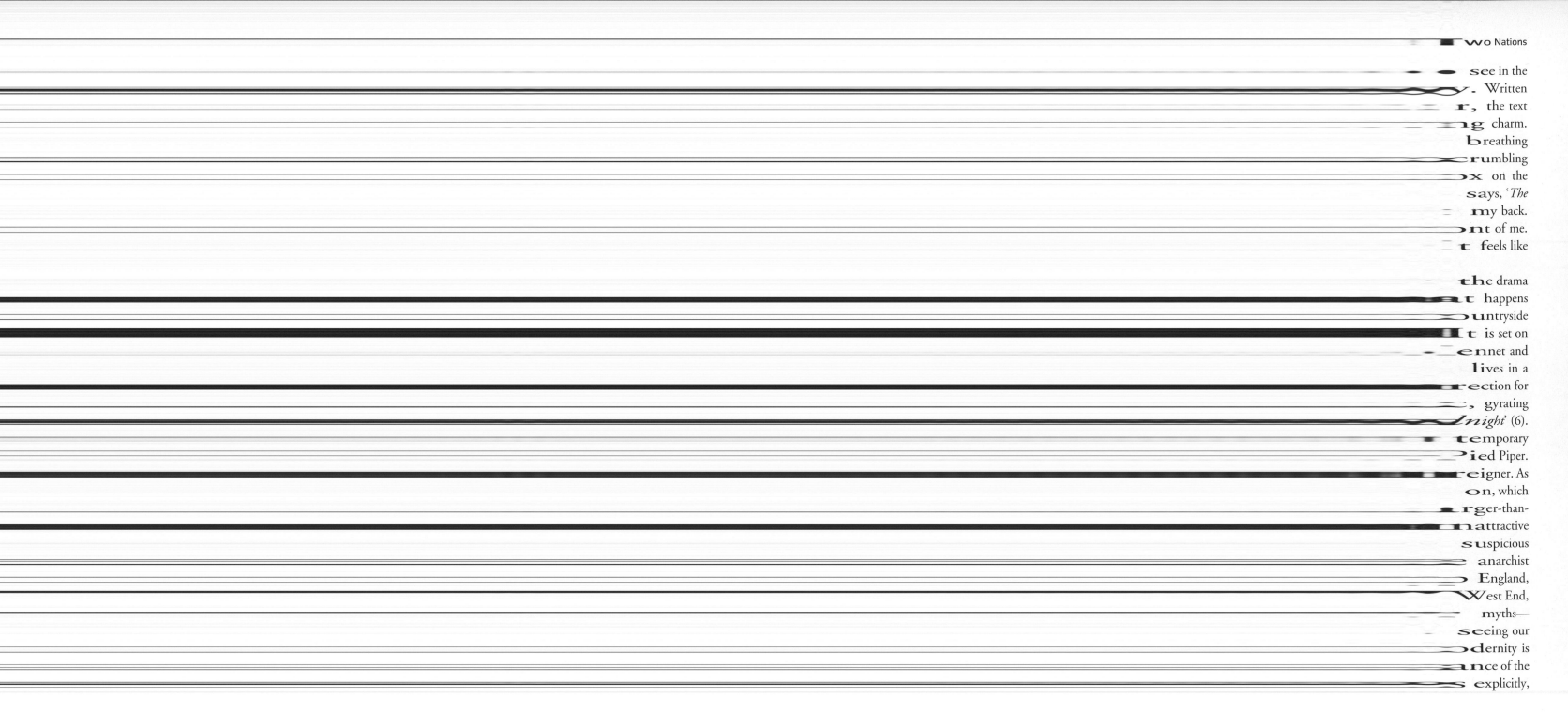

as the play's title re...

whose time is up: as...

sits up, wipes the de...

dark place?" And she...

By the end of the play...

it's a funeral pyre for...

In *Jerusalem*, the...

sex-mad bunch. If, i...

nation of storytellers'...

'The prevailing "co...

deliciously fuzzy opt...

crisis.[25] It's an Eng...

creations and where t...

countryside beyond r...

is just as crime-ridden...

landscape. All three...

Heron, with its me...

huge picture – made...

saints, starred Ray W...

complete with deep...

doomy production,...

crash of passing mil...

drums. With a crack i...

Daniel Mays (Patsy)...

example of a deeply i...

profane. Best of all, *Je*...

blitzy music, starred...

Mackenzie Crook an...

petrol filled the air, R...

made you hope that...

the operative word is...

Some rural plays...

temptation by urban i...

life seriously. Nell Le...

(Hampstead, 2005)...

farm, and equates the...

a whole way of life, symbolised by the family story of the Apple Tree Man, who is both a symbol of fertility and of death, when the 'world is cold and dark and flat' (78). This autumnal, visceral production, directed by Lucy Bailey, with Anna Calder-Marshall as the seventy-something matriarch, ended with the image of her lying down in despair, along with her brother, and covering themselves in fallen leaves. In David Harrower's *Dark Earth* (Traverse, 2003), a pair of townies get lost in the Scottish countryside, and meet a farming family, who have had to sell their farmland. Although the young couple and the family are initially drawn to each other, in different ways, they end up completely divided: as the farmer concludes, 'They dinnae understand us' (92). Several plays responded to the decade's rural crises: Lance Woodman's *Red Skies over the Severn* (Swan, Worcester, 2001) looked at the foot and mouth epidemic in Worcester while Nell Leyshon's *The Farm* (Southwark, 2002) did the same for mad cow disease in Somerset. Others focused on teenagers: Molly Davies's *A Miracle* (Royal Court, 2009) showed the effect of a young returning soldier on a teen mother in a Norfolk village, in a production whose set made use of dark, deep-smelling soil. Joel Horwood's *I Caught Crabs in Walberswick* (Eastern Angles, 2008) squinted at rural Suffolk through the eyes of three sixteen-year-olds. At the end of a wild party night, two of them, Wheeler and Fitz, find that what they have in common, a desire to leave their 'backwater villages' (44) for the bright lights, is less strong than their class differences, summed up by the phrase that in the future, 'They will be on opposite sides of the pub' (52). In plays such as these, Britain's countryside is not a green and pleasant land, but a place riven with class conflict and blasted with strange imaginings.

Segregated communities

The most serious controversies in the 2000s were caused by plays about segregated communities, and especially those which are defined, in some way, by their religious beliefs. In 2003, Julia Pascal's *Crossing Jerusalem* (Tricycle), which shows an Israeli family uneasily celebrating a birthday in an Arab restaurant in Jerusalem at the height of the Intifada, attracted angry reactions from both pro-Israelis and pro-Palestinians. A year later, *Behzti* was stopped by a riot. In 2009, Caryl Churchill's *Seven Jewish Children* offended supporters of the state of Israel and Richard Bean's *England People Very Nice* was offensive to some Asians. But offence was not limited to questions of race. *Jerry Springer: The Opera* (National, 2003), a musical about white trash on reality TV, offended fundamentalist Christians, and the national tour was cut short because of theatres pulling out after protests against the show. In each of these cases, the controversy proved that theatre could be a powerful way of showing us who we are, and that disagreement about such depictions were arguments about our national identity. Incidents such as these also illustrated the fact that prevailing ideas about the tolerance of British culture were under strain.

The most painful example was Gurpreet Kaur Bhatti's *Behzti*, a play about the Sikh community by a British-born playwright from a Sikh background. Set partly in a Gurdwara (temple), the story begins with the disabled but comically foul-mouthed Balbir's attempts to marry off her fun-loving daughter Min. Very soon we see how these two are locked in a mutually torturous relationship. But one part of the story, the fifty-five-year-old Gurdwara elder Mr Sandhu's sexual predations, was even darker, more visceral, and part of Bhatti's attack on religious hypocrisy. Shockingly, his rape of Min (which is not shown) results in the play's older women seeing her as dishonoured rather than abused. On stage, they beat her. Traditional culture comes into conflict with contemporary sensibility. Most provocatively, Mr Sanhu was once in love with Min's father, who is now dead, and his assault on her is like a necrophiliac consummation of a lost love. In the scene in which she is beaten, Min is also gagged – an uncanny symbol of the playwright's own silencing.[27] Yet the work also brimmed with other issues. As Dawinder Bansal, one of the few critics who reviewed the show before it closed, writes: 'Bhatti has not shied away from exploring topical subjects such as homosexuality, corruption, social status and acceptance, suppression, drugs, domestic violence, rape, murder, mixed race relationships and paedophilia.'[28] The name of the play, which means dishonour, obviously touched a raw nerve and one report stated that 'There are people in the Asian community who are more afraid of dishonour – *behzti* – than actually confronting injustice.'[29] Sadly, the *Behzti* incident contributed to an atmosphere in which all religious belief was seen as fanatical and all discussion of the faith of a segregated community as a vulgar provocation. On the other hand, the play is also hopeful in its delightful comedy and energetic moments of dance. Members of a segregated community can rock as well as suffer.

Despite 9/11 and 7/7, it took a while before British playwrights tackled Muslim identity, and the best part of a decade passed before writers such as Alia Bano and Aitha Sen Gupta answered one critic's call for 'a play telling us what it is like to be a Muslim living in Britain'.[30] Before that, Pravesh Kumar wrote two sparky comedies, *The Deranged Marriage* (Rifco, 2004) and *There's Something about Simmy* (Rifco, 2007), which suggest that you can mix the best of both Punjabi and English culture – a kind of masala beans on toast.[31] Female Asian playwrights also grappled with ideas about national identity in flux: the roll-call includes Yasmin Whittaker-Khan, whose controversial courtesan-club drama *Bells* (Kali, 2005) painted a picture of Pakistani men, including religious leaders, as hypocritical and predatory: they advocate tradition but exploit women. In Dolly Dhingra's *Unsuitable Girls* (Leicester/Pilot, 2002), Chumpa appears dressed in a traditional sari while her mobile phone rings unanswered, a neat mix of tradition and modernity that summed up this engagingly contemporary look at young Asian women in search of a mate. Similarly, Alia Bano's award-winning *Shades* (Royal Court, 2009) showed the single Sabrina's search for love getting a helping hand from Zain, her gay flatmate. But when she meets Reza, their mutual attraction is held back by his strong Muslim beliefs, which turn the path of true love into a bumpy ride, as humorous as it is engaging.

Urban ghettos could be segregated by race as well as religion, and one of the success stories of the decade was the greater visibility of black playwrights. For example, Roy Williams's brilliant play *Fallout* offers a vivid snapshot of a group of black teenagers who are completely alienated from mainstream society. Written as a response to the murder of ten-year-old Damilola Taylor in Peckham, south

London, in 2000, it begins with the brutal killing of a studious young African boy, Kwame, by teenagers Emile, Dwayne, Clinton and Perry, and then the rest of the play shows the fallout from this murder. Along with the bad boys are two teenage girls, Shanice and Ronnie. What emerges is a complex account of black youth culture, with its males jockeying for position and respect – one of Emile's motives for kicking Kwame to death is to prove how hard he is. Masculine competition is the organising principle of the ready give-and-take of the teenagers' banter, the heat of their spicy language. And as well as enjoying the delicious texture of their own subcultural chat, these kids also love the highs of drugs and the buzz of committing crime. For them, the posse is an alternative family. Williams describes his mission as going beyond the headline image of black kids as muggers or killers to 'show where these kids are coming from, and to say that this concerns everyone because these are British kids'.[32]

Williams peoples *Fallout* with a variety of characters. Dwayne comes across as the real hard man, the leader. Emile is more unstable, less secure, quicker to loss his cool. Clinton – who, unlike the others, is taking a BTEC – and Perry are Dwayne's sidekicks. At the same time, Shanice and Ronnie have a complex relationship, which Williams shows with a typical mixture of tenderness and force, with Ronnie jealous of Shanice's attractiveness, and Shanice, full of self-doubt, embarrassed by Ronnie's intense feelings towards her. Both girls are aggressive yet insecure. Williams deftly shows how the police investigation – led by Matt, a white liberal, and Joe, a black maverick – makes little headway until Joe focuses on Shanice and Emile, both of whom suffer from a bad conscience. Joe, who comes from the same sink estate, identifies with Kwame because he sees him as someone who, like himself, was working hard to leave poverty behind. Desperate to get a conviction, he coaches Ronnie into making a false witness statement: when the deception is discovered, Joe's taken off the case. At the same time, the sexually insecure Emile is provoked into attacking Dwayne, who responds by threatening him with a gun.

Both Matt and Joe are working in a police force deeply affected by the 1999 Macpherson Report, which accused the Metropolitan Police of being institutionally racist in the wake of the poorly investigated killing of black teenager Stephen Lawrence. Matt is politically correct, but also detached; Joe is contemptuous of the black boys and of the niceties of best practice. He mixes cynicism and truth-telling, mocking Matt's *Guardian*-reading 'wishy-washy liberal crap', and resenting his own role as 'poster boy' for the post-Macpherson Met (97, 50). His provocations suggest that black police officers can be as racist as their white colleagues. Although the teenagers call him a slave as a wind-up, he does indeed have less power than Matt, who finally puts an end to his unorthodox investigations. As Harry Derbyshire points out, 'The root of [Joe's] problems is the same societal division which has given rise to the murder itself.'[33] The play not only vividly portrays a black subculture, it also shows a group of youngsters that have been failed by the system. As well as being about race, this is also a story about class, the underclass. With bad education and poor employment, these kidults drift into gangs in search of self-esteem. But although Joe questions this loser mindset, his method – taking the law into his own hands – proves to be no solution. The class difference between cops and kids is of course expressed in language: one uses standard English, the other a streetsmart semi-patois. For example, when Joe asks, 'Why don't you enlighten me?', Emile answers, 'We ain't tellin yu shit' (39). Joe, however, slips into youth-speak whenever he wants to make a point with the kids.

The original production was directed by Ian Rickson, and Kwame's murder happened just offstage at the start of the play in the cavernous entrance to designer Ultz's stark oval set. With its wire-mesh baseball court fencing separating the actors and audience, this world of dirty-white tiles created a dispiriting sense of human beings caged by their environment. This staging, argues Deirdre Osborne, 'served to replicate a surveillance camera', but also tended to 'alienate the audience'.[34] But not always. Near the end, Joe (played by Lennie James) loses his temper and throws Emile against the fence, a shocking moment when, to quote *Time Out*, 'You don't watch the actors, you watch the frightened punters.'[35] While black commentators were often more critical of the play than white, these kinds of disagreements prove that Williams was dealing with a hot issue, and one which defines our sense of the identity of British black youth.

Fallout was staged at the same time as another successful play about black-on-black violence. Kwame Kwei-Armah's sizzling *Elmina's Kitchen* (National, 2003) transferred in 2005 to the Garrick Theatre, and was widely hyped as the first black British play to be staged in the West End. Kwei-Armah was as newsworthy as his work, being a star of the TV series *Casualty*, graduate of *Fame Academy*, *Newsnight Review* pundit, recording artist and award-winning playwright. His play was the first in a trilogy that looks at the institutions of the black British experience, and continued with *Fix-Up* (National, 2004), about a radical bookshop, and *Statement of Regret*. Set in Elmina's Kitchen, a Caribbean eatery on Hackney's Murder Mile, it is both a powerful family drama and a state-of-theblack-diaspora play. Its historical resonance begins with its title, which echoes the name of an African fort, Elmina Castle, used during the slave trade. In this family story, Deli is a black Briton who's been in prison, but now believes in doing the right thing. However, his son, nineteen-year-old rudeboy Ashley, is tempted by easy loot and peer pressure, and falls prey to his father's mate Digger, a hard West Indian gangsta. Add a couple more characters – Anastasia (a gutsy woman who works in the cafe) and Clifton (Deli's dad) – and the brew begins to bubble. Kwei-Armah takes the theme of personal responsibility in a racist society and cleverly grafts it onto the stomping West Indian comedy, a theatre genre which convulses its audiences with rude innuendo and lewd suggestiveness. With its salty dialogue, and lines as sharp as chilli and as fast as a takeaway, the play rarely lingers too long on the issues it raises. For example, the notion of national identity obsesses Digger, who repeatedly mocks 'You British blacks' (7). When Deli reminds him that he has lived in the UK since he was fourteen, Digger shoots back: 'I was born in Grenada and I've lived in jailhouse all over the world', to which Deli replies, 'Five years in a New York jail don't make you a citizen of the world, motherfucker' (16–17). At another point, Clifton sings a calypso which rhymes 'In England what you must understand' with 'You's a black man in a cold cold land' (55).

In fact, Clifton's character is as pivotal as Deli's to the play's central theme of masculine identity. Having walked out on Elmina, Deli's mother, Clifton represents the irresponsible father who's more interested in sexual adventure than in parenting. By contrast, Deli is the good father who spends time with Ashley, even if he can't keep him out of trouble. Being black means having an absent father, and trying to live up to the images of masculine violence that saturate street culture. Even Anastasia, who tries to save Deli's business by giving it a makeover – beautifully realised by Bunny Christie's design for Angus Jackson's production – asks, 'Why are my men too weak to raise their head above the fucking water' (45). In the end, Deli fails and Digger shoots Ashley. So the play ends on more of a cry of despair than a call for change. The black Britain shown here is a place of violence and despair. Not surprisingly, Kwei-Armah contests this reading, saying that when Ashley dies, 'It is the spirit of Africa saying you need to overcome the shackles [of slavery].'[36]

Many other plays looked at divisions within the black community. One of the freshest was Bola Agbaje's *Gone Too Far!* The two main protagonists, sixteen-year-old British-born Yemi and his older brother Ikudayisi, who has recently arrived from Nigeria, embark on an odyssey across the metropolis. From their first argument with an Asian shopkeeper – 'I LOVE THIS COUNTRY. I NO TERRORIST' (11) – to their tense confrontations with street life that goes by the name of Razer, Flamer and Blazer, the play examines identity and climaxes with Ikudayisi's cry of 'We are all BLACK! WE ARE ALL BLACK AND YOU ARE ACTING LIKE WE ARE ALL DIVIDED! It needs to stop now' (79). Agbaje writes with a freshness and energy that is delightful, and has a clarity of observation that shows how the girls, especially the noisy and posturing Armani, provoke the boys into aggression. Behind the male who draws a knife stands a female egging him on. Director Bijan Sheibani's beautifully evocative production used dance moves to portray violence and emphasised the play's humour. And his final image of Yemi mixing traditional African dress with American street fashion offered an optimistic glimpse of hybrid black British identity.

As Agboluaje's *The Christ of Coldharbour Lane* makes clear, stories about divided communities – in this case between believers and non-believers – are also stories about national identity. Another example of the issue of racial identity being tackled with wry humour is Levi

David Addai's comic *Oxford Street* (Royal Court, 2008), in which Kofi asserts, 'Despite my name I will always be a British-Jamaican.' To which his Ghanaian colleague Emmanuel replies, 'Wid a Ghanaian-shaped head' (54). Other work showed the complexity of the new national mix: Cosh Omar's excellent *The Battle of Green Lanes* (Stratford, 2004) is set in north London and examines the resentments within the Cypriot community. For although the middle-aged Greek-Cypriot Anastasia looks back to Cyprus as 'an ethnographical fruit cake in which the Geek and Turkish currants were mixed up' (57), the new generation has re-created the hatred of the Turk and Greek communities, and moreover the Muslims are split between the easygoing and the fundamentalist. By contrast, in Toby Whithouse's *Jump Mr Malinoff, Jump* (Soho, 2000), about Russian expats in Southend-on-Sea, the two nations are generational, with the intensely moral Pasha, a fifty-five-year-old Russian immigrant, opposing his amoral teenage nephews. Last but not least, David Edgar's *Playing with Fire* examined the political context of a situation in a post-industrial northern town where, in the words of the chair of the public enquiry into local riot, 'There was a series of events, over many months, provoked by, or enacted by, both the white and Asian populations' (96). In an echo of the 2001 Oldham riots – when Asians and white youngsters fought running battles – the council is accused of contributing to 'the segregation of its white and Asian communities by its housing policies' (105), and the riot is race-specific: 'Asians going for white stores in Broughton Moor and whites selecting Asian targets in Thawston' (129). As Edgar says, 'Everything that raises barriers between groups is bad for finding ways for us to look at ourselves and our society.'[37] In general, British playwrights provided few images of hope when creating their portraits of segregated communities.

Racial tensions

One persistant theme was racism. Although, under New Labour, public awareness of this issue was more acute than in previous decades, racial prejudice remained a potent source of social division. One of the most powerful accounts of racism old and new is Roy Williams's much-revived *Sing Yer Heart Out for the Lads*, set in a pub during the 2000 football World Cup qualifier between England and Germany (here sport is an index of national identity). As a pack of England supporters watch their team go down to Germany by one goal, history is being made: this was the last match played at Wembley before the stadium's rebuilding, and defeat precipitated the resignation of England manager Kevin Keegan. 'For an England fan like me, it was bad,' says Williams, 'but, for a dramatist, it was better than winning – the fans' reaction against the Germans was very aggressive and very theatrical.' He was 'keen to write a state-of-the-nation play that asked hard questions about multiculturalism. Whenever we talk about race, we dismiss it too easily with wishy-washy liberal clichés. If we're going to talk about race, let's get ugly.'[38] Although Williams is black, this time most of his characters are white.[39] The King George pub, decorated with St George flags, is run by Gina: her father Jimmy, little son Glen, friends Lee and his brother Lawrie are all white, as are regulars Alan, Becks, Phil and Jason. The black characters are brothers Mark and Barry, plus some minor parts. Most of the regulars are members of a local footie team, and the play focuses on two sets of brothers, Lee and Lawrie as well as Mark and Barry. The key is contrast: black Mark is an embittered ex-soldier while his brother Barry is the team's star player and has painted his face with the St George flag, as well as getting a bulldog tattoo. White Lee is a conscientious policeman while Lawrie is an unemployed hooligan. Support for the England team is the index of identity. As the thuggish Lawrie says, talking about another match, 'It was fuckin war on the streets. Argies, Krauts, coppers, didn't fuckin matter. We were England!' (164). Likewise, Barry is quick to counter any idea that he's 'not white enuff for England' (194). The play's grim ending, in which young Glen stabs Mark to death, shows the result of racial hatred.

The theme of racism is mediated through family conflict. For example, when Jimmy and Gina disagree about immigration, it's also a conflict between father and daughter (187–88). The rivalry between brothers Mark and Barry, and Lee and Lawrie, is also fuelled by domestic tensions. The keynote is complexity. As Professor John

Stokes says, 'Because he works so close to the street, Williams shares his topics with the tabloids – prison conditions, football fans, teenage gangs, racial divides – but he looks for complexity.'[40] In the play, racism takes many forms. The older Alan is a political racist, Lawrie an in-yer-face yob and the others are casual racists, or quickly become racist when pushed. Yet some characters also have sexual relationships across race lines: Mark and Lee have both been Gina's lovers. But when Mark accuses Gina of dumping him because he's black, she replies that the reason was because he was 'boring' (208). Typically, Gina, after abusing some black kids for stealing her son's phone, tells Alan, who has alluded to Enoch Powell's 'Rivers of Blood' speech, 'I don't want to hear that kind of talk in my pub' (186). Adding to the complexity is the way young white kids imitate black street culture: Glen's speech is peppered with 'awrights', 'wass ups' and 'ennits'. At the same time, the black kids have been picking on a young Asian boy: each ethnic group puts down another. And the blacks mock the whites. Most provocatively, Williams gives Alan, the respectable suit-and-tie racist, plenty of room to express his ideas about white supremacy. For example, Alan condemns the thuggish racism of Lawrie, describing a football riot: 'That wasn't been [sic] English, you were acting like a bunch of savages. You were no better than the coons' (197). With his advice to read – 'You want to hide something from the black man, put it in a book' (198) – and his insidious needling of Barry and Mark, Alan is crafty racism personified. Despite that, Mark agrees with some of what he says, saying that some black people 'make me sick to be black' (216).

Sing Yer Heart Out for the Lads was first staged as part of Trevor Nunn's *Transformation* season, directed by Simon Usher, then restaged at the National in 2004 with Ashley Walters (former So Solid Crew rapper) as Barry. (It was also memorably revived by Pilot theatre company in 2006.) Running at about ninety minutes, the play was like a real-time football match. For the 2004 version, director Paul Miller and designer Hayden Griffin placed tables on the stage, allowing audience members to be close to the beer-swigging, slogan-chanting action. Although the play leaves a taste of bitterness, what is its message? 'At the end,' says Howe Kritzer, 'all nuances of individual identity dissolve in the division between black and white. The play offers little hope for progress in race relations.'[41] Such a view is countered by Professor D. Keith Peacock, who argues, somewhat idealistically, that 'awareness' of the complexity of racial relations 'may be a first step in transforming Britain from a multiracial to a multi-cultural society'.[42]

This is certainly a play about national identity. Barry, for example, was born in Britain so he's got as much right to act as a typical football hooligan as anyone else. He's British and his view of being English is as atavistic as that of any white youth. He buys into the national obsession with the Second World War, where victory in the past compensates for defeat in the present. (His team is beaten by the Germans.) This contrasts with Mark's disillusionment with the army, which Barry sees as a patriotic career. Of course, Alan sees British identity as exclusively white, although he despises Lawrie's violence. His idea that white supremacy has to win the argument by appealing to Middle Britain is politically dangerous. By contrast, Lawrie, a defender of the white working class, uses violence for male bonding and sees it as a final solution: whites and blacks must fight it out until 'Lass one standing at the final whistle, wins England' (231). In the end, because of his brother's death, the horrified Barry rubs the flag of St George from his face. But the Britain these men love is not only lost in the past, it never existed even during the days of Empire. They are fighting for a mythical land. By showing this, Williams poses the urgent question: what kind of Britain do we want to live in now?

Racism was tackled in a variety of ways. For example, Kwame Kwei-Armah's *Statement of Regret* is set in a black think-tank and articulates a passionate debate about contemporary racism and how best to fight it. Idrissa, a black Briton of West African heritage, argues that it's self-defeating to 'always blame the white man for our every fucking woe' (183), and comes into conflict with traditional black activist Kwaku, son of a West Indian migrant. When, in a desperate attempt to get publicity for his failing organisation, Kwaku argues that reparations for slavery should be paid to West Indians rather than to Africans, he stirs up a huge controversy. The play is packed full of ideas, and buzzes with appealing characters and provocative theories about 'post-traumatic slave syndrome' (195, 220), as well as the right way forward for the race-relations industry. Other plays explored similar subjects. Most ambitious of all was the Tricycle's 2009 *Not Black & White* season, which consisted of Kwei-Armah's hectic *Seize the Day*, which created a fiction in which a black TV personality could run for the office of Mayor of London; Roy Williams's *Category B*, which examined power hierarchies in a prison where most of the inmates are black or Asian; and Bola Agbaje's *Detaining Justice*, about a migrant's trials and tribulations. As indicated by its title, the season presented an engagingly nuanced, powerfully written and complex picture of race in Britain today. Similarly strong was debbie tucker green's *Random* (Royal Court, 2008), where the family of the knife-crime victim is initially reluctant to let the police into their home: 'Dad always said / 'Don't bring no Polices back — / don't let no Polices in' / same thing he'd say bout white people —' (30). Depressingly, all of the guys on the victim's posters are, his sister says, 'as young and black and dead as he is now' (48).[43] Although the family is black, and the parents have been written as if they were migrants rather than British-born, it is interesting that their grieving is so typically English. Heads down, dumb with shock and despair, both Mum and Dad prefer silence and solitude to cussing and company. It's a dignified and quietly devastating account of British society today.

Equally contemporary was Ryan Craig's *The Glass Room*, a play which debated the issue of holocaust denial, partly inspired by the case of historian David Irving, who was condemned in 2000 as racist for denying the Nazi Holocaust of European Jewry. In Craig's play, Jewish human-rights lawyer Myles agrees to defend Elena, a controversy-seeking historian. She claims that doubting established accounts of the Holocaust is not racist, but good history: history is 'a constant reassessment of events' (28). She also attacks the hypocrisy of prosecuting historians when leaders such as Bush and Blair mislead their people. 'Our government and our media create a tapestry of lies and people are dazzled into submission. And they call me a denier. The whole country's in denial' (107). But when Myles realises just how much of a racist she is, he also understands his own identity better. *The Glass Room* presents a flattering picture of Britain as a land where the best minds are tolerant, open-minded, slow to anger, but righteous when roused.

Other plays explored racism in local contexts. Joy Wilkinson's excellent *Fair* (Finborough, 2005), for example, is set in Lancashire and shows what happens when Melanie meets Railton at a fairground, and they end up in bed. Soon after, she discovers that he's a racist and the play accurately explores the resentments of the white working class, often using the ghost of Railton's dead dad as a third character. For while Melanie campaigns for a multiracial mela, Railton wants an English St George's Fair. At one point, Railton mocks Melanie's middle-class bohemian identity: 'Northerner? Londoner? English? British? European? Westerner? Earthling? Some liberal pick 'n' mix bag' (26). Here the white working class is seen as the problem. Similarly, in Atiha Sen Gupta's thoughtful *What Fatima Did* . . . (Hampstead, 2009), the teenage Fatima throws her friends and family into confusion when she decides to start wearing the hijab, and the climactic scene comes when her white ex-boyfriend George arrives at her fancy-dress eighteenth-birthday party draped in the flag of St George (although his folks are Irish) and then provocatively turns the flag into a hijab (79–85). Likewise, D. C. Moore's *Alaska* (Royal Court, 2007) looks at how a twenty-four-year-old failure, Frank, who works at a cinema kiosk, racially abuses Mamta, his new supervisor. In their final confrontation, Frank provocatively argues that black and Asian peoples commit worse crimes on each other than they suffered under British imperialism: 'Cos I'm white, you care more about what I say than what all those billions of black and brown fuckers actually do' (48). Like Williams, Moore introduces complex cross-currents, and shows how Frank's insecurities about his sexual identity are part of his racist mindset. Plays such as these illustrate the fact that there is no such thing as racial purity, and argue that racism in Britain results from a mix of social failure and sexual anxiety.

Devolved identities

In the past decade, the United Kingdom was divided not merely into two nations, however class obsessed and racially segregated, but four:

England, Scotland, Wales and Northern Ireland. As you'd expect, playwrights did tackle political devolution, although not explicitly. The foremost dramatist of Scottish identity, David Greig, wrote two plays which examined Scotland's history in the twentieth century. *Victoria* (RSC, 2000) looked at the life of a rural coastal community in 1936, 1974 and 1996, while *Outlying Islands* (Traverse, 2002) shows what happens when two English ornithologists visit a remote Scottish island in 1939. In these plays, history is a special place where a discussion of national identity is performed, and, in the words of Steve Blandford, the recurrent sense is of a 'conversation' which refuses 'any attempt to "fix" a new post-devolutionary identity'.[44] Ideas remain fluid and changeable; being Scottish is a work in progress. The plays are also, says Nadine Holdsworth, examples of the trend to depict the Highlands and Islands as 'places that exist on the edge, on the border of the nation [. . .] that throw questions of personal and national identity into sharp relief'.[45] Such work, along with Greig's *Damascus*, exemplifies his characteristic stance, which is, in Professor Dan Rebellato's words, 'always at least two things at once': it 'insists on a global perspective as well as local engagement, sees what divides us as well as what connects us'.[46] In *Damascus*, Paul, a Scottish writer who sells English-language texts, travels to Syria and meets Muna, his Syrian contact, Wasim, her boss, and receptionist Zakaria. His dealings with them are full of linguistic and cultural misunderstandings. Despite his gauche attempts to make friends, he is condemned to be an 'Englishman' abroad, divided from the rest of the world partly because the locals insist on seeing him as English rather than Scottish. The play is a profoundly rich text which, in Philip Howard's original production, was nimbly performed and included moments of magical music making. With its ideas about a 'Damascus of the mind' in which layers of history make a 'place of infinite possibility' (65, 64), the play suggests that national identity is infinitely malleable. In the end, its portrait of a blundering Brit who glimpses, if only for a moment, the possibility of a different kind of life serves as a metaphor for the state of the nation as a whole, and especially its Scottish part. Greig has, in Peter Billingham's words, 'distanced himself from the simplistic and reductive politics of national or nationalist identity', and here he deals with the theme in an allusive, poetic and tantalisingly thought-provoking fashion.[47] By contrast with this view of a morphing nationhood, English national identity seems depressingly fixed in the past.

Likewise, Douglas Maxwell's grimly hilarious *If Destroyed True* (Paines/Dundee, 2005) exemplifies both a distinctly Scottish the-atricality, with its direct address to the audience and big vaudeville acting, and a satirical appraisal of the new nation. Set in a fictional New Flood, the play is looks at what happens to Vincent, born when his junkie mum committed suicide by jumping off a building, as he reacts to his birthplace winning the Worst Town in Scotland award. The place is certainly in a parlous state: 'All the traditional social ills are iller here than anywhere else: unemployment, health, income, education, crime' (76). The solution offered is a high-tech quick-fix: universal internet connection, plus the demented rhetoric of progress. But, as Vincent points out, this will only make everyone lonelier: 'You're taking away the only thing we had going for us: that we're all stuck here geographically, physically, a community cos we have to be' (84). As directed by John Tiffany, the play had a comic and verbal inventiveness that itself suggested a forward-looking nation. As Nadine Holdsworth argues, the best new plays from Scotland 'propose a nation that is never static, always in process, proud of its heritage as well as its increasing heterogeneity and, above all, one that can surprise and provoke engagement beyond the confines of a restrictive and potentially damaging nationalism'.[48] Similarly, David Pattie argues that Scottish writers such as Greig, Gregory Burke and David Harrower all tend 'to suggest that national and cultural identity is always in the process of formation, that it is always up for grabs', always fluid.[49]

In Wales, local writers have made a similar point. Welsh play-wright Gary Owen's exhilarating *Crazy Gary's Mobile Disco* (Paines/Sgript Cymru, 2001), for example, is both a wild account of a group of small-town losers, and an acerbic comment on life in a national backwater. Set on a Saturday night in an unnamed Welsh town, it focuses on three lads in their mid-twenties, each of which is still tethered to their school reputations: psycho-bully Gary, mentally challenged Mathew and brainy dreamer Russell. In three interlocking monologues, the piece – which is written with an energy that makes the lines leap off the page and ricochet around the room – tells the story of Gary's night out at a local pub. When he gatecrashes a party, he spots Mary, who is 'major-league fuckable' (13). Yet just as Gary connects with Mary, Mathew's monologue takes over and we learn of his vivid fantasy life, his problems at the job centre and his religious ideals which make him feel guilty for dropping a coke bottle in the street. In the final monologue, Russell – who lives with Mary – insists on leaving her, until he sees Gary chatting her up at the party. Incensed, he provokes a fight in the street, during the course of which he picks up the bottle that Mathew dropped – and slashes Gary's neck with it. As Gary dies in Mary's arms, Russell leaves town. Although this a play about masculinity, it is also about story-telling and the text sings joyfully of the contours of its own lurid imagination, leavened by moments of spectacular grossness, as when Mathew stuffs a dead cat into a post box. At the same time, *Crazy Gary's Mobile Disco* paints a striking picture, all acid-glow colours and purple-shadow effects, of dead-end life in smalltown Wales. With its petty resentments, vulgar emotions and mindless violence, it's such a suffocatingly awful place that Russell's final escape has all the glory of a rebirth. Owen is clearly one of the most confident playwrights to emerge from Wales in the 2000s and his English-language work is an example of British new writing, all verbal acrobatics and in-yer-face ferocity. His *Ghost City* (Chapter Arts, 2004), for example, in the words of Heike Roms, 'depicts fragmentation, failed communications and latent violence as the defining experience of contemporary urban life'.[50] Although Owen has written plays in Welsh, he has, in Steve Blandford's analysis, 'escaped' the 'burden' of having to explicitly represent his nation.[51]

Like Owen, a playwright such as Catherine Tregenna is symptomatic of a 'stir around Welsh playwriting getting in on the "Cool Cymru" act'.[52] Tregenna's *Art and Guff* (Sgript Cymru/Soho, 2001) features two 'dull boys from Kidwelly', once again smalltown escapees, in a squalid flat in London, where the locals see them as 'provincial', calling them 'Bill and Ben' (38, 96). But their vision of everyday life in Wales is grim: 'I don't want to listen to no ticking clocks above diamond patterned carpets telling me it's time to take a queen cake from the tin and warm the bastard pot' (51). The two young men then fulfil the prophecy articulated by another character: 'Show a Welshman a hundred doors and he will go through the one marked "Self-Destruct"' (63). These kind of plays are, as Steve Blandford accurately points out, more about masculinity in general than Wales in particular. Other Welsh theatre-makers, such as Ed Thomas and Mike Pearson, have, says Heike Roms, a 'bleak view' of national identity, which sees being Welsh as a 'malady'.[53]

Turning to Northern Ireland, the work of Gary Mitchell has strong local roots. In particular, his award-winning *The Force of Change* (Royal Court, 2000) and *Loyal Women* (Royal Court, 2003) powerfully explored the culture of Loyalism. Both plays use the structure of a finely plotted thriller to peer into the heart of a rapidly changing part of the UK: the first examines the role of Royal Ulster Constabulary and the second a Belfast family with links to the paramilitary Ulster Defence Association (UDA). In *The Force of Change*, the police are shown not only to be collude with the Loyalist paramilitaries but also to be confused about their changing role, and by new splits in their community. As one of them says, 'The IRA must be laughing their heads off at us. Loyalist feuds in Portadown. The LVF taking on the UVF and now this. UDA members threatening police officers. Where will it end?' (81–2). The question goes unanswered. In *Loyal Women*, four generations are shown: thirty-something Brenda, her old mother-in-law, her teenage daughter and her daughter's daughter. When the local Women's UDA decides to meet in her house, her desire to protect her daughter from involvement with Loyalist violence comes into conflict with her loyalties to the group. In a long interrogation scene, the women question Adele, who has a Catholic boyfriend and is considered a security risk. The codes of conduct are rigid: as Brenda says about her husband's infidelity, 'One mistake is all it takes [. . .] Once a man is unfaithful . . . disloyal to you [her daughter] or me, that's it' (78). And although Brenda is promoted in the UDA because of her adaptability to change, she wants to quit: 'I used to have a list it read like this: protestants, Ulster, the Queen, Britain and fuck everything else but I changed that list to me, my mum, my daughter and her daughter' (85). The two loves of her life were her husband and her country, 'and both of them have let me down' (86). While Mitchell's work portrays a traditional community adapting, however unwillingly, to political change, it also shows how, in Nadine Holdsworth's words, 'The largest threat to the Loyalist community is itself and the masculinist culture of allegiance, confrontation, intimidation, interrogation and violent reprisal.'[54] Or as Amelia Howe Kritzer puts it, 'People trapped in this unending division find their world limited.'[55] Northern Irish identity is shown as crisis-ridden, a leftover from the past.

Equally ambitious are the plays of Owen McCafferty, especially *Closing Time* (National, 2002) and *Scenes from the Big Picture* (National, 2003), which together give memorable impressions of Belfast life today. If *Closing Time* deals mainly with the personal misery of emotionally damaged drunks, *Scenes from the Big Picture* covers twenty-four hours of city life during a Belfast summer. Once again, recent politics have left their mark; as *The Times* reported:

> After all, there aren't many parts of the United Kingdom where a drug-dealer may get kneecapped, or brothers find a cache of arms buried in their dead da's allotment, or the authorities finally fulfil an obsessive father's hopes by discovering the body of the son who was murdered 15 years ago.[56]

But this panorama, given a bold production by Peter Gill on a bare set full of blue furniture, also conveys more common agonies: a man married to a woman he doesn't love, a junkie beaten up by her dealer, harassed shopkeepers and troubled abattoir workers. Because McCafferty doesn't say who is Protestant and who is Catholic, he implicitly indicates that such divisions are becoming less important, and that economic background, and class, are the main determinants of individual life chances. Just like the rest of the UK. In a world of poverty, where 'the only thing these people's interested in – the colour of yer readies' and 'unless ya have the money to back it up you'll be treated like a joke' (50), there's not much time to spend on musing about national identity. Like Tinderbox's multi-authored, site-specific *convictions* (Crumlin Road Courthouse, 2000), such plays are examples of theatre-makers, in Tom Maguire's words, 'reimagining Northern Ireland, challenging the clichés of the Troubles play and the stereotypes to which it has contributed'.[57]

If Northern Irish writers, working in a culture squeezed between the Republic of Ireland and the British mainland, sometimes write with a greater sense of urgency, one of the best post-Peace Process plays was written by south London-born Martin McDonagh, a hugely talented British playwright and film-maker. His award-winning comedy *The Lieutenant of Inishmore* (RSC, 2001) is one of the wildest black farces of the decade, and justly, in Wilson Milan's splatterfest production, enjoyed a West End transfer. Set in the early 1990s, this time the focus shifts onto the Irish Republicans. Enter young Padraig, a crazed member of a Republican splinter group, who tortures drug dealers and leaves bombs in chip shops, while at the same time having a grossly sentimental attachment to his cat, Wee Thomas. It's a joke that reverberates through the play. At one point, a group of Republicans debate the role of cats in the reunification of Ireland: 'I don't remember agreeing to batter cats when I joined the INLA' (28); 'Is it happy cats or is it an Ireland free we're after?' (30). This mockery of the rhetoric of Republicanism is followed by a climactic bloodbath – which turns out to have been totally unnecessary. As one survivor glumly exclaims, 'So all this terror has been for absolutely nothing?' (68). Although this eye-poppingly satirical play passed off without provoking a response from Republicans, academics were divided on its significance. While Mary Luckhurst attacked McDonagh for pouring 'contempt on the peace process', and questioned the radicality of his 'excess' and 'his use of stereotypes' to undermine British ideas of Irishness, Catherine Rees praised the comedy for being 'a clear and absolute political satire'.[58] But while this debate confirmed the play's timeliness, it is also true that, in Blandford's words, it 'is one of the most direct dramatic responses to the changing shape of the country'.[59] The ability to laugh at the ideology of Republican paramilitaries – and the embattled mind-set of splinter groups – is surely a sign of the strength of the new Northern Ireland. And isn't a changing national identity enhanced by a comic response to the tragedies of history?

If the best post-devolution theatre from the three corners of the disunited kingdom did not always address questions of national identity directly, its growing confidence, willingness to experiment and openness to diverse influences was itself surely a mark of an independence of spirit. But while the three nations seemed to be moving, England often felt as if it was immobile, stuck in a rut of old ideas of a split nation.

In the past decade, plays about a divided nation were a staple of British theatre, and they took a huge variety of forms, speaking in a babble of voices. Generally, they were better at providing vivid images of social fissure, whether by class or by religion or by race, than at offering solutions. Cultural and racial segregation became the number one social ill. With its stage images of ugly chavs, impoverished mums, feckless dads, thuggish kids, crims and gangstas, it was only the flashes of humour or glimmers of hope that prevented total despair. Even the countryside was awash with urban ills. These images of a divided Britain meant that while we knew that we were living in an unjust society, we didn't know how to fix it. If the glum resignation of grinding poverty was only glimpsed when someone was stabbed, or when a riot resulted from social segregation, does that mean that we just don't want to know? Have we apathetically come to accept social division as just another fact of life? After all, isn't the personal more important than the political?

6 LOVE HURTS

Flora   Our families hate each other.
George   Our families can go to hell.

(Charlotte Jones, *Humble Boy*, 89)

Britain in the 2000s was a place where love not only tore you apart, but also scattered the fragments to the winds. Marriage was never less popular. In 2007, for the first time the number of births to unmarried couples exceeded those to married ones. If the traditional family was dead, the new extended families developed in eye-wateringly complex ways, with a plethora of relationships, from single motherhood to multiple varieties of step-parenthood. Every new lover brought a handful of strangers into your life. These blended families were complex, chaotic and child-centred. Despite an epidemic of teen mums, most mothers have never been older. Women, as ever, were good at multi-tasking (they have to be); men, as ever, were in crisis (still). More kids lived at home, and we were told that every child matters, even if some matter more than others. A new social divide opened between Grandboomers, who have everything, and youth, who have nothing. Old divisions take new forms: boys, with their toys, were kidults. Girls were loud, or cheeky, had one-track minds, and wouldn't be held down. Women enjoy their middle youth. Female bloggers such as Bitchy Jones and Belle de Jour developed clit lit with online sex stories. Speed dating became popular. But despite the bootie calls, what most people were looking for is love, actually. In the sex war, both women and men claimed victim status. Desire continued to diversify. So metrosexuals, transgendered queens, gays, queers and post-gays partied on, and many were now in civil partnerships. Others offer wisdom from the frontline of bedroom wars: while therapist Susie Orbach points out how 'the sexual today has been hyper-stimulated', playwright Tim Fountain discovers that 'many of our strongest national obsessions were as present in people's sex lives as they are in their everyday lives'.[1]

Family favourites

In the 2000s, new writing rediscovered the family play. In the previous decade, the typical drama had been about 'me and my mates', with parents typically represented as absent fathers or their surrogates. With the return of the family play, British theatre rediscovered conflicts between generations, divided loyalties and emotional density. A fine example is Charlotte Jones's award-winning and much-revived *Humble Boy* (National, 2001), a tragi-comedy about the relationships of Felix, a thirty-five-year-old Cambridge astrophysicist who, following the sudden death of his father, returns to stay with his mother, Flora, in her Middle England home. Shocked by bereavement, Felix is suicidal. Added to the mix are Flora's best friend, Mercy Lott, Jim the gardener, Flora's not-so-secret lover George Pye and George's daughter, Rosie. While Felix struggles to reconcile himself to his loss, his mother is thinking about marrying George, and it also emerges that Felix and Rosie were once lovers. By the end of the play, Rosie reveals that she was pregnant with Felix's child when he left her to go to Cambridge and that the seven-year-old is called Felicity. As the couple consider an uneasy reconciliation, Jim – with whom Felix has been chatting throughout the play – turns out to be the ghost of his father.

A former actress, Jones emerged as a playwright in the 1990s with a characteristic style of gutsy realism laced with affectionate loopiness, and *Humble Boy* is partly a delightful comedy of English middle-class manners and partly a richly allusive masterpiece. Both amusing and quirky, the text's metaphors come bouncing at you with zesty confidence. Talking about the way Flora had her entomologist husband's bees removed immediately after his death, Jim says, 'Very sad. A hive without its bees. It says it all, doesn't it?' (10), a delicate reference not only to loss but to the dominance of Flora as Queen Bee of the family. Then Felix's description of his family draws beautifully on scientific metaphors: 'It's like my mother was the big force – gently warping everything around her. And my father was the little force, fizzing away quietly on a microscopic level. But I can't bring them together' (44) – neither can he, as a scientist, bring about a reconciliation between relativity theory and quantum mechanics, the much-sought-after 'theory of everything'. For Felix, mum is a 'black hole' (30), who warps anything in her orbit. But when the refreshingly down-to-earth Rosie talks about her daughter, she borrows an image from Felix's work: 'My life is full of Eureka moments' (85). As Jones says, 'What really attracted me to string theory was the language in which it is described: almost religious. All about dwelling in possibility and questing after the unknowable, living in between doubt and fear.'[2] The play uses science as a metaphor for emotional choices, and represents Middle England as divided between the desire to be exceptional and the challenges of the ordinary.

Set in '*a pretty country garden*' (1), the play not only fizzes with witty dialogue, it also includes some positively cannibalistic symbolism. For example, the central scene, a family lunch party, begins with Mercy mistaking the urn holding Jim's ashes for pepper, and adding some to the gazpacho. For the rest of the scene, the audience waits for the cast to start eating a soup garnished with a dead man's ashes. It's a brilliantly theatrical episode. Then, when Felix arrives, he is wearing one of his father's old suits, which is much too small for him, a metaphor of his desire to achieve more than his father did. As a family drama, the conflict between Felix and his mother is written with wit and precision, from Flora's sarcastic point that 'Everything that goes wrong in your child's life can be laid squarely at your feet' (34) to Felix's exhausted 'We have all said enough' (78).

Humble Boy has its origins in the National's 2000 production of *Hamlet*, in which Jones's husband, Paul Bazely, played Guildenstern. Jones says that she also had 'this image of a golden boy', whose prospects are marred by depression,[3] and her references to Shakespeare's play deepen its resonance as a picture of Englishness. The casting reflected the connections: Simon Russell Beale played Hamlet and Felix; Denis Quilley Polonius and George, and Cathryn Bradshaw Ophelia and Rosie. Diana Rigg starred as Flora. One critic felicitously summed up the acting:

Diana Rigg plays Felix's mother Flora Humble, all hard heart, sharp heels, and back copies of *Vogue*; Marcia Warren portrays a scene-stealing Mercy, a family friend evocative of a church mouse that has bought its assertiveness from Oxfam, and Simon Russell Beale becomes the hapless Felix with a donnish bitchiness which can lapse quite suddenly into heart-rending pathos.[4]

In director John Caird and designer Tim Hatley's production the set was a plant-filled summer garden, with an empty beehive looming over the patio, and long grasses stroking the feet of the audience. Here the family life of Middle England is eccentric, ruled by strong women and riven by parental infidelity. Yet it also shows the refreshing power of hope and happiness (the names Felix and Felicity are no accident); in a nation of broken homes, *Humble Boy* offered images of emotional healing.

Elsewhere, happy families were an endangered species. In Michael Wynne's *The People Are Friendly* (Royal Court, 2002), Michelle is an ambitious business executive who holds a housewarming on her return to Birkenhead after years in London. Her family is completely contemporary. The older generation, unemployed shipwright John and religious Kathleen, contrast with their children, Michelle and her stay-at-home sister Donna, who had her first child, Kirsty, at the age of sixteen. Her second, Eddie, is mute, and Kirsty, a gobby teenager who deals drugs and wants to be famous, already has her own sprog. By contrast, Michelle is having trouble conceiving. Another contrast is the sisters' relationship to their father: Michelle is daddy's 'girlie', his favourite (40, 70, 72). When she left home, he 'had to put up with your mother and Donna ganging up on me' (71). The two sisters agree that men – Michelle's classy Robert and Donna's streetsmart Brian – are useless, even if they can't agree about the future of Birkenhead. For while John dreams of the Cammell Laird shipyard reopening, Michelle has been employed as a consultant to manage its closure. In the sisters' final showdown, Wynne stages a debate between nostalgia for the town's shipbuilding past and concern for its post-industrial present. Like the Slippery Nipple cocktail that fuels Michelle's party,

Wynne's style is heartwarming, with a hidden kick and a cruel after-taste. At times, the sheer exuberance of the mouthy humour drowns out the clichés, and the play's snarls of genuine anger subvert its pre-dictability. Zestfully directed by Dominic Cooke, with Sally Rogers (Michelle) and Michelle Butterly (Donna), the play, as Amelia Howe Kritzer points out, focuses 'on the less tangible loss of pride in doing something worthwhile. This sense of pride has linked Michelle and her father, but now it divides them.'⁵ Cooke adds, 'It's basically a metaphor for Blair's Britain and the conflict between old Labour or working-class values and "the third way".'⁶ The depressing idea of the distressed family as metaphor for a nation torn apart by class is slightly mitigated by the fact that, alone at the end, Michelle comforts Kirsty's baby, which has been forgotten when the rest of her family walked out.

Comfort is also central to Simon Stephens's award-winning *On the Shore of the Wide World* (Manchester, 2005), which examines three generations of a Stockport family over nine months, a time pregnant with meaning. As the title's allusion to Keats's sonnet 'When I Have Fears that I May Cease To Be' suggests, it's also a play about the fear of dying before you've experienced love. For each generation of the Holmes family – sixtysomethings Charlie and Ellen, thirtysomethings Peter and Alice, and their teenage children Alex and Christopher – the family is problematic. As Alex's girlfriend, Sarah, says, 'Marriage is odd [. . .] sometimes I think it's a completely insane idea' (117). Similarly, when grandad Charlie tells Alex that, in each generation, the quality of parenting improves, his grandson responds, 'I'm not sure' (123). The play is sprinkled with ideas which question optimistic notions of monogamy, and love in every generation emerges only after a struggle with more selfish passions, and even then it feels provisional, fleeting. Inspired perhaps by the tightness of Keats's sonnet, Stephens's play is divided into four sections, each of which focuses on one family member: Christopher, Alex, Alice and Peter. At the end of section one, fifteen-year-old Christopher is killed in a road accident. The incident casts a deep shadow over the rest of the play. You feel it's always in the thoughts of the characters, especially when – in a scene which stretches credulity to the limit – Alice meets and then contemplates having a fling with the man who drove the car that killed her son. In this play, Stephens's writing style recognises, in the words of Professor Dan Rebellato, evasions but also imagines 'moments when people reach out to say just what they mean'.[7] At the end of the play, the whole family cook Sunday lunch together, and the show – delicately directed by Sarah Frankcom – ended with the men quietly preparing the table. The British family, despite its moments of masculine violence or emotional cowardice, somehow survives the worst. Love might shrink, but most people are decent.

Many family dramas dealt with familiar domestic issues, from the school run to running out of milk, but some also came up with memorable visual images: in Amelia Bullmore's ever-popular *Mammals* (Bush, 2005), Jane and Kev's children – four-year-old Betty and six-year-old Jess – were played by adults (Helena Lymbery and Jane Hazlegrove in Anna Mackmin's production). The effect was to physically enlarge their chaotic effect on the harassed adults. In Lucinda Coxon's excellent *Happy Now?* (National, 2008), Johnny's wife Kitty meets the charismatic Michael at a conference hotel. When she ends up in his room, the tensions between the two of them explode into a pillow fight which, in Thea Sharrock's production, was a glorious moment of fluff-billowing anarchy. But if plays such as these cast a rueful eye on post-feminist clichés about women being able to 'have it all', they seemed only to offer a stoical endurance. Mike Leigh's stimulating ensemble piece *Two Thousand Years* (National, 2005) added a political element to domestic tensions: here a north London Jewish family, proud of its own secular traditions, is threatened by the fact that one of its children, Josh, has become a devout Jew. 'It's like having a Muslim in the house,' says his exasperated father (20). If Josh is, in one critic's words, 'another in Leigh's line of unresponsive and resentful children', the final image is of father and son sitting down to play chess, a symbol of their reconciliation, however uneasy.[8] In Bryony Lavery's lovely *A Wedding Story* (Birmingham/Sphinx, 2000), a hilariously farting whoopee cushion deflates traditional ideas of pure heterosexual courtship in a play where the disintegrating marriage of Peter and Evelyn (affected by her Alzheimer's) is balanced by the newly flowering love of their daughter

Sally for Grace, a woman she meets at a wedding.[9] Elsewhere, reconciliation could prove elusive. Gurpreet Khar Bhatti's *Behsharam* (*Shameless*) (Birmingham/Soho, 2001) examines two generations of an Asian family in Birmingham. After their ineffectual father remarries, his two daughters, Jaspal and Sati, react in different ways: Jaspal starts having sex for money and getting out of her head while Sati carries a cardboard cutout of Arsenal footballer Ian Wright, and chats to that. More seriously, debbie tucker green's *Born Bad* (Hampstead, 2003) shows a religious, hymn-humming family where the sexual abuse of Dawta by her Dad has been organised by his wife and witnessed by her sister, while another sister and a brother have different views about what happened. As directed by Kathy Burke, this account of power relationships in a black family used the stage image of a circle of chairs which, in Amelia Howe Kritzer's words, 'never opens to permit the characters to exit the situation' – there is no way out of the abusive family.[10]

Some domestic dramas evoked a genre as familiar as curled-edge sandwiches and blended whisky – the family reunion play. Simon Mendes da Costa's comedy *Losing Louis* (Hampstead, 2005), for example, is set in Louis and Bobbie's marital bedroom and shows how the secrets of past infidelity are discovered when their children, Tony and Reggie, plus their wives Sheila and Elizabeth, come to the funeral of Louis, a widower whose philandering in the 1950s results in present upheavals. Robin Lefèvre's production starred Alison Steadman as the vulgar Sheila, proving that an Estuary whine is all that's needed to raise a laugh, while Lynda Bellingham's Elizabeth had a nice line in frosty contempt. Truth-telling results in a predictable conclusion: Reggie tells Tony, 'We obviously hate the sight of each other. It seems we've always hated each other' (98). Yes, this is a nation of explosive families.

Like many contemporary black plays, Michael Bhim's *Pure Gold* is also a family drama. When Simon, an ex-bus driver, messes up an interview for a menial job, his wife Marsha is unimpressed. Even worse, he's been hanging around with his cousin Paul, a no-good criminal. Added to this, the couple's young son Anthony has a birthday coming up and Simon is determined to treat him. Bhim's play, directed by Indhu Rubasingham, began with a riveting scene which compellingly explores family life and managed to convey, without being banal or predictable, what it feels like to be black and poor. Simon's experience of having no money feels as if 'every way you turn, you can feel that noose, turning tighter round your neck' (17). But his aspiration to be the 'captain' of his family 'ship' (10) is compromised by the temptation offered by crime.

In the plethora of plays about family crises some moments stood out as sharply as a mangled wedding ring. In Kevin Elyot's *Forty Winks* (Royal Court, 2004), one character says, 'Families! If there's one thing worse than your own, it's other people's. All those secret signs and codes – like the fucking Masons' (26), and in Nick Stafford's *Love Me Tonight* (Hampstead, 2004), by the time Moira says 'This family's a mess and we always shall be' (68), the death of one of her children, sixteen-year-old Vince, has exposed the cracks in her relationship with Roy. In Winsome Pinnock's *One Under*, the main character's declaration that 'Family, that's what it's all about, ennit?' (109) is contrasted with the desire of the main male characters to escape. Similarly, when Maurice, in Matt Charman's *The Five Wives of Maurice Pinder* (National, 2007), says, 'The most important thing in the world is family' (38), this sentiment is underscored by the fact that he is a polygamist! In Mike Bartlett's tightly scripted *My Child* a separated couple fight for the affections of their increasingly confused nine-year-old son: the crisis comes when the Man, inspired by the pressure group Fathers for Justice, kidnaps his Child. As the playwright comments, 'A family is somewhere you find the most unconditional love but it's also the place where you find the most violence, the most danger.'[11] Likewise, in Lucy Caldwell's award-winning *Leaves* (Royal Court/ Druid, 2007), nineteen-year-old Lori bleakly concludes, 'I don't think that things ever really get any better' (101). One is tempted to sympathise with Deirdra in Che Walker's *Flesh Wound* (Royal Court, 2003) when she says, 'Biological don't matter. Iss a lie that you can't pick your family, you can. And you can unpick it. And thass what I'm choosing to do' (57). Hearing dialogue such as this, you could be forgiven for thinking that the disputatious family was sometimes a metaphor for a conflicted nation.[12]

Couples in crisis

Although family plays made a comeback, the couples-in-crisis play certainly lost no ground in the 2000s. One of the most wicked, and most successful, of these was *Dinner*, by Moira Buffini, a playwright whose work in the 1990s immediately attracted attention because of its wit and flair. In this bittersweet fantasy about one woman's revenge on her deceitful spouse, Paige, a rich woman, is hosting a celebration for Lars, her self-help guru husband who has just published another book. Served by a silent Waiter, the guests are a cross-section of British society: politically correct artist Wynne, gloomy scientist Hal and his newsreader wife Siân.

As Paige attacks the conceited Lars, insults her guests and forms a bond with Mike, an intruding cockney van-man, the result is a wonderfully humorous, gobsmackingly offensive and surreal satire on social mores. More than half its pleasure lies in hearing Paige saying things that polite society habitually keeps quite. As Jonathan Croll observes, 'intelligent, cynical and savagely witty, Paige is the hostess from hell'.[13] So, as the dishes appear, starting with Primordial Soup and followed by Apocalypse of Lobster, the play mocks the self-satisfied Lars, with his ideas about the 'psyche-drive' (26), as well as the middle-class Wynne, and her New Age banalities. Microbiologist Hal and his 'newsbabe' (19) get similar treatment, while Mike's down-to-earth charm adds a dash of real life. But although the main conflict is between Paige and Lars, Hal and Siân also lock horns. As things turn 'really ugly' (71), Paige serves her final tribute to her husband, a symbolic dish composed of ice and rubbish from the dustbin.

Lovingly directed by Buffini's sister, Fiona, the play starred Harriet Walter, a contemporary Cruella wrapped in a scarlet dress to die for, a woman who mixes herself a cocktail of bitter melancholy and sweet irony. The end is suffused with ambiguity: has Paige really paid the Waiter to help her commit suicide, or did she originally plan to kill Lars? Why does he refuse to kill her? And why does she long to die in the first place? In fact, Buffini rewrote the ending. In the original, the innocent Mike dies, a working-class pawn of rich folk's games; in the second version, the hostess kills herself. In Buffini's words, 'Ultimately, greed eats itself. Paige engineers her pact with the eternal footman.'[14] The revelation that Lars plans to divorce Paige explains her pre-emptive strike, if not the couple's collapse. By not revealing exactly what split them apart, Buffini suggests that crisis is a natural state and that the longer the marriage, the more violent the explosion. When the play transferred to the West End, there was no consensus over its meaning. While the *Guardian* said it conveyed 'a real understanding of the despair that haunts the empty lives of the rich and successful', *The Times* opined that it 'isn't very trenchant [. . .] as a study of representative Britons'.[15] A fantasy evocation of contemporary Britain, it is also allegorical, recalling the medieval myth of Death coming to the banquet and taking one of the revellers. As an image of the nation, it is hardly optimistic.

Some couples-in-crisis plays gave conventional theatre form a slap in the face: the best example was Anthony Neilson's storming *Stitching* (Bush, 2002), the intense love story of Stu and Abby, an argumentative couple who are first seen discussing whether to keep the child she has just conceived. Flashing forward and back, the fragmentary play shows how they decide to have the baby to bring them closer. But, while the parents argue, the child is killed by a car: 'We were too busy fighting to hear him die,' says Abby grimly (44). Grief splits them up, then reunites them. This dark material is delivered through dialogues that are psychological double-binds, intricately written and excruciatingly familiar. As Stu says, 'We can't be what we're not. And we can't be what we were' (45). Certainly, this grieving couple find themselves at the extremes of experience, and their attempts to recapture their original feelings are desperate. At one point, Stu claims that he had his first orgasm when he was looking at 'a book about Auschwitz. All these naked women in a line, waiting to go into a gas chamber. I remember thinking how hairy their cunts were' (29). At another terrible moment, Abby sews up her vagina. As she sings a song, 'We will fix it, we will mend it' (47), the horrific irony of the play's title becomes clear.[16] As Kathleen Stark writes, Abby stitching herself has 'entirely lost its meaning of repairing and restoring, but is transformed into its opposite – destruction of the body'.[17] Equally subversive of expectations is the role play of the couple, with Abby acting the whore and Stu the macho man. As directed by Neilson, *Stitching* was as exciting as it was disturbing. The actors, Selina Boyack and Phil McKee, seemed to be hurling down a spiral, with each scene more shocking than the last. At one point, both rolled around tickling each other, then they fell into 'violent sexual passion' (33) to the pounding sound of Iggy Pop's 'I Wanna Be Your Dog'. Love can sometimes be bestial.

Similarly, Georgia Fitch's *Adrenalin . . . Heart* (Bush, 2002) was a roller-coaster which charted the relationship of a white single-mother, Leigh, and a black drug-dealer, Angel. From their first awkward meetings, and embarrassed silences, to their intensely passionate embraces, the play uses a variety of theatrical devices, with both Leigh and Angel completing each other's sentences, mixing acting with dialogue, narration and direct address to the audience. Fitch's characters talk to each other, across each other, commenting on each other and on themselves. For example, Leigh visits Angel in his council-estate flat:

> **Leigh** I am a mother, I am a Catholic, I am a sinner. I flirt with my . . . urban angel.
> **Angel** I think she definitely is a bit nutty tonight. Weird fucking energy man. (29)

As well as jokes and insights, Fitch slips her big themes – race, drugs, parenthood – easily in between the sheets. At one point, someone mouths 'Nigger lover' at Leigh on the bus, but her response is 'Yeah I am and I am proud of it mate' (39). As both Angel and Leigh become increasing obsessed with the other, their love affair blossoms and then withers during one long hot summer. Their relationship is played out in isolation: avoiding their friends, and her kids, the couple meet in his flat at night, creating a parallel reality to that of the ordinary world. The irony, of course, is that while Leigh is fascinated by Angel's world, with her voice taking on his tone, Angel is set on escaping it. The result of their passion for each other, and for drugs – from speed to Es to crack to smack – is expressed by Leigh's confusion: 'I am starting to feel so fucking strange. Nothing's piecing together – with a constant state of . . . arousal. Hardcore exhaustion now man' (53). As she plunges deeper, drugs turn into depression, and the dialogues split and fragment. When everything goes wrong, the language of the text breaks down. The final word is an eloquent stage direction: '*Enuff*' (75). As directed by Mike Bradwell, with Mark Moreno and Julia Ford, this glorious seventy minutes showed how love can be both addictive and devastating.

By contrast, Laura Wade's hugely enjoyable *Other Hands* (Soho, 2006) imagined a couple's problems by means of the metaphor of physical disability. Having written two plays in 2005 – *Colder than Here* (Soho) and *Breathing Corpses* – on the subject of death, it was clear with *Other Hands* that her main interest was in how people communicate, or fail to. Having been together for years, computer geek Steve and management consultant Hayley barely speak to each other. 'Everything I say feels like I've said it before,' she complains (31). Worse, the unresolved tensions in their relationship – which include the disparity in their earnings (she's a high-flyer and he's a lazy freelancer) – manifest themselves in a painful affliction of their hands. It might be Repetitive Strain Injury or Carpal Tunnel Syndrome, or just a psychosomatic paralysis. With quirky humour and a loving attention to detail, Wade shows how both Steve and Hayley drift towards strangers: he gets interested in Lydia, one of his clients; she flirts with Greg, a man she met through work. In one of the most erotic moments in this decade's drama, Hayley and Greg describe having sex with each other, a purely verbal game of desire, which takes place in a coffee bar. But although this sexy encounter leads Hayley to realise that: 'Oh my god the grass isn't just greener I mean it's got ten-foot sunflowers I can I can *smell* them' (70), it also confirms her feeling that she can't have an affair. In the end, neither Steve nor Hayley is unfaithful, and his conclusion – 'I just think we've got to be braver' (95) – applies to both of them. Bijan Sheibani's production, with Anna Maxwell Martin as Hayley, brought out Wade's characteristic mix of brutality and tenderness, leaving you with the feeling that this couple had pulled back from the abyss.[18]

Other plays also used intriguing metaphors. In *Pyrenees* (Paines/Tron, 2005), David Greig looked at a married couple, and the relationship between individual and national identity. A fiftysomething Man is found in snow at the foot of the Pyrenees: he has lost his memory and doesn't know who he is. In the first half, he attempts to re-create his own identity, helped by Anna, a British Consulate official. But although these two are drawn to each other, their attraction is interrupted by the arrival of Vivienne, the man's wife. In the second half, it emerges that Man, now identified as Keith, faked his own death, and ran away from his marriage. He has had a mid-life crisis, bought a motorbike and been unfaithful; she is faithful and forgiving, and in a wonderfully fantastical narrative tells how she followed him across Europe. With its setting in the neutral space of a mountain hotel, this is a play that, with Greig's admirably light touch, argues that some locations allow us to loosen our rigid identities. Keith, who fantasised about being a seafaring English loner from Bristol, turns out to be a married Scotsman from Edinburgh. And, from the cheerfully anarchic hotel Proprietor come comments on national identity. At one point, he says, 'There's no vanity like an Englishman's concern for his conscience' (102). At another, he claims Englishmen like 'to spank or be spanked' (32). Meanwhile, Anna admits, 'I'm Welsh but I'm so bloody English' (35). Tightly directed by Vicky Featherstone, with Hugh Ross (Keith) and Paola Dionisotti (Vivienne), *Pyrenees* was a meditation on human communication, national identity and feelings of connection which ended on a note of muted reconciliation.

The idea of crisis-struck couples took many different shapes. In Abi Morgan's *Tender* (Birmingham, etc., 2001), Gloria is a fortysomething woman who only gradually accepts her husband's sudden disappearance. Morgan, who gives marvellous accounts of, in the words of one of her characters, 'the intimacy of strangers' (22), shows in this play how even the most stable couple, Al and Hen, can find themselves in crisis, after the man deceives his pregnant partner. Similarly, in Bryony Lavery's *Stockholm* (Frantic/Plymouth, 2007), the couple is seen as a prison with two jailers. The title alludes to the Stockholm Syndrome, in which hostages become emotionally tied to their captors. In the play, Todd and Kali's happiness is disturbed by her irrational jealousy, although every time they fight their reconciliation is a beautiful moment of joy. At one point, in Frantic Assembly's original production, the couple use kitchen utensils to show how both are consumed by sexual desire, a touch of marital cannibalism. By contrast, in Leo Butler's *Lucky Dog*, Eddie and Sue – an old married couple in Sheffield – are having a very unseasonable time. Over Christmas dinner, while Sue chatters away, it slowly emerges that the uncommunicative Eddie – who likes going for long walks with his dog – also visits Pam, his bit on the side. Butler's bleak drama allows the truth about their loveless marriage to seep out like a bad smell.

Often, an innovative form highlighted the life and death of a marriage: Richard Bean's *Honeymoon Suite* (ETT/Royal Court, 2004) is set in a Bridlington hotel and shows Eddie and Irene as eighteen-year-old newly weds, then at age forty-three and finally as sixty-seven-year-olds, using six different actors and with the action often happening simultaneously. Sarah Phelps's *Modern Dance for Beginners* (Soho, 2002) also starts in a hotel bedroom, and the same two actors – Justin Salinger and Nicola Walker – played four disparate couples in a play with enough anguish to fill a dozen condoms. Like *Losing Louis*, Alexi Kaye Campbell's award-winning *The Pride* (Royal Court, 2008), is set in two eras, the 1950s and the present, and shows how the 1958 marriage of Philip and Sylvia is corroded by his love for Oliver, and by his inability to face the truth about his desires. Finally, Jez Butterworth's grimly hilarious *Parlour Song* (Almeida, 2009) gave a deliciously surreal spin on marital infidelity in a new-built suburb. As the husband Ned returns from business trips, he keeps finding items missing from his home, some of which are symbolic: gold cufflinks his wife bought him, a stone birdbath acquired on their honeymoon, a tandem bicycle purchased for their wedding anniversary. Ned's nightmare – 'Suddenly I see walls growing up around me. Brick by brick' (61) – perfectly suggests the anxiety that marriage cannot banish. But if couples-in-crisis plays suggest a nation in constant disagreement, they also picture the British as a passionate lot.

Unsuitable suitors

The acutest crises were represented by the unsuitable couple play. David Harrower's award-winning *Blackbird* (EIF, 2005) is an excellent example. The central relationship is summed up neatly in the play's publicity: 'Ray, 56, is confronted with his past when Una, 27, arrives unannounced at his office. Guilt, anger and raw emotions run high as they recollect the passionate love affair they had 15 years earlier.'[19] If you do the maths, that makes Ray forty-one, and Una twelve, at the time of their 'affair'. Set in a works canteen, Harrower shows how Una confronts Ray about the way he exploited her. But the play is much more than a simple drama about abuse; it is also a dangerous account – provocative, disturbing and unpleasant – of something that, judging by the way the characters remember their emotions and shower each other in recriminations, does resemble a love story. Like any love story, the play radiates neediness, loneliness and fear, as well as obsession, infatuation and desire. And guilt, and regret and depression. Because Una and Ray are adults on stage, it's hard to remember that she was still a girl when Ray first started sniffing around. Here, the paedophile appears to be charming and credible – until the end, when '*a Girl of twelve enters*', the daughter of Ray's current lover (82). Suddenly, Una realises that he has deceived her once again.

Harrower, a Scottish playwright, whose 1995 debut *Knives in Hens* was sublimely written and widely influential, gives *Blackbird* a compellingly poetic rhythm, as, for example, when Una describes her loyalty after their relationship was discovered:

I protected you.
Defended you.
Stayed
stayed true.
I told the police you hadn't touched me. (57)

Harrower avoids cliché by making it clear that Ray was never abused as a child and has pretended to participate in his rehabilitation without actually changing. It's also clear that Una, the woman, has paid the greater price. Not only did he mercilessly exploit her girlish crush on him but, as she says, '*I did the sentence. / I did your sentence. / For fifteen years. / I lost everything. / I lost more than you ever did*' (28). She's the loser. But, despite its questionable sexual politics, *Blackbird*, in German director Peter Stein's production, was a thrilling two-hour drama. Under Stein's control, it felt at times like an epic of human feelings, good ones, bad ones and ugly ones too. Instead of naturalistic acting, what we got from Jodhi May and Roger Allam were big gestures and large sweeps of the stage, whose design emphasised the chaos of an astonishingly litter-strewn canteen. At times, May was like a fury from a Greek tragedy, a woman confident of having Athena at her back; and when Allam bent under her onslaught, he was Atlas, carrying the weight of the world. Here, a dirty little tale becomes a state-of-humanity play. Yet Stein obviously felt that the final revelation provided by Harrower was not dramatic enough because he added an extra scene, in which the set flew away and the stage became an underground car park in which Una and Ray fought over the ignition keys to an onstage car. As they grappled on the ground to the thunder of a Patti Smith song, the play ended in emotional darkness.

The relationship of an older man and a young woman was also explored in Lucy Prebble's award-winning debut *The Sugar Syndrome* (Royal Court, 2003), a daring journey into the black heart of British solitude. Bright seventeen-year-old Dani has parent issues, and has been treated for food disorders. A lonely soul, she searches the internet and meets two very different blokes, Lewis, a nerdish, wannabe rock journalist, and Tim, a balding, middle-aged man who has been in prison for molesting boys. When they first meet, he's disappointed that she's not, as he expected from her cyber chat, an eleven-year-old boy. But because Dani has problems, she sees in him a kindred spirit. 'I'm generation X,' she tells him, 'we don't judge anything anyone does' (14). Although this odd couple clicks, and Dani encourages Tim's fascination with under-age kids, her discovery of violent kiddy porn on his laptop provides a salutary conclusion to their rapport. In Marianne Elliott's original production, the alienation of what the *Independent* called 'the recurring image of faces bathed in the ghostly radiance of computer screens' contrasted with the humanity of what the *Daily Telegraph* saw as 'the sight of the pair slowly dancing together to Bob Dylan's Simple Twist of Fate'.[20] With an appealing mix of intelligence and irony, and provocative because she refuses to judge her characters, Prebble shows the attractions of perverse behaviour – and its emotional costs.

Tim is an ex-teacher, and British teachers could be portrayed as exploitative rather than caring. At the centre of Terry Johnson's icily witty *Hitchcock Blonde* (Royal Court, 2003), for example, is the relationship between media lecturer Alex and his student Nicola. When she accepts his invitation to a Greek island to catalogue an old film archive, he manipulates her into having sex with him by pretending to have a fatal disease. But he can't develop a relationship with her because of his obsession with images: when Nicola realises this, she says, 'You never intended to touch me again, did you, Alex?' because 'Touching me wakes you from the dream of someone else you'd rather touch' (90). Similarly, Fiona Evans's *Scarborough* (Northern Firebrand/Royal Court, 2008) is set in a seaside bed and breakfast: in the first half, a female teacher is there with a fifteen-year-old boy; in the second, it's a male teacher with a fifteen-year-old girl. The trick is that the dialogue is identical for both situations, which are sad rather than overtly abusive. The English come across as riddled with guilt and fear.

Simon Vinnicombe's *Cradle Me* (Finborough, 2008) also looks at the older woman. In it, forty-eight-year-old Marion has lost her son Nick, and in her grief she has a brief fling with seventeen-year-old Dan, one of Nick's friends. When Marion says 'Kiss my wrists' (63) or Dan says 'I'm going to cradle you' (69), what emerges is a very tender account of neediness and love, both young and old. In the end, despite some graphic outbursts, the family stays firm, and Dan is squeezed out. By contrast, the older man in Philip Ridley's excruciatingly painful *Vincent River* (Hampstead, 2000) never appears on stage. Instead, we see the confrontation between his mother, Anita, and the boy, seventeen-year-old Davey, who was once briefly his lover. It turns out that schoolboy Davey picked up thirtysomething Vincent, who was later viciously murdered by a homophobic gang. But the play is mainly about, in Ridley's words, what happens 'when you break away from the pack': 'the pack attacks you. And of course the family works like that'.[21] At one point, talking about his encounters with Vincent, Davey kisses Anita, and she has to stop him going any further. Desire always prefers the warm body to the cold memory.

Equally unsuitable is the central relationship in Jonathan Harvey's *Out in the Open* (Hampstead/Birmingham, 2001). At the start of the play, Tony – a thirty-three-year-old gay man – is grieving for Frankie, his lover, who died six months earlier. As a distraction, he gets off with Iggy (played in Kathy Burke's production by James McAvoy), who it turns out was having a secret affair with Frankie at the time of the latter's death. In a plot with more twists than a stretch of crazy paving, it finally emerges that Tony knew about the affair all along, and who Iggy was. 'I just wanted to be near you,' he tells Iggy. 'Because you'd been near to him' (93). To which, Iggy shrugs and says, 'Snap' (93). Desire for a lost love here seems to enhance, rather than destroy, a current affair. But knowledge of betrayal also casts a pall over the past, and when Tony realises that all his friends knew of Frankie's affair, and didn't tell him, there's an explosion of feeling. Like so many characters in 2000s plays, Tony realises he is essentially alone.

One extreme cure for loneliness is incest. In Judy Upton's *Sliding with Suzanne*, for example, Suzanne is a thirty-five-year-old whose life is on the skids. But although she is certainly feckless and foul-mouthed, her despair comes from, in Rebecca D'Monté's words, a 'mismatch between the promise and reality' of a country where her A-levels only qualify her to work in a coffee bar.[22] She's also a foster mother to sixteen-year-old Luka. And soon a lover as well as a mother. At one point she says, 'I still feel kind of maternal towards you. I know it's fucked up but there it is' (57). Her incestuous love affair gets out of control when she becomes pregnant and he is set to be a teen father. In despair, she threatens to have an abortion, but it's Luka who insists on her keeping the baby. Written in furious, rasping dialogues, with a gut-wrenching subtext of naked neediness and lashings of acidic humour, this piece of stonking in-yer-face theatre was directed by Max-Stafford Clark, with Monica Dolan as the lipstick-smeared Suzanne, typical British tabloid fodder.

Several playwrights explored similar territory, often in a middle-class setting. Kevin Elyot, the master of fractured theatre form, used the juxtapositions and revelations available from telling a story unchrono-logically to produce memorable stage suggestions of incestuous and other dark feelings. In *Mouth to Mouth* (Royal Court, 2001), fifteen-year-old

Phillip returns from holiday to tell his mother Laura about a holiday romance he's had with an older Spanish woman, well twenty-two to be precise. But Mum's more outraged by the fact that he's had his bottom tattooed: as she says, 'The thought of some greasy old man pricking my son's thigh with needles, and that harlot leering in the background with a fag in her mouth' (287). To calm her down, Phillip leads her in a tango, taught to him by his girlfriend, a moment in Ian Rickson's production (with Lindsay Duncan as Laura) which felt disturbingly incestuous. Suddenly, her concern for her son seemed like wanton jealousy. At another point, middle-aged Frank, a family friend who's suffering from AIDS, also snogs Phillip. In a final twist, it turns out that Phillip's father is not her husband but Roger, a lover she had a brief fling with when he was seventeen and she twenty-eight. In Elyot's *Forty Winks*, Don is obsessed with Diana, who was once his girlfriend, but then married someone else. It becomes apparent that he has seduced her fourteen-year-old daughter Hermia, who reminds him of her mother, and the play ends on a sinister note as, in a flash forward, he's introduced to Hermia's thirteen-year-old daughter, also a spitting image of her mother (in Katie Mitchell's production both were played by Carey Mulligan). Elyot's teasing structure opens the play with a scene in which Don prevents Diana from coming into his hotel room, and uses a later scene to show that Hermia was concealed in the room while this was happening. In this play, amid mentions of Englishness, from cricket to croquet, Don's obsession – 'She's here, all the time,' he says, touching his head (29) – comes across as a kind of frozen half-life. Those who dwell on the past are condemned to relive it, and there's nothing so British as addiction to the past.

Like Elyot's plays, Polly Stenham's instantly appealing hit *That Face* (Royal Court, 2007) has a middle-class setting and focuses on a dysfunctional family. Martha, a nice middle-class mum with a not-so-nice drink-and-drug problem, lives with her son Henry, who's dropped out of school to become an artist. Meanwhile, her daughter Mia is threatened with expulsion from her boarding school when an initiation ceremony goes badly wrong. Stenham clearly has empathy with both older and younger generations, and her point is that although Mia and Henry are rich in material goods, they are poor parents, with Dad absent and Mum acting like a needy child. This role reversal, as well as Martha's incestuous attraction to her son, which at one point leads her to cut up his clothes in a jealous rage, gives the play its emotional depth. Like a party drug, Stenham's writing is exhilaratingly heady: images of addiction, abuse and aggravation pepper the text. Her portrait of Martha, played by Lindsay Duncan (both pussy cat and vicious lioness) in Jeremy Herrin's production, is sympathetic in its account of her chronic neediness, with its hints of forbidden love. Vivid stage images included the opening ritual in the boarding-school dorm, with the initiation ceremony looking like a terrorist kidnap, and the climactic appearance of Martha in a scarlet dress and jewels while her son wears her silky slip and pisses on her bed. A similar emotional buzz was captured by In-Sook Chappell's *This Isn't Romance* (Soho, 2009), which explored the sexual attraction of two siblings, the Korean-born Miso and Han, who were separated as children but meet again as adults. One of Chappell's provocative suggestions was that our sense of identity is genetic, in our blood. As she travels to Seoul, Miso discovers that she has feelings that are foreign to her in their intensity: Korean feelings. And if you share someone's blood, you're inevitably drawn to them. But, just as Martha discovers in *That Face*, the sheer intensity of incestuous emotions is too much to bear, and both plays end in separation, with hope muted.

The prize for the most unsuitable relationship of all must go to Kate Betts's *On the Third Day*. In it, Claire (Maxine Peake) is a presenter at Greenwich Planetarium, who goes to a bar one night and brings home Mike, with whom she plans to finally lose her virginity. What she doesn't know, but soon finds out, is that he claims to be Jesus. Unsuitable or not, Mike has a nice line in spiritual healing. Here, as in so many other plays, breaking taboos seemed to be a national characteristic. And both the cause and the result of unsuitable coupling was solitude, which evoked the sense of a nation of loners.

Desperate females

Women were often portrayed not just as lonely, but as desperate. One of the very best of this genre was Emma Frost's *Airsick*, a debut play about two young women on the edge. Lucy, an artist, has an American boyfriend and a domineering father, whose wife has left him. Her best friend Scarlet is a wild spirit who can't stand still; she was abused by her father when she was five years old. As Scarlet comments, 'Lucy and I used to play Crap Family Poker. Lucy would call a Bullying-Father and a Mother-On-Valium, and I'd match her Mother-On-Valium and raise her a Bastard-Stepfather-Who-Charges-Me-Rent' (32). One of the most delicious plays of the decade, *Airsick* is delirious in its storytelling panache and, amid its hilarity, offers images of sexual despair. At one point, Lucy says, 'Show me a man with a serious psychosis and I'm the one he's sleeping with' (7); Scarlet's most successful sexual encounter is with Lucy's Dad, whom she's known since childhood. The play is full of references to the stars (Lucy was born on the same day in 1968 as Black Holes were named) and to the colour yellow (Lucy eventually dies of liver disease which turns her body this colour; as she gets ill, there's a blast of Coldplay's 'Yellow').[23] With its metaphorical overkill and filthy sex stories, the play's production, directed by Mike Bradwell, was an unalloyed joy. And although both Lucy and Scarlet are each, in their way, desperate, *Airsick* also shows how female friendship can give an optimistic shine to even the most dreadful situations.

Similarly, and from its first scene, Georgia Fitch's *I Like Mine with a Kiss* (Bush, 2007) grabs you by the pubes. Louise is entertaining friends with her party piece, a drunken lapdance routine, gyrating to pounding music. Celebrating her thirty-ninth birthday, she and her best friend Annie go out, get plastered, have sex with men and end up pregnant. Both of them. Annie, who already has a teen daughter, decides to keep her baby while Louise has an abortion. Despite this, Louise is desperate because her biological clock is ticking so loudly. As she puts it, 'I know this is the last bus now isn't it [. . .] jump on now [. . .] to motherhood, being a mum, mummy land' (35). Although the play is crammed a bit too full of issues, the character of the hard-drinking and tough-talking Louise, played by Michelle Butterly in Mike Bradwell's vivid production, was so engaging that you wanted her to stay on stage for ever. Desperation can sometimes be so attractive. The theme of yearning for motherhood was also central to Shelley Silas's *Falling* (Bush, 2002). This time, forty-two-year Linda is finding it hard to get pregnant, having suffered five miscarriages. She aches for a child: 'To have a fuss made, to never be the same person again, to have a new identity, to be a mother, a mum' (42). Her sister Kate has had three kids and one of them, teenager Grace, who's still at school, gets pregnant with barely a thought. Although Grace's sexual precocity is portrayed as fun, her decision to give her baby to Linda spreads as much anguish as it alleviates. In the end, Linda refuses the offer and settles for just being herself, 'funny, amusing, intelligent, can look quite pretty if she tries' (106). With its foetal heartbeat thumping during the scene changes, John Tiffany's slick production was both intelligent and heartwarming.

Men also tried their hands at desperate female plays. Simon Stephens's *Harper Regan* (National, 2008) charts the journey of self-discovery of Harper, an Uxbridge-based working mother, whose daughter is in college and whose husband may or may not have an unhealthy interest in underage girls. As she decides to visit her dying father in Manchester, thus walking out on her family, and her job, she discovers the truth about herself. What the play succeeds in doing beautifully is in showing how fear and grief can knock us off balance, making us do things we normally avoid. Harper, played by Lesley Sharp in Marianne Elliot's enjoyable production, appears in every scene, and drifts from one situation to another in a shell-shocked but open-eyed way that invites us to share her feelings. In the programme, Stephens says that he originally wrote the play with the idea of using a man as his lead character, and then changed his mind.[24] In fact, the family scenes are much more convincing that the scenes in which Harper meets strangers, glasses a man in a bar and has casual sex. The play's ending restores harmony in this splintered family through the device of fantasy – the husband's dream of happiness heals the conflict. By contrast, Terry Johnson's *Piano/Forte* blazes with fury from beginning to end. When Louise returns to the family home, a highly metaphorical country house, her sister Abigail is hardly overjoyed. The sisters are opposites – Abigail is agoraphobic, repressed and could have been a concert pianist; Louise is adventurous, loud-mouthed and very angry. You can see why their father has banned her from coming home. In Kelly Reilly's screaming performance, directed by Johnson himself, Louise roars onto the stage, upturning the applecart and full-frontally confronting all the family secrets. On the occasion of her father's third marriage, to a B-list celebrity airhead, she stamps into view, a spitfire hollering for revenge. Johnson stages the Oedipal conflict between the powerful Tory father (Oliver Cotton) and his two daughters, both of whom have been damaged by the suicide of their mother, his first wife. As Abigail, Alicia Witt played an Ingrid-Bergman-type character in a world that was two parts *Rebecca* to one part *Jane Eyre*. There are plenty of bitter jokes about family life, unrequited love and emotional incontinence, and there are passages of spiky writing, which will make prigs blush and bring heat to sluggish spirits. Similarly, Michael Wynne's *The Priory* (Royal Court, 2009) stages a fateful New Year's Eve party to show the desperate measures that Kate, a thirty-six-year-old writer, takes to get her man, in order to prove that she – like her media friends – is also a success. Last but not least, Jack Thorne's *2nd May 2007* (Nabokov/Bush, 2009) takes the prize for one of the most excruciating scenes of the whole decade: when the shy Ian takes a very drunk Sarah home, he finds that her sexual advances are a turn-off. Not only is the episode a study in embarrassment as Sarah realises that she's gone home with the wrong man, but there's a daringly theatrical moment when she whispers her secret thoughts into Ian's ear as a thumping Donna Summer track prevents the audience from hearing them (38). Clearly Sarah uses sex to cover her desperation, and in that she's not alone.

Other depictions of desperate females included Nina Raine's award-winning *Rabbit* (Old Red Lion, 2006), whose main character, Bella, celebrates her twenty-eighth birthday in a bar with friends. Intercut with these scenes of gossip and verbal sex war were glimpses of her dying father, the source of much of her desperation. Sometimes metaphor offered a way into psychology. Joy Wilkinson's excellent *Felt Effects* (503, 2006) used the image of an earthquake to measure the growing emotional intensity of its female characters, and in Gary Young's *Running Girl* (Boilerhouse, 2002) a young woman (played by Kate Dickie) spends most of the seventy-minute show on a treadmill, exemplifying the way that today's twentysomething women are running to stand still. But sometimes love offered healing: when, during a performance of Liz Lochhead's rom-com *Good Things* (Borderline, etc., 2004) at the Tron in Glasgow, forty-nine-year-old Susan realises her dreams of love there was a collective sigh of delight. Otherwise, female desperation showed a nation where the sexes were more equal than ever, even if that equality was expressed either in bad behaviour or chronic loneliness.

Worried men

The crisis of masculinity, a staple subject of much 1990s drama, continued to exert its fascination, especially on male playwrights. What David Hare calls 'the melancholy of maleness' made several notable appearances.[25] For example, veteran Doug Lucie's quietly beautiful *The Green Man* (Plymouth, 2003), named after its pub setting, is about a group of men preparing for a night of carp fishing. Led by Mitch, their developer boss, the men – middle-aged builder Lou, young surveyor Greg, plus landlord Bernie – plan to enjoy a couple of drinks before setting off in the small hours but are stranded because their van-driver fails to show up. So they get drunk and bicker until dawn. The men are well aware of how they hold reality at bay by compulsive joking: as Lou says to Bernie, 'That's your way of putting people off though, innit? [. . .] 'Cause you don't want no one getting near the real Bernie' (8). The main conflict is between two competing ideas of masculinity, hardman Mitch's know-it-all sexism and soft-at-heart Lou's sensitive soul. Mitch sees Lou as 'half a man' who compensates by feeling superior (20), and his view of women – 'dozy tarts' who are only good at 'fucking nattering' and can only be placated by 'money and sex' (25–6) – is old-fashioned verging on Neanderthal. Yet Lou's socialist principles seem equally out-of-date. The men are pathetically unable to deal with contemporary life: as Bernie points out, they're 'not fantastically in tune with the modern world' (35). Late in the play, Bernie's wife Linda arrives and delivers some home truths. She tells Lou to get in touch with his estranged daughter, and gives a hilarious account of how a former barmaid 'decided quite young that she was going to sit on her fat arse and do nothing except drink, take drugs and sleep with anything that stood up in her presence' (52).

Lucie's forte is integrity: he loves all his characters and it shows. If his vision of masculinity is soaked in the bitter gall of middle-aged experience, each of his characters is admirable as well as flawed – even Mitch, who is full of life and generosity. In Simon Stokes's production, which was headed by Phil Daniels (Lou) and Danny Webb (Mitch), this was a noisy evening which, rather like getting drunk, felt like fun at the time. As the *Daily Telegraph* put it, 'bitter humour gathers into noxious antagonism', for, as *What's On in London* pointed out, both Mitch and Lou are dinosaurs: 'Lou is a genuinely committed socialist and man of nature whose compassion for humanity and contempt for materialism sit ill in the age of New Labour', and the same is true for Mitch's Thatcherite 'loadsamoney acquisitiveness'.[26] In this decade, traditional British masculinity was past its sell-by date.

Other plays showed masculinity as an emotion-fraught grapple of antagonism. Scottish writer Grae Cleugh's *Fucking Games* (Royal Court, 2001) is set in the tasteful Chelsea flat of the older Terrence and younger Jonah. When Terrence's secret lover Jude turns up with his new boyfriend Danny, the older man tries to break them up. But although Terrence and Jonah have agreed that monogamy is only for 'the breeders' (30), they are confronted by Danny's point that in an open relationship one partner always has more power than the other. If some of the play's issues are specific to the gay community, its snapshot of competing men, each of whom needs someone to trust, is of wider resonance. In Mark Norfolk's *Wrong Place* (Soho, 2003), Trevor, a young black man, is confused because his adopted father Roddy is a respectable West Indian who came over in the 1960s and works on the railways, but his biological father 'Uncle' Monty – an old friend of Roddy's – is an ageing playboy and career criminal. When Trevor finds himself facing twelve years in prison after a drugs bust, both his fathers are implicated. The final stage picture of Roddy, a tired old man playing with a train set, struggling to connect with his large and awkward gangsta son, was heartbreaking. Just as desperate was Scottish writer Simon Farquhar's *Rainbow Kiss* (Royal Court, 2006), in which Keith, a single parent recovering from a failed relationship, has a solution to loneliness: find a woman. So when he manages to pull Shazza at a local bar, he is after love rather than sex. For Shazza, however, a one-night stand is just a one-night stand. Keith's neediness is clear when he asks Shazza just to hold him, and her incredulous face reveals her appalled reaction (65). As she admits, she has 'warm hands cold heart eh?' (61). How disarming is that?

Sport, drugs and gambling have always made male hearts beat faster. In Matt Charman's award-winning *A Night at the Dogs* (Soho, 2005), five losers pin their hopes on a racing greyhound. Although no women appear onstage, the men are defined by them: one has lost his wife and kids in an acrimonious divorce, another lets his wife wear the trousers and a third has a crush on his Estonian lodger. When a crisis hits them, these men all turn out to be ineffectual. Similarly, in Henry Adam's *Among Unbroken Hearts* (Traverse, 2000), the junkies Ray and Neil are, in the Scotsman's words, paralysed 'by the fear of growing up, the perennial Peter Pan impulse to remain a boy and refuse responsibility', and by the time that Ray realises that 'I want to grow up and be a man' (67), it's too late.[27] In David Dipper's *Flush* (Soho, 2004), three poker players tell filthy stories – all 'pump-pump-squirt jobs' (20) – partly for fun, and partly as a tactic to distract the others in the game. Full of metaphors of male power play, this account of wounded men revisits the dark world of Britflick gangsters. Likewise, the connection between masculinity and the playground was neatly encapsulated by the cover of the playtext of Mike Bartlett's *My Child*, which showed an action-man toy. By contrast, in Jack Thorne's excruciating monologue *Stacy* (Arcola, 2007) the protagonist Rob, played by Ralph Little in the West End transfer, seems at first like a confused young man, until gradually the truth comes out: he's a rapist and a very unpleasant individual. Sometimes the connection between maleness and Englishness was explicit. In Richard Bean's *Mr England* (Sheffield, 2000), Stephen England is a Mondeo-man who works as a sales rep. As his name implies, he believes in Middle England, free enterprise and male heroism. But he goes off the rails. At the start of the play, he narrates his breakdown: 'Wednesday night, middle of the night. I got up, went downstairs, had a shit on the mat, and pissed on the sofa' (81). As Jack Bradley, then literary manager at the National, said, 'He is not the hero he needed to be and so, by his Middle England values, deserves everything that comes to him.'[28]

Terrible teens

The 2000s saw the rise and rise of the teen angst play. As these plays proliferated, teenagers appeared on stage in the guise of problems crying out for a solution, part of society's general fear of young people. For example, in Suzy Almond's *School Play* (Soho, 2001), three disrespectful and motorbike-obsessed teens – led by fifteen-year-old Charlie (Brooke Kinsella) – indulge in some bolshy behaviour, but when Charlie's music teacher, her foul-mouthed equal, discovers her talent, she helps to bring her back from the brink. Problem solved, at least temporarily. Some situations, however, were more intractable. Kerry Hood's *Meeting Myself Coming Back* conveys the personality of its traumatised protagonist – Catherine, who refuses to speak and has been disabled since the death of her parents when she was thirteen – with a fine mix of linguistic inventiveness and fractured narrative. Although the character is mute, the play allows us to hear her internal monologues. The English essay she writes at school sums up her experiences:

> My family by Catherine Hope Swan. I lived with my sister, mother and father in Enid Blyton life until two years ago when my mother lost a nearly-baby, we went to Cyprus and came back not exactly My Family. My house got cleaner [. . .] I do not like shouting and bruisey skin. (50)

Gradually, it emerges that the reason for her damaged hips and for her refusal to say anything other than 'Thank you' stems from her father, an ex-military man, who 'jumps on my pelvis, both feet on it' (59). The trauma is intensified by the fact that her mother has protected neither her nor her sister Meg from similar violence. As Catherine revisits her childhood home, she re-enacts the primal scene of her family tragedy. But Catherine is not just a victim, she is also, in the words of one critic, a 'warm, witty, brilliant young woman whom horror has robbed of a voice'.[29] In this account of the damage wrought by an abusive father, recovery is slowly and partially won by a constant day-to-day struggle. But far from being depressing, this emotionally excruciating but wonderfully written play gleams at the end with more than just a twinkle of hope.

In Matthew Dunster's richly imagined coming-of-age monologue *You Can See the Hills* (Manchester, 2008), the Oldham adolescent Adam (William Ash) finds growing up hard, and his stories cover adolescent sex, teen pregnancy, gang violence and family life. He's lucky, his parents are decent; another adolescent has to knife his violent father to save his mother from a beating (76–7). At one point, Adam asks himself, 'When does it stop? / When you have kids I suppose and have something proper to worry about . . .' (80). Like many teen plays, this one was as much about family as about being a boy in search of sex and fun. Two plays by Chloe Moss – *How Love Is Spelt* (Bush, 2004) and *Christmas Is Miles Away* (Manchester/Bush, 2005) – further delved into the world of the northern teenager: Petra in the earlier play moves to London, and Christie and Luke in the latter stay at home, one signing up for the army. In these plays, the youngsters appear as both endearingly fragile and remarkably resilient. Likewise, in Ali Taylor's *Cotton Wool* (503, 2008), two brothers – sixteen-year-old Gussie and eighteen-year-old Callum – have recently lost their mother, but their intense bond comes under pressure when the older one meets seventeen-year-old Harriet, a runaway with her own family problems. If teen love does eventually heal the rifts, the two brothers first have to suffer intense feelings of jealousy.

The teens in Simon Stephens's beautifully well-rounded dramas *Herons* (Royal Court, 2001) and *Port* (Manchester, 2002) express, in the words of Dan Rebellato, 'a childlike sense of wonder at the world', but experience their 'adolescence as almost intolerably brutal and cruel'.[30] Similarly, David Eldridge's *M.A.D.* (Bush, 2004) explores the metaphor of a Cold War conflict by applying it to the parents of eleven-year-old John, son of Romford market trader Kelly and his wife Alice. While he's fascinated by the Mutually Assured Destruction of the nuclear arms race, he hopes that his parents' mutual aggression guarantees that they will stay together, until one night he overhears one particularly titanic argument and realises that his family is no longer safe. Occasionally young feelings found a visual metaphor: in Jess Walters's *Terracotta* (Hampstead, 2000), which lifted the lid on the life of fretful teen Nicola, the stage gradually became littered with dead fish, dollops of paint and splashes of cherry yoghurt, an apt image for the messy emotional confusion of growing up. Otherwise, narrative could be therapeutic. In Richard Cameron's immensely enjoyable *Gong Donkeys* (Bush, 2004), fourteen-year-old David spends his holidays in Doncaster with his cousin Charlene, and her two twentysomething mates: the mentally challenged Wink and Gobbo. Both adults and kids tell stories to combat the boredom of everyday life. After all, fantasy is preferable to facing the pain of reality.

Some teen plays ran right up to the very edge of reason. Dennis Kelly's extravagantly comic debut *Debris* (Latchmere, 2003), for example, begins with one sibling, Michael, narrating the utterly outrageous story of how, on his sixteenth birthday, he returned from school to find that his father had crucified himself in the family home. As the shell-shocked teen remarks, 'My coming of age' (15). Then, in an extended flashback – as Michael's monologues alternate with those of his sister Michelle – Kelly tells the fantastical story of how things came to such a ridiculously surreal pass. As their mother expires on her daughter's birth, the kids are threatened with being sold to a sinister sugar daddy, but discover their own emotional satisfaction when Michael finds an abandoned baby, which he names Debris. The play's big themes – parental responsibility and the normalising influence of television – jostle for space in a text that oozes bodily fluids, gross violence and gut-burning feeling, all in the acidic glow of magic realism. Drinking from the same pool, although with a more realistic structure that was part psychological thriller and part childhood fantasy, Polly Stenham's *Tusk Tusk* (Royal Court, 2009) shows what happens when two teens and their younger brother are abandoned by their mother. The absent parents, which include a dead father as well as the AWOL mother, still structure the lives of their children. And Stenham is especially observant in her account of the gender wars that occur in each family, and the different bonds that bind mother and son, and mother and daughter. Without the adults, the kids live in a wonderland of total freedom. So they stay up all night, smoke to their heart's content and eat junk food. Instead of their five-a-days, they feast on crisps and cold takeaways. As in her *That Face*, loyalty is a key theme, and child's play becomes a tactic in the power game between siblings in a world that mixes the imagination of *Peter Pan* with the viciousness of *Lord of the Flies*. Britain is a fantasy island. The appeal of all these plays was their fascination with the extreme intensity of youthful feelings. If Britain really was, according to New Labour, a young country, its young were almost a country to themselves.

In the 2000s, plays that celebrated love, such as Chris Chibnall's warmhearted *Kiss Me Like You Mean It* (Soho, 2001), were comparatively rare. More common were plays that gazed across a panorama of lonely souls. For example, actor-turned-writer DeObia Oparei's high-energy extravaganza *Crazyblackmuthafuckin'self* (Royal Court, 2002) looked at Femi, a mixed-race gay man who works by day as an actor called Laurence and then, by night, turns into rentboy Big Black Jungle Nigga or pre-op trannie Shaneequa. In the livid red flat of Josie Rourke's production, he was joined by Kareema, a pregnant Asian glam girl and her Jewish blackney boyfriend Danny, plus assorted theatre-people. A similar landscape was imagined by Australian-born Samuel Adamson's cheery comedy *Southwark Fair* (National, 2006), which featured a gay IT consultant, a dotty aged actress, a bitter rock chick who has lost a hand in an accident, a black, pompous, deputy Mayor of London, an Adelaide busker and an Eastern European waiter. However empty the lives of these characters, together they presented in Nicholas Hytner's production a memorable snapshot of London as a metrosexual metropolis which is emerging, a touch hungover perhaps, blinking in amazement at the new millennium. As one critic wrote, its central motif was 'confused identities', personal and national.[31] Similarly, one of the strongest plays about sexual confusion was Mike Bartlett's superbly written *Cock* (Royal Court, 2009). In it, John, played by Ben Whishaw, cannot decide between his male lover or a woman he has just met. Because he is confused about his own identity, and doesn't really know who he is, he cannot make a choice. Was this a metaphor for a nation unsure of itself?

In the past decade, plays about love offered contradictory conclusions: whether they featured desperate females, miserable men or traumatised teens, they often resulted in a reaffirmation of the family. Or they offered the consolations of loneliness. If individualism is a national characteristic, plays about love showed individuals who were solitary, or in agony. Wherever these plays were set, the keynote was naturalism – the aim of most of them was to entertain by means of realistic accounts of what relationships are like; writers strived for veracity in their pictures of families and partners. The more intimate the play, the more real the aesthetic. But few plays accurately represented the full complexity of family life in 2000s Britain: where, for example, were the step-dads and step-mums? So, as Brits shrugged off their inhibitions, Britain emerged as a country full of fractured families, unfaithful spouses, childless women, troubled teens and perverted desire. Instability was the key. Maybe the answer was to take refuge in fantasy.

7 RIVAL REALITIES

> It's not a metaphor, it's a simile, but even if it were, the defining
> feature of a metaphor is that it's real.
>
> (Sarah Kane, *4.48 Psychosis*, 211)

The arts of the 2000s were rich in visions, imagination and fantasy. It
was the quantum decade, the metaphor-rich decade. If the notion of
globalisation suggested a world that is shrinking ever more rapidly,
British theatre seemed to have taken a mind-expanding drug, encouraging us to go beyond the normal confines of daily life. Sure, theatre
usually reflects the economic, social and political life of the country, but
sometimes it does much more: it creates different realities; it explores
imaginative worlds; it ascends to heaven or stumbles into hell. Weird
scenes inside the cool mine, and oh the senseless facts of beauty. More
bathetically, the creative industries and creativity became New Labour
buzzwords – and policy wonks generated more hot air than sense. Still,
politicians wanted the arts to deliver. As Munira Mirza, the Mayor of
London's cultural adviser, says, 'Aesthetic excellence is simply not
enough. Artists and cultural organizations are under greater pressure to
prove they can transform society.'[1] On a smaller scale, one tool of
transformation is metaphor. 'Metaphor is analogous to fiction, because
it floats a rival reality. It is the entire imaginative process in one move,'
says one literary critic; or, as one blogger puts it, 'When there are few
locations left to explore, the strangest undiscovered territory may be
within our own troubled heads.'[2]

Inner space

British playwrights in the 2000s explored the inner space of the
individual mind. In the first year of the new millennium, the Royal

Court staged *4.48 Psychosis* by Sarah Kane, the most outstanding playwright of the previous decade. Like Joe Penhall's *Blue/Orange*, *4.48 Psychosis* is about mental health; unlike Penhall, Kane takes a completely subjective route into the subject. Following her suicide on 20 February 1999, this was a posthumous production directed by James Macdonald, her most loyal interpreter. Since her five-play career had been a vigorous grapple with traditional notions of naturalistic form, it is fitting that in her last play she kissed goodbye to realistic play-making and embraced instead a much freer style: the text looks like a modernist poem. As Graham Saunders points out, the content is a series of discourses which 'express the boundaries between reality, fantasy and different mental states'.[3] There are short passages of fine writing, internal monologues, diary entries, dialogues between patient and doctor, examples of medical questionnaires, excerpts from self-help books and gasps of spirituality. Admittedly, some of the text has a juvenile feel to it, but other parts explore the sensibility of an agonised self-consciousness: 'It is myself I have never met, whose face is pasted on the underside of my mind' (245). Yet all is not bleak: jokes jostle with despair; irony cohabits with disbelief. The effect is theatrically thrilling. As David Ian Rabey says, '*4.48 Psychosis* is profoundly (perhaps uniquely) self-dramatising', a text which invites the audience 'to acknowledge an imaginative kinship with a self they have never met (Kane's) or at most briefly confronted (their own self-destructive impulses)'.[4] As usual, the action takes place inside the audience's heads.

When the Royal Court announced its intention to stage *4.48 Psychosis*, there was media speculation about the fact that its subject matter was mental breakdown and suicidal psychosis – the play's themes were linked rather too glibly with Kane's mental anguish. With admirable restraint, the Court advertised the play by using a minimalist black square for a poster, while Simon Kane, Sarah's brother and in charge of her literary estate, pointed out that the piece is 'about suicidal despair, so it is understandable that some people will interpret the play as a thinly veiled suicide note', but, he added, 'this simplistic view does both the play and my sister's motivation for writing it an injustice'.[5] Quite. Nevertheless, it is fair to argue, as

Professor Christopher Innes does, that in this work a personal despair bleeds into political resignation, with the important proviso that 'liberating the irrational' offers a way 'to free the subconscious'.[6]

There was an air of reverence about the memorial performance of *4.48 Psychosis* on Saturday, 24 June 2000. The audience included family, colleagues and invited guests. As we filed in, the atmosphere was funereal. The production began, with a long, agonising silence – broken by a mobile phone going off. As its owner struggled to silence it, Vince O'Connell – Kane's mentor and friend since her teenage years – let out a long growl: 'Arseholes.' After this tribune to Kane's no-nonsense personality, the performance continued in a wonderful version which brought out its dark humour as well as its moments of spiritual awe. The superbly imaginative staging by designer Jeremy Herbert made good use of a large mirror and projections of street scenes and static to emphasise the disjunction of the inner life from external reality. The actors – Daniel Evans, Jo McInnes and Madeleine Potter – wore causal urban wear, and often lounged around the stage, using, according to the *Daily Telegraph*, 'all kinds of tone – bitter, ironic, placid – to make the lines jump free of mawkishness'.[7] The emotional effect was of a long conversation with a deeply disturbed person which culminated in a blaze of dark glory: 'Remember the light and believe the light' (229). At the end of the show, which was staged in the claustrophobic Theatre Upstairs, a window was opened and sounds from the summer street outside floated into the theatre, a reminder that whatever happens inside your head, life flows on regardless.

If this suggests that the Brits are a level-headed lot, there were plenty of other plays that explored the inner space of subjectivity. One of the best was Anthony Neilson's highly successful *The Wonderful World of Dissocia*. In fact, after laying aside his original in-yer-face style, Neilson spent most of the decade 'exploring the internal life of the mind', which presents a challenge to traditional notions of form because 'the mind works on many levels'.[8] This play, directed by the playwright, is split into two acts. In Act One, thirtysomething Lisa suffers a psychotic episode, with paranoid delusions and strange distortions of time. In Act Two, she's in hospital, visited by medical staff and people she knows. What Neilson does is to present this material subjectively in first part and objectively in the second. So Act One is vividly imaginative, with Lisa talking to weird and wonderful characters such as insecurity guards, a scapegoat, a do-gooding council employee and some argumentative individuals: all the colours are deliberately heightened, the language is lush and the incidents farcical. Puns abound, cars can fly. At the same time, there is a sense of danger: the Goat threatens Lisa with sexual assault and another woman is attacked. An hour of Lisa's life is lost. The air is paranoid. But some moments are deliciously pleasurable: when a polar bear appears and sings a song – 'Who'll hold your paw when you die?' (46) – it was one of the decade's most memorable moments of perfect bliss. Act Two was a complete contrast: Lisa's hospital room; arctic sterility, sparse dialogue, depressed feeling. Even the solitary footsteps sounded muted and alien. The patient is seen through the eyes of others.

In Act One Neilson is not showing what a psychotic breakdown is literally like – most people don't have delusions featuring cuddly bears or argumentative hotdog eaters. Instead he conveys a feeling of the manic exhilaration often experienced by patients, some of their fears and the heightened sensations they experience. He is, after all, a master of experiential theatre. His metaphor for psychosis is the idea of another world, called Dissocia, with its own borders, rituals and mores. It's a kind of *Alice in Wonderland* on acid. The most contentious point is that psychosis – like drugs – has an enjoyable side. Fed up with the dulling effects of the pills that control her mania, Lisa hears an inner siren that tempts her to stop taking them. Of course, even in the confusion of runaway psychosis, reality is not far away: Lisa communicates excruciatingly with her boyfriend Vince by mobile phone, and aspects of the imaginary world are clearly echoes of the real: its Tube, airport, motorways and eateries. The shocking change to the more anodyne environment of the hospital in the second part is a visual embodiment of the idea that while medication can stabilise uncontrollable emotions, it can also deaden feelings and slow down thoughts. Lisa is helped by hospitalisation, but at a cost. This scepticism about medical help for mental patients, and the suggestion that manic episodes have pleasurable as well as distressing aspects, led to some negative reactions to the play's NTS revival in 2007. The

Guardian, for example, attacked Neilson for suggesting that 'there is something life-denying about the curative treatment of mental disorder – a notion that strikes me as a late 1960s sentimental fallacy' and the *Evening Standard* dismissed 'the false notion that her madness is more seductive than sanity'.[9] When it comes to mental health, the Brits are a disputatious lot.

A companion piece to the play is Neilson's *Realism*, which is similarly subjective in form, and shows a day in the life of Stuart, whose thoughts, feelings and inner contradictions are highlighted as he lazes around his flat. In doing so, distinctions between reality and surreality, childhood and adulthood, are blurred. Both these plays suggest, in the words of Trish Reid, that Neilson is 'a Scottish playwright and director able to draw, in his work, on the richly varied, populist and eclectic traditions of the Scottish stage'.[10] The politics of his plays, which assert human values in a culture that sometimes seems dedicated to suppressing them, is expressed in terms of both form and content. Similarly, few playwrights have explored the connections between inner and outer world as intelligently as Martin Crimp. His *Fewer Emergencies*, given a memorably atmospheric production by James Macdonald, is a series of fractured narratives which maybe take place inside the playwright's head, while his *The City*, beautifully realised in Katie Mitchell's production, plays deliciously wicked games with audience expectations, and with the metaphor of the city as a space of creativity.[11]

Other examples of intrepid explorations of inner space include Welsh playwright Ed Thomas's *Stone City Blue* (Clwyd Theatr Cymru, 2004), which explores, in the words of David Ian Rabey, the 'themes of memory, personal and national identity, belonging and love' in a series of internal monologues, voices speaking about loss and desolation, with the intention that 'its *form* might permit a partial transcendence of the dislocation and isolation that are its *matter*'.[12] Other plays which lingered on an absurd or surreal subjectivity include Nick Grosso's highly enjoyable crazy-one-liner fest *Kosher Harry*, set in a quirky restaurant, and Patrick Marber's *Howard Katz*, which, says its author, 'should seem as if the protagonist is in a dream – though he isn't'.[13] Similarly, David Eldridge has experimented with subjective dramas, which foreground the inner life of their central character. In his *Incomplete and Random Acts of Kindness* (Royal Court, 2005), the thirty-nine scenes of fractured narrative clearly take place inside the head of Joey, who suffers a breakdown. He rejects his girlfriend; his mother dies and his father falls for another woman; a young black boy he's been teaching to read is murdered; the Iraq War impinges. A fine mixture of delicate naturalist dialogue and a bold approach to theatre form, the play gives a powerful impression of what it's like to have your world fragment around you, a metaphor for our anxieties about the stability of the world, and of the nation.

Dystopian visions

When British playwrights squinted into the future, they saw bleak vistas. At times, the work of Caryl Churchill or Mark Ravenhill seemed to be preparing us for disaster. Likewise, Philip Ridley, one of the most truly exceptional playwrights of the past two decades, wrote *Mercury Fur*, a controversial play which expresses the full fury of his vivid and visionary imagination. Part of Paines Plough's *This Other England* season, the dark beauty of Ridley's words certainly conjure up a post-apocalyptic London. Set on a run-down council estate, the play imagines a country where a government has bombed its own population with a mixture of sand and butterfly cocoons. Once ingested, these butterflies allow the individual to vividly hallucinate fantasy scenarios, such as being part of Kennedy's assassination. But repeated use of these experiential drugs results in massive memory loss. In this anarchic place, two teen brothers, Elliott and Darren, survive by dealing butterflies and organising sex parties for rich clients. When the young 'party piece', a ten-year-old Asian boy they have procured for a City trader to act out his murderous Vietnam War fantasy, dies before the party starts, they turn on Naz, a local teen. Dressed in a gold Elvis suit, he is presented to the 'party guest' for sacrifice. While this is happening, the brothers come into conflict with gang leader Spinx, Elliott's genderbending lover Lola and the Duchess, their mother.

In the past, the two brothers lived in a pub called the Dover Castle, a clear signal of a state-of-the nation play. As such, it is also a provocation. The age of the victim suggests prevalent child abuse, and the drama's language is deliberately in-yer-face: the boys' incantatory insults are variations on 'ya nigger, Catholic, Yid, Christian, Paki, spic, wop, Muslim, shit, cunt' (86). But Ridley's main theme is that 'the stories we tell make sense of our lives', and his play is a dystopia where our ability to tell stories has broken down.[14] At one point, Darren garbles a mishmash history of the Second World War which mixes up Kennedy, Monroe, Hitler and 'a couple of atom bombs' which 'turned all the Germans into Chinkies' (114). It's both hilarious and desolate. More generally, the play is about what happens to people when you take away their history. 'The first thing that goes,' argues Ridley, 'is a sense of identity. And once your identity and storytelling starts to go, the next thing that goes is a sense of morality [. . .] Storytelling is our morality.'[15] If the play dramatises the decay of historical memory, it also shows its characters struggling to make meaning in a meaningless world. Particularly graphic examples of storytelling include Naz's young sister Stacey being chopped by machetes and raped by a rampaging gang in a supermarket (108–9) and the outrageous drug-addled Kennedy-assassination fantasy (115).

The play was provocative in performance. When John Tiffany's production (with Ben Whishaw playing Elliott) visited the Menier Chocolate Factory, the audience was led by torchlight into the main auditorium through a dark side room, an abandoned kid's bedroom: old wallpaper, toys and rubbish, smell of decay. Sounds of children. Later, at the climax of this two-hour piece, when the sacrificial victim is led into the room to be eviscerated, the audience had a stark mental image of the room in which the atrocity was happening – even if the violence took place out of sight, we remembered its look, feel and smell.

But the play is much more than a shock-fest: it deals starkly with our contemporary fears about social collapse, the decay of historical memory and the vulnerability of children. Its world is tinged by both echoes of Greek tragedy and visions of a sci-fi futurama. With its vision of violent anarchy, the play affronts liberal sensibilities, but it also warns us about unaccountable leaders. It questions our ability to educate future generations, and, finally, the strange family it assembles both illustrates the damage done to children when society breaks down and suggests new ways of bonding in adversity. Predictably, the play divided critics, with some being outraged by what they saw as its nihilism, while others praised the power of its writing. Certainly, its meaning was affected by the visceral disgust it provoked, and the fury of the reaction testifies to its intensity. So frank were its horrors that audience walk-outs took place almost every night. Yet its emotional effect on audiences was its meaning: the world is full of atrocity. Moreover, Ridley points out that the two brothers in the end decide not to kill anyone: they break the cycle of violence. In fact, his other England is a land of hope, despite its horrors. As when Elliott says, 'The power's still in our hands' (141). While the play explores the logical conclusion of our society's fantasies about violence, by enacting them it utters a plea for sanity in an insane world. You can't get much more ethical than that.

Darkness held an irresistible attraction for British playwrights. In autumn 2004, the RSC's *New Work Festival* featured two finely written dramas about a post-apocalyptic future when war has not only ravaged the land, but has also fractured language. In Edinburgh writer Zinnie Harris's *Midwinter*, a ten-year conflict has left survivors eager to rebuild their lives. One of them, Maud, swaps a dead horse for a very young boy. But despite this altruistic act, war has brutalised her soldier husband, the child and herself. On stage, the recurring refrain of 'the war is over' conjured up images of the Iraq War, and a crazy vision, articulated at the end, of 'a war without soldiers' (76) resonated with our fears about shock and awe, and anticipated another play, Joe Penhall's *Landscape with Weapon*, which also imagined metallic drones fighting humans in a world of terror. Similarly, Joanna Laurens's *Poor Beck* showed what happens when survivors of an apocalypse, who now live underground, turn to an itinerant tinker, Poor Beck, for news of the world above ground. While he claims that 'the surface is safe' (32), the survivors think, correctly as it turns out, that 'There a stain on the land' (14). Laurens's strange, lilting dialogue conveys their sense of estrangement, and her play also warns against trusting demagogic politicians. Just as Harris's play is a morality tale about telling the truth, so Laurens's piece is a grim account of human gullibility, and about our need for wishful thinking. Both suggested that Britain was a vulnerable place, fragile in the face of global conflict. Similarly intense was Leo Butler's *I'll Be the Devil* (RSC, 2008), which looked at the British occupation of Ireland during the 1760s, and examined how British soldiers, who had originally been born Irish Catholics, experienced the loss of their own traditions when they renounced their religion to take up the king's shilling. More a dystopia than a history play, Ramin Gray's satanically dark production showed the bedevilled family life of the characters in an orgy of tangled and twisted language, difficult to follow but rich in resonance. Such plays were a troubling antidote to the national myth of 'a progression of what you could describe as British values – freedom, fairness, decency – which have been fought for, won and kept across the centuries,' as David Edgar put it.[16]

Other dystopian visions included Gary Owen's *The Drowned World* (Paines/Traverse, 2003), a thrilling play which imagined a world divided between 'radiants' (beautiful elite) and 'citizens' (deformed masses), and where the underprivileged hunted down the gifted. As its director, Vicky Featherstone, says, metaphor can 'speak louder' than realism, and the play is an 'example of masterful, apparently seamless storytelling, which shocks and reviles us with the need and brutality at its core'.[17] Similarly, Fraser Grace's *The Lifesavers* (503, 2009) examined a society where it is illegal to bring up children privately, and shows what happens when one family decides to break the law. A nightmare of extreme surveillance, it challenged our complacency with today's social controls. Equally provocative, Kay Adshead's *Animal* (Soho, 2003) pictured Britain's green but unpleasant land being tormented by mass demonstrations against the government's war policy. As female protesters are beaten by truncheon-wielding riot police, anger spills over – in one hotspot, a woman who has lost both her hands holds a silent vigil. But not every dystopia was deadly serious. Savan Kent's comedy *Another Paradise* (Kali, 2008) is set in the near future when biometric identity cards have become compulsory, and shows what happens when the system malfunctions and tells people who they are, even when they know they're somebody else. What's notable about these visions of society is that they were as class-conscious as contemporary Britain. Although seen through a glass darkly, this was still recognisably our country.

Spooky coincidences

Rival realities can also be represented by devices such as coincidences and ghostly presences, which tease out strands of meaning from the texture of everyday normality, and suggest that the Brits are, in Peter Ackroyd's words, characterised by 'the love of the marvellous'.[18] One of the best examples of the marvellous is Abi Morgan's masterpiece *Tiny Dynamite* (Paines, etc., 2001), a tender story about two men, Lucien and Anthony, who have been friends since childhood. When they were boys, a freak lightning strike hit Anthony in the chest and, although he survived, he's a deeply troubled man who often sleeps rough. Lucien works as a risk assessor. One summer holiday, they meet Madeleine, and a love triangle develops which echoes a previous affair, which ended in the woman's suicide. History is in danger of repeating itself. The play asks whether Lucien and Anthony can break the cycle of repetition – and whether Madeleine can survive meeting these emotional lightning conductors. As the story blooms, its circular structure beautifully reflects the themes of repetition, risk and recurrent loneliness. Morgan is a master of subtext and this gentle play has a placid surface which barely conceals its strong undercurrents. Written with enormous elegance, the play uses words like musical motifs – such as the 'kapow' of a lightning strike – and an abundance of quirky humour. The mood of a summer break is lovingly conveyed, and if the text is sometimes obscure, in performance the play made perfect sense.

Directed with great delicacy by Vicky Featherstone, the production was acted by Frantic Assembly's Scott Graham and Steven Hoggett, plus Jasmine Hyde. The mix of imaginative storytelling, dance moves and evocative music inspired by English electronica band Zero 7 left you feeling elated. Using video projects and joyful theatre tricks, this was a magical experience: a metal fork floats down on a mini-parachute to illustrate a joke about forked lightning; Anthony's chest glows to show how his trauma has been imprinted on his body; a galaxy of light bulbs hanging above the simple deck stage buzz quietly; a strawberry suddenly appears from a mouth. So beguiling was the production that you almost believed that the spooky coincidence of feelings at its heart was perfectly reasonable.[19]

Tiny Dynamite is full of stories about freakish accidents, and is shot through with evocative metaphors, which often generate meanings and connections which are wordless but full of feeling. The tales of accidental deaths, such as the woman killed by a sandwich thrown off the Empire State Building, create an ambiance for the contrasting undertow about how Anthony and Lucien lost their first love: she told them she was going to commit suicide but they didn't believe her. When she asked Lucian, 'Who loves me the most?', he answered 'Anthony' (75). Taking this as bad faith, she killed herself. Lucien was, of course, trying not to hurt his friend. But when Lucian and Anthony both fall for Madeleine, the play not only suggests that lightning can sometimes strike twice, it also shows how life can come up with a second chance, in which the grip of the past can be eased just enough to enable you to move on. Towards the end, all three retell the story of the suicide and invent a healing ending. And, the second time around, Lucien is not afraid to show Madeleine he loves her. But this moment, Morgan suggests, requires the courage of a leap in the dark. Until then, Madeleine says she's 'never been so happy and never been so lonely in all my life' (71–2). *Tiny Dynamite* suggests that being British involves an openness to taking a risk to overcome individual repression.

Glyn Cannon's *On Blindness* (Graeae, etc., 2004) got a similarly inventive staging. It is about two couples who discover that there's more to perception than just the evidence of our eyes. Edward and Shona both work for a company that produces audio versions of films for the visually impaired. When the shy Edward is invited on a hot date by the sexy Maria, a blind woman, he struggles to reconcile his desire with his sense of her vulnerability. By contrast, the sassy Shona has to confront her own upfront attitudes when Gaetano, a painter, unveils a portrait of her in the nude in front of her new boyfriend. If love can help you see the truth, the play suggests, desire can blind you to the facts. And Maria's experiences with Edward show that the main problem with disability is the attitudes to it of the able-bodied. The production's mixture of signing, projected captions and voiceovers meant that simple words and actions became loaded with added meaning as we could imagine what it's like to be deprived of one of our senses. As Edward eventually realises, 'In the darkness you could see everything' (82). The oxymoron of enlightening darkness suggests a different way of being.

Spooky coincidences are also at the heart of Laura Wade's brilliant *Breathing Corpses*, the story of how the discovery of one corpse leads to other deaths, which is told by using a structure in which some scenes are chronological and some not, a device which creates a sense of dislocation that emphasises the inability of the characters to communicate. Amy, a hotel chambermaid, finds a corpse on two occasions while cleaning a room. It turns out that the second corpse is that of Jim, a storage facility manager whose depression has worsened after he himself found a corpse of a woman in a box at work. And that dead body turns out to be a woman killed after a quarrel with her boyfriend, during which it emerges that she – in a 'surreal' (55) turn of events – found a corpse in the park while walking the dog. Because of the play's fragmented structure, the story only fully emerges in the final scene. Similarly unsettling is Winsome Pinnock's underrated *One Under*, in which train driver Cyrus is so shocked by the experience of his first 'one under' that he quits his job and tries to find out why the victim, Sonny, killed himself. Meanwhile, we watch the last twenty-four hours in the life of the suicide. When Cyrus becomes spookily convinced that Sonny is his long-lost son, he tries to atone for abandoning him by calling on his adoptive mother, Nella. This mirrors Sonny's desire to make recompense for accidentally running over a child. By playing with coincidence, Pinnock creates a satisfying thriller out of a domestic drama. In this dark landscape, national unease is expressed through fear of murder, and plot dislocations mirror identity confusion.

Equally daring was Caryl Churchill's exceptionally cogent *A Number*, which looked at the issue of genetic engineering by staging encounters between an aged father and his son, and with two clones of his son. One actor, Daniel Craig in Stephen Daldry's production, plays all of the sons, thus underlining the point about the confusions of genetic manipulation (164). First we see the father (Michael Gambon) with Bernard, his favourite of a number of cloned replicas of an original Bernard, who had been taken into care after his mother's suicide and his father's descent into alcoholism. Then we see the original Bernard, and finally another of the clones (after the original Bernard kills the favoured clone). Although the emotional heart of play is about father–son relationships, the spookiness of seeing the same actor portraying three very different characters gave the text an added punch. As well as being a play, in Daldry's words, about the 'conflict between nature and nurture', it is also, argues Amelia Howe Kritzer, yet another example of 'a dysfunctional family once again serving as metaphor for a nation in conflict'.[20]

Plays featuring ghosts were also a feature of the decade. A ghost or spirit presence is a theatrical device which quietly questions British secular identity. Of course, spirits are a paradoxical stage presence: by nature incorporeal, they are embodied by flesh-and-blood actors who defy the audience to question their ghostliness. For example, Tanika Gupta's heartfelt *The Waiting Room* (National, 2000) opens with Priya (a Bengali mother living in England) waking up but not realising that she is dead. After seeing her corpse in an open coffin she successfully persuades her spirit guide, in the guise of Bollywood idol Dilip, to grant her spirit three days on earth to clear up some unfinished family business. In David Farr's hauntingly redemptive *Night of the Soul* (RSC, 2002), Francis, a forty-year-old market-research guru, meets Joanna, a fourteenth-century ghost and bubonic plague survivor, in his hotel bedroom. She is visible only to him, and needs his cooperation to find release from purgatory. By contrast, Moira Buffini's amusing *Loveplay* (RSC, 2001) is set on the same patch of land 'which moves through time from the past to the present', covering incidents from AD 79 up to now, while in Roy Williams's *Little Sweet Thing* (Ipswich, etc., 2005), the medieval figure of Death lurks behind a contemporary hoodie.[21] Finally, the first prize for celestial drama must go to Frantic Assembly's *Heavenly* (2002), based on an idea by Gary Owen and set entirely in heaven. Plays such as these contest the materialism of British society with intimations of a spirit world, and suggest that the Brits are less earthbound than they sometimes like to think. While in this decade few plays seriously got to grips with the reality of the upsurge in contemporary religious feeling, whether Christian or Muslim, fiction was a place where vaguer spiritual longings could be expressed.

Parallel worlds

Closely related to spooky coincidences was the device of parallel worlds, in which playwrights evoked lives which run side-by-side with our own, either simultaneously or at a distance. For example, Zinnie Harris's *Further than the Furthest Thing* (Tron/National, 2000) is a history play whose language evokes a whole new world. Based on real events on Tristan da Cunha, an island in the South Atlantic whose 268 inhabitants were evacuated by the British government in 1961 after a volcanic eruption, the play dreamily creates a society that time forgot. Their isolation, according to Harris, means 'that the islanders are an odd hybrid of cultures and periods, part Napoleonic, part Victorian and part modern in dress, accent and attitude'.[22] But she is careful not to turn her island into a lost paradise. Its community is poor, ignorant and suspicious of strangers; strong friendships rub shoulders with ancient feuds; pidgin is the common tongue. Two main plotlines twist like creepers among the island rocks: in one, Mill, who is married to Bill, tries to keep her sister's son Francis, who she has brought up, on the island despite his desire to leave. When the family is evacuated to Southampton, Mill gradually becomes the leader of the campaign to return home. In the other plotline, Francis falls in love with Rebecca, a young woman who's pregnant after being raped by sailors. He emerges as a man unable to commit himself to love because he's always dreaming of living in another place. At the same time, the play also explores a wider issue, with its imaginative account of how a guilty secret in the island's past – Mill reveals that when the supply ship was delayed by world war, the islanders let some starve so that others could live – can both cement and threaten the foundations of this remote community. Mill's description of how those condemned to starve, including her sister (Francis's mother), looked when they were packed into boats is typically haunting:

> And they is all sat there – rows and rows
> Empty faces, old old faces
> Is got so old all of a sudden
> Even though my sister is younger than me, her face is all bone
> And we is said good bye on the shore (159)

The play also explores different attitudes to identity: the British government wants the islanders to 'feel like Britons' 'even when you are undressed' (133), but Mill refuses, and becomes a stronger, more determined islander while in exile. By contrast, Francis adopts an English identity, and tries to speak standard English. Although he insists that he no longer feels alone because 'out there is all of H'england' (128), Mill mockingly asks Rebecca to 'Be pouring Francis some H'england tea out of the H'england teapot' (137). Britain is shown to deceive the islanders by pretending that their land has sunk beneath the waves, while using it as a base for atom-bomb tests. With its poetic text, its fully imagined characters and its nuanced approach to the big issues of colonialism and community, *Further than the Furthest Thing* is a triumph of ambitious theatricality and affectionate empathy.

Sometimes parallel worlds are divided by centuries. In Mark Ravenhill's epic and highly entertaining play with music, *Mother Clap's Molly House* (National, 2001), Act One is set in the eighteenth century and tells the story of Mrs Tull (Deborah Findlay), who after the death of her husband manages his dress-hire shop and eventually turns it into a molly house, a kind of 1720s same-sex club, which, says the playwright, 'wasn't a brothel, you didn't pay for sex, but you did pay for the beer, and it was a good place for men to gather'. Based on this 'hidden history',[23] Ravenhill begins with the sexual ethos and the spirit of capitalism, in which sex increasingly becomes a commodity. In this Hogarthian London, whores and backstreet abortions counterpoint the joyful frolics of the mollies. By contrast, Act Two looks at gay identity in contemporary London. Here gay men, plus a dealer and his woman friend, lose themselves in the party atmosphere: drugs are consumed, sex acts are filmed and porn videos watched; partners are swapped. This is more critical than Act One, and Ravenhill is sceptical of the current idea of gayness as an identity based simply on shopping and fucking. While we tend to think of the past as sexually repressed, what fascinates him is its tolerance. And the absence of restrictive labels, such as 'gay'. The molly house is an urban oasis where activities include sexual pleasure, transvestitism and even a game in which a man 'gives birth' to a baby doll. It is a metaphor for flexible gender identity.

Both the eighteenth-century characters and their contemporary counterparts have created a world in which anything is possible, but some of them – eighteenth-century Martin and twenty-first-century Will – still long for traditional one-to-one relationships, and the play dramatises the contradictions between freedom and fidelity. But critical reactions to it focused less on questions of monogamy and more on stage images of sex. Ravenhill clearly wanted to get away from the 1990s trope of equating anal sex with violence. He says:

> In fact, anal sex is much like any other sex – nearly always consensual, often a bit messy, a bit embarrassing, a bit funny, a bit moving, sometimes boring but usually amazingly enjoyable. Let's see men on the British stage having anal sex much as they do in life – frequently and for fun.[24]

Some critics agreed that the play 'celebrates Sodom like there's no Gomorrah' and that 'buggery is often a Good Thing', while others argued that he was 'less a serious playwright than a clever sensationalist' or condemned his 'decadent self-indulgence'.[25]

In the end, it is music that joins the two parallel worlds. Throughout Nicholas Hytner's production, Matthew Scott's baroque fanfares and lively song settings lifted the spirits, culminating in the final moments when a molly-house scene morphs into a rave. Although Ravenhill has no easy answers to the problems of gay culture, and refuses to hark back nostalgically to the past, he does suggest that the joys of music and the pleasure of desire offer an affirmation of the human spirit: as one character says, 'Now dance, you buggers, dance' (109). Being staged at the National, and directed by its artistic director, *Mother Clap's Molly House* confirmed the assimilation by the liberal elite of contemporary notions of queer identity.

Although the 2000s were not vintage years for Howard Barker, one of British theatre's most imaginative playwrights, his *Dead Hands* (Wrestling School, 2004) is proof that, in the words of David Rabey, he has not only 'questioned and extended the possibilities of theatre so restlessly, eloquently and purposefully', but also retains the ability to create a world suffused by the 'gratingly beautiful and the desperately erotic'.[26] The play is a powerful psychodrama: a father lies in his coffin, and his two sons, Eff and Istvan, arrive. Eff is drawn to Sopron, his father's mistress, and soon discovers that Istvan has already had sex with her. When she offers herself to Eff, he struggles to accept his father's strange legacy. Using a style of writing and staging he calls 'Theatre of Catastrophe', Barker eschews naturalism and offers instead a fascinating meditation on loss and longing, and on the intimate coupling of sexuality and death. His ideas on the erotic energy that emanates from the body of a widow are provocative, macabre and oddly appealing. In this parallel world of the aroused imagination, it feels as if he's torn open our psyche and shone a light into the darkness. Barker's characters don't just talk – they spill out streams of words, which are sometimes poetic, sometimes incantatory, sometimes crude. The effect of the production, directed by Barker himself, was emotionally cold yet strangely compelling. Although the action felt as if it was at a great distance, the gleam of an acute speculative intelligence illuminated this murky tale and, as the characters buckled under the weight of their feelings, you ended up with a sense of having survived a long psychological journey. Yes, Barker's work is a reminder that there is more to British theatre than soap-opera naturalism.

Similarly, the work of Lin Coghlan infuses elements of magic realism into tales of underclass life. An Irish playwright who works in Britain, Coghlan says, 'I've always been interested in magical realism [. . .] and the idea of having different realities happening at the same time.'[27] Her *Mercy* (Soho, 2004), for instance, is about a group of underclass kids who find themselves, for various reasons, in the open countryside. Mac and his brother Cookie have teemed up with Deccy for some petty crime, but their plans have gone awry, and they're on the run. Meanwhile, Terry is helping fifteen-year-old Jean escape from her care home. Finally, Rory, a probation officer who's sick of both his job and his marriage, joins the youngsters. In a wonderfully freewheeling story – which mixes bold dialogue, direct-address narrative and surreal imagery – Coghlan brings her characters together as a flood of biblical proportions suddenly overwhelms the country. London, it seems, has been hit by a terrorist attack and nature has gone haywire. In this post-apocalyptic landscape, Coghlan, with a lovely lightness of touch, gives *Mercy* a redemption tone, arguing for the innate goodness of even the worst underclass tearaway. Thrown together by disaster, each of them reacts with a touch of true humanity.

If Coghlan's play has elements of magic realism, so does Fin Kennedy's award-winning *How To Disappear Completely and Never Be Found*, which shows two parallel worlds: in one, the stressed out executive Charlie lives out his last day on earth; in the other, a pathologist repeatedly tells him he is already dead. The result is a spooky take on the theme of identity. Set in the no man's land between Christmas and the New Year, the play, with its focus on the invisible economy of branding and banking, seems to anticipate the credit crunch, and Charlie's decision to drop out and change his identity, acquiring forged documents and being tutored in how to disappear and create a new life, clearly touched a contemporary nerve. But this rich play also rippled with many other ideas. At one point, a man who looks after lost property for London Transport asks himself what the 'armfuls and armfuls' of mislaid umbrellas say about Britain: 'It says caution, it says preparation, it says pragmatism. Quiet, ordered lives in which nothing could be more distressing than to get rained on. The umbrella, the safety net of the nation' (11). In the end, this excellent morality play, directed by Ellie Jones, shows that we can escape everything but ourselves.

Medium messages

Paradoxical storytelling – and the world of the arts and media – were another fertile ground for playwrights. A fabulous example is Martin McDonagh's *The Pillowman* (National, 2003). Set in police cells in an unnamed totalitarian state, it focuses on Katurian (K), a writer whose stories about children meeting horrible deaths seem to have inspired a rash of copycat killings. Two cops, the wily Tupolski and the dim Ariel, interrogate him and his retarded brother Michal. It turns out that both brothers have been victims of an experiment performed by their parents: in an effort to turn K into a genius, they tortured Michal every night, making his brother listen to his screams. After Michal is revealed as the child killer, K murders him, in an enactment of 'The Pillowman' story, which imagines a friendly executioner who helps children destined to become suicidal by murdering them in childhood. He then confesses so that he can make a deal and preserve his writings for posterity. At the end, K is executed and Tupolski tells him he will burn his stories. But, in a final twist, Ariel preserves the manuscript. All this is shown amid dizzying flights of storytelling which include readings of K's short stories and narratives about the lives of the brothers.

As a meditation on storytelling, this is a theatrically compelling extravaganza which plays with ideas about the relationship of art and life. For while K is the main storyteller, with such horrid gems as 'The Little Apple Men' and 'The Tale of the Three Gibbet Crossroads', it is clear that he does not approve of real-life killings. It is the damaged Michal, the audience of these gruesome tales, who acts them out. On stage, K tells Michal two stories, 'The Little Green Pig' and 'The Pillowman', while Tupolski joins in this festival of narratives by telling his own tale: the hilarious 'Story of the Little Deaf Boy on the Big Long Railroad Tracks. In China'. As Catherine Rees observes, the storytelling follows the changes in power relations between the men. At the start of the play, K is interrogated by Tupolski and has no power; if knowledge is power, then Tupolski is all-powerful, and he initially uses one of K's stories to argue that it has a hidden agenda 'underneath the surface' (19). When he makes K read out his 'best' story, 'The Tale of the Town on the River', K comments that this feels like being at school. Tupolski's reply – 'Except at school they didn't execute you at the end' (19–20) – shows that his power is total. Later, after K is condemned to death and has nothing to lose, this is reversed when the cop solicits the prisoner's approval for his story (90–1).[28]

McDonagh makes fictional and metaphorical truth more meaningful than literal truth. For example, at the end of Act One, K's autobiographical story 'The Writer and the Writer's Brother' is not literally true – K alters the literal truth of the story, making it a 'happy ending' for Michal. This attitude leads to K's instruction to his brother, that the 'first rule of storytelling [is] "Don't believe everything you read in the newspapers"' (40) and his belief that 'There are no happy endings in real life' (34, 59–60). Originally directed by John Crowley, with a cast led by David Tennant (K), Jim Broadbent (Tupolski), Nigel Lindsay (Ariel) and Adam Godley (Michal), the play featured tableaux which illustrated the tortured childhood of the brothers. At one point, a seemingly dead character jumps up (34) – and the gasp of the audience seared the memory.

Equally fascinating was Terry Johnson's highly successful *Hitchcock Blonde*. The play spans three different eras: in 1999, Alex takes one of his students, Nicola, to a Greek island, where they unearth fragments of a lost Alfred Hitchcock movie. In 1959, Hitchcock is filming *Psycho*, using Blonde as a body double for Janet Leigh. In 1919, the date of the film fragment uncovered by Alex and Nicola, the director's trademark obsession with blondes is already taking shape. The tawdry tale of Alex's mid-life crisis, and his manipulative seduction of the blonde Nicola, fuse with the triangle of Hitch, Blonde and her husband, which illustrates Hitch's power to make and unmake stars. Blonde understands this, and expects to graduate from body double to star by way of the casting couch. To her surprise, Hitch just wants to watch, to film but not to touch her. When she tells her husband of how she felt on the set, with all eyes on her naked body, and her growing awareness of the power of her beauty, he attacks her. In the end, both Alex and Hitch are men who prefer to watch rather than touch, to control rather than feel. Their love of sexual images comes from their fear of intimacy; it's safer to gaze than to get involved. For them, blondes are childlike women – less of a threat. And, for Hitch, the blonde has to be cool, unsexed. For the women, each with their distinctive voice, their compliance in male sexual fantasy ends in self-mutilation and disappointment. Directed by the author, the production featured David Haig (Alex), Fiona Glascott (Nicola), William Hootkins (Hitch) and Rosamund Pike (Blonde), and its multimedia elements – projections created by William Dudley – were beguiling.[29]

Other playwrights were also inspired by the lives of artists. For example, Rebecca Lenkiewicz's *Shoreditch Madonna* (Soho, 2005) shines a light on youngsters Michael, Nick and Hodge, who run a squatted art-space in London's East End. They invite fiftysomething Devlin – once an inspiring painter, now a washed-up drunk – to a Happening. When he arrives, he meets Martha, an old flame. Meanwhile, on the other side of town, Christina is devastated by the suicide of her lover, Devlin's son. Although the play is full of snippets about art, from Hodge's evocation of a woman as 'Venus de Milo. Plus arms' (39) to Martha's habit of staring at the figures in Leonardo's 'Virgin and St Anne' 'until they start to move' (71), it's the domineering Devlin, played by Leigh Lawson, who was the most memorable part of the show. He is an amazing, larger-than-life creation, with his wryly disillusioned declarations, such as 'I have as little desire to show my work as my genitals' (16), and his hopelessness. In him is embodied the idea of the artist as madman. And next to craziness is belief. In Tim Crouch's *An Oak Tree* (Traverse, 2005) and, especially, *England* (Traverse/Fruitmarket, 2007), the world of art comes across as a substitute faith. Both pieces not only question the definition of theatre, but also suggest that the Brits can be defined by a passion for art. Similarly, questions about the relationship between art and life are deftly handled in Stephen Jeffreys's engaging and original *I Just Stopped by To See the Man* (Royal Court, 2000), in which a 1970s white rock star meets a mythical Delta bluesman in a confrontation that explores superstition and authenticity in popular music. In Bryony Lavery's captivating *A Wedding Story*, the iconic 1942 film *Casablanca* provides a romantic counterpoint to the more down-to-earth story about love, marriage and its discontents, while David Greig and Gordon McIntyre's uplifting

Midsummer used songs to chart the highs and lows of falling in love in a play which also has joyously satirical references to rom-coms, as well as a hilarious episode ('The Song of Bob's Cock') in which a man's penis chats to him (21)!

If film or art was often used as a metaphor for the problems of creativity, Helen Cooper's lyrical and humane *Three Women and a Piano Tuner* uses classical music in a similar way. Here all is not what it seems: halfway through, the piano tuner turns out to be the son of one of three sisters; by the end, the three sisters turn out to be one person (their names – Ella, Beth and Liz – are variations of Elizabeth). It's a play about the three possible outcomes of a daughter's decision, after being impregnated by her father, about whether to have the baby. In this dream play, Ella, who lives her son, a piano tuner, has composed a piano concerto, and to get it publicly performed she enlists the help of Liz, a professional pianist, and Beth, whose husband is immensely rich. If you have been brought up to play an instrument – 'before we were eighteen we had already practised more than 15,000 hours' (47) – how difficult, the play asks, is it to have a different career? Cooper is as creative in her attitude to theatre form as her characters are in musical composition.

The delight of writing plays that allude to other media led to some vivid stagings. Anthony Neilson's explorations of dreams and nightmares have, in some instances, involved using parodies of established theatre forms. In Edward Gant's *Amazing Feats of Loneliness!* (Plymouth, 2002), the set is that most English of entertainments, a Victorian freakshow, but the theme is at first loneliness, and then the tensions between realism and absurdism, 'real life as it is lived' versus 'all that is superfluous to survival: love and dreams and imagination' (67–8). Another Neilson play, *The Lying Kind* (Royal Court, 2002), is a black farce about two policemen who are not brave enough to break some bad news to an old couple at Christmas. Once again, the farce form is used to make serious points about how trying too hard to be kind, a very English vice, can be more cruel than direct communication.

Direct communication is also much needed in Dan Rebellato's *Static* (Suspect/Graeae, 2008), a story about Sarah, a young woman who loses her husband. As she grieves, barely consoled by her geeky friend Martin, she comes across a compilation tape of songs recorded by her husband. Knocked off balance by her loss, Sarah begins to think that the tape holds a secret message for her. But, when she can't work out what it is, she starts imagining that her husband is visiting her in spirit and communicating from beyond the grave. In fact, the cassette does have a message – but it has nothing to do with spirits. Instead, the titles of the songs spell out a message of love to her. The whole play is full of delightfully nerdy stuff about pop music, and features a game of fantasy concerts in which long-dead musicians or bands that have split up return for an imaginary gig. And the compilation tape is aptly described as a two-act drama (50). Music is a metaphor for life's glory. 'Music isn't just music. Music is also everything else' (82). The play is also a meditation on fallibility as Martin proves that Sarah's memory of first meeting Chris is fictional, even if it has an emotional truth.

Media means cameras and screens, and the sinister nature of surveillance was emphasised by Rob Evans's *A Girl in a Car with a Man* (Royal Court, 2004), which doesn't show the child abduction suggested by the title, but instead illustrates its effect on gay clubber Alex (Andrew Scott), shopping-channel presenter Stella, ex-photographer David and troubled mother Paula. And rarely can a theatrical absence so strongly affect what we see on stage. Paula, who's fascinated by the CCTV footage of the abduction, struggles to connect with the reality behind the images, while Alex finds that when a club screens the surveillance footage during a dance, it simply reminds him of his terrible loneliness. Meanwhile, Stella is so haunted by the same pictures that she flees her job and bursts in on the unsuspecting David, a loner nursing photos of his dead girlfriend. Although reminiscent of Simon Stephens's *One Minute*, which handled a similar situation with more concision, Evans's play is both a powerful account of the effect of images on the lonely mind and a representation of contemporary Britain, not only the surveillance capital of the world, but a place that delights in all forms of media.

Imagined communities

One powerful aspect of fantasy is imagining national identity, and British playwrights sometimes produced metaphors to help us understand the changing image of the nation. One of these was the classroom, in which people from different backgrounds struggle to learn about the United Kingdom. The best example was David Edgar's *Testing the Echo*, one of the few plays that staged the full cacophony of voices in contemporary Britain. At its start, cast members speak in a variety of foreign languages, reflecting the cultural mix that makes up today's Britain. The title refers to the way that tourists once tested the echo in the old domed library at the British Museum by shouting loudly – how very unBritish.[30] As such, it is a powerful metaphor: the outsider might be encouraged to test the echo, just to see if it really exists, but then they might be taken aback by the response of the natives. More practically, they might want to test how far they can go in our increasingly illiberal society. Central to the play is New Labour's citizenship test. As anxieties about what it means to be British have intensified, it is surely a characteristic irony that the test we expect foreigners to take is so difficult that most natives couldn't pass it.

The play's main conflict is between Emma, a teacher of English for Speakers of Other Languages, and one of her students, a Muslim woman called Nasim. While the idealistic Emma tries to treat every student equally, her liberal values clash with Nasim's religious beliefs. Emma asks Nasim to discuss a picture of an English breakfast, which includes pork, and to play devil's advocate by arguing against a student's right to wear a jilbab in school. For her part, Nasim won't say things she doesn't believe in, and she objects to gays. Is any compromise possible between Emma's ideas of openness, tolerance and decency, and Nasim's deeply held religious commitment? Edgar offers no simple solution. At the same time, this is only one plot strand in a complex play that also includes a passionate discussion between two Muslims about the meaning of Islam, the story of Tetyana, who needs British citizenship to solve a marriage problem, and Chong, whose workmates tease him about the citizenship test. Added to this is a running debate about British history, comments by bloggers on the citizenship website, and a heated dinner-party conversation about values and rights. In this way, the play perfectly reflects the confusing mess of reality. In fact, here the confusion is positively thrilling. Politically, Edgar underlines the irony that many of the things that attract people to Britain, such as personal freedoms, are now in danger of being taken away by a government which cannot resist public pressure to 'do something' about immigration. He also shows how the citizenship test raises more questions than it answers.

The strength of Matthew Dunster's Out of Joint production was that it ended with the whole cast on stage performing a minute of clapping, in which some actors clapped one rhythm and others clapped a different one. This referred back to the scene in which Emma got her class to clap to illustrate the idea of stress. At the end of the play, all these different rhythms coalesced into one. Although *Testing the Echo* offers no solutions to the problems of culture clash, its staging did suggest the possibility of harmony, however temporary and however stressful. As journalist Abdul-Rehman Malik wrote in the programme:

> In the handwringing over national values, we forget that nations and nationalisms are not static. Values are best developed as a result of vigorous debate, not social engineering. I believe that Britain is, and always will be, a work in progress. The reality of 'Middle England' is not my reality [. . .] Britain is formed and re-formed every day by her citizens. It seems we 'newcomers' have embraced the mongrel character of this English race.[31]

Richard Bean was one of the few playwrights who grappled with this idea of a mongrel England, or Britain. In his introduction to Bean's *Plays Three*, Chris Campbell points out that three of his plays 'feature the word "England" or its cognates in the title' (9). Most of his plays – but especially *The God Botherers*, *The English Game* and *England People Very Nice* – are full of humorous insights into the way the Brits imagine themselves. As Keith says in *The God Botherers*:

'Without the rule of law you're fucked. That's what Britain gave to the world, and from that one idea, flows everything. Equal rights for all men, Shakespeare, cricket, The Clash. Look at the sports we invented: football, rugby, swimming – ' (187). Or cricket. Unlike most of the decade's dramas, Bean's *The English Game* is a play about sport. Focusing on the Nightwatchmen, an amateur London cricket team, it watches the eleven men play a Sunday match against their opponents. The picture of England at the start is contemporary in its squalor: the pitch has been fouled by dogs, the pavilion burnt down by vandals, so the team has to change in the open air, leaving on the ground their valuables, which are then stolen by a chav. It's such a familiar sketch of national life. The characters too are instantly recognisable: Will the opinionated captain, Theo the understanding GP, Sean the cricket-mad journalist, Thiz the aged rock star, Reg the Little Englander, Clive the egotistical actor, plus a plumber, a gay Hindu and a black British Council penpusher.

Playing cricket is a powerful metaphor: very little is said explicitly about England or Britain, and although Tory politician Norman Tebbit's notorious 'cricket test' is rebuffed implicitly, it is never mentioned directly.[32] Instead, Bean takes an indirect approach. At the climax, Sean and his ideals of fair play are exposed as selfishness (225), and Bean shows how the Iraq War has divided the country into satirists and tolerants. The satirists, embodied by Will, are old lefties who are prepared to mock militant Islam as well as the rich and powerful. The tolerants, embodied by Theo, stand for the old British values of benign toleration. Near the end of the play, Will argues that 'self-hatred is the cancer at the heart of our nation' (220) and, upset by 7/7, rants against Islamic fundamentalism, while Theo protests, 'What's happened to tolerance?' (221). Britain is a nation divided. Cricket is no longer a symbol of national unity, but a place where male anxieties flourish. When I saw Sean Holmes's touring production at a matinee at the Rose in Kingston upon Thames, the audience laughed at the dirty humour, muttered at Theo's speech about quitting the country and tut-tutted the Muslim jokes. Then they clapped the summer rainstorm which ends the play. Bad weather provided a moment of self-recognition. How very English.

Fantasy about the future often addresses the issue of national identity, and the way we imagine ourselves behaving in a crisis says a lot about who we want to be. Steve Waters's *The Contingency Plan* (Bush, 2009) was a rare attempt to tackle the subject of climate change. It comprises two plays about how flooding induced by global warming will affect Britain. In the first, *On the Beach*, Will, a glaciologist working in Antarctica, returns to his East Anglian coastal home to introduce his new girlfriend, Sarika, a top civil servant, to his parents. He also needs to tell his father Robin that he has accepted a job advising the government about climate change. This is tricky because some forty years previously his father had fallen out with a fellow-scientist, Colin, about the causes of global warming. Colin has gone on to become the top government expert while the bitterly disillusioned Robin has retired by the sea, whose levels are relentlessly rising. In the second play, *Resilience*, the location is Whitehall and, Sarika introduces Will to the two new Conservative ministers, Tessa and Chris. As they struggle to mitigate the immediate effects of extreme weather conditions, Will and Colin fight over the contingency plan. For while Colin believes that small measures will be enough, Will insists that only drastic action – creating a carbon-free lifestyle – will have any effect. Waters's portrait of the Brits in adversity is very familiar: Robin is an eccentric figure who is so disillusioned with politics – 'suck the good out of you' (63) – that he deliberately remains in his flood-threatened house. The younger generation, Will and Sarika, are more idealistic while the politicians are either opportunistic moralists or simply lazy. Colin, the scientific expert, is a passionate pragmatist. In the original production, the doubling of Robin Soans as Robin and his rival Colin enforced this picture of English eccentricity. Soans also performed the most theatrical moments of the plays: in *On the Beach*, directed by Michael Longhust, he wheeled out a small transparent tank which, using real water, shows the effects of rising sea levels on a small model landscape. In *Resilience*, directed by Tamara Harvey, he illustrates the interdependence of nature by using several metres of bright green twine.

The subject of national identity also attracted leftfield plays. The most beautifully bizarre must be Lucy Kirkwood's *Tinderbox*, which is set in an Empire-building butcher's shop and features a running joke about rewriting British history in a pornographic register: Churchill's speech becomes a film called *We Will Fuck Them on the Beaches*; Sir Francis Drake tackles *The Spanish Arse-mada* and Horatio becomes *Fellatio Nelson* (22). If an Englishman's home is his castle, 'an Englishman's shop is his Empire' (10)! Another example, Ron Hutchinson's *Head/Case* (Coventry, 2004), is set in a halfway house for brain-damaged patients and features Irish Tracy who, after being hit on the head, can't stop talking, and English Julia who, after surviving a car crash, can barely get a word out. Given their nationalities, the clash between the verbose emotionality of the one and the repressed stiffness of the other acquires a political edge, as exemplified by asides such as: 'There's your Irish joke and your Scots joke and your Welsh joke but the English joke? [. . .] the English are just the English' (73). If both Tracy and Julia typify national stereotypes – the hard-drinking, song-singing and life-loving Celt versus the dreary, Laura Ashley Englishwoman – then how are their personal identities affected by their accidents? When Tracy says, 'Tracy; I'm Irish' (42), you can feel she's hanging onto this idea for dear life. But since Julia is stuck in the past, and can't feel anything, there's no way she can change her essential Englishness, or update it, or respond to anyone. Both women have found that their most intimate sense of self has been affected by brain damage. And without a sense of self, how can you be either English or Irish?

Stage images can sometimes picture the nation. In Anne Downie's *Parking Lot in Pittsburgh* (Byre, St Andrews, 2001), the legacy of a Scotswoman in her seventies is contested by her sisters in an allegory of Scotland's position in the new millennium, and conveyed by a set that was a cluster of coloured windows which gradually turn into a fragmented Union Jack. Thrown across the footlights, stage images can also be tellingly ambiguous: in Catherine Czerkawska's *Quartz* (Traverse, 2000) a mysterious statue is washed ashore – it looks like a woman roughly carved by the sea: depending on who is looking, it might be a gift from nature, a miraculous Madonna or a Protestant shrine. Which poses the question: are we a nation of nature worshippers, renegade Catholics or good Protestants? And who is the 'we' here? Similarly, Marisa Carnesky's 'House of Knives', a sketch that was part of the *Everything Must Go!* review (Soho, 2009), used a stage trick to convey the agonies of mortgage madness, a national obsession during the run-up to the credit crunch. A 'volunteer' from the audience was put into a bright-red doll's house and then Carnesky, dressed in a bold-red flouncy frock, skewered them with a dozen huge knives. Once again, the nation is seen as fragmented, ambiguous or skewered.

Sometimes the whole cast of a play, such as Che Walker's *The Frontline* (Globe, 2008), presented a panorama of today's rainbow Britain in all its vibrant confusion. Set in Camden, north London, its twenty-three-strong cast of lonely souls showed how the mean streets shake with the howls and exaltations of the lost, the sad, the good and the evil. Walker's parade of characters included Beth the born-again Christian, Erkenwald the Scottish hot-dog vendor, Violet the lap-dancer and Marcus the bouncer. One running joke concerned Mordechai Thurrock, a self-obsessed playwright. Another followed an eccentric old gent called Ragdale, who thinks that he is related to every young woman he comes across. Yet another was about Babydoll, Violet's daughter, the quintessential gobby teen. There is an Afghan coffee salesman, a Polish immigrant, a suit-wearing racist, a chav teen and a valium-addled mum. What is true of London is not true of the rest of Britain, but few other plays showed the kaleidoscopic sense of national identity in flux as effectively as this. Welcome to your nation, mongrel and proud of it.

When British theatre lets its hair down, and starts to loosen up, a whole world of experiment becomes available to writers of every generation: imaginative visions, from inner space to parallel universes, and from spooky coincidences to exploring other media. Art and media might occasionally appear to be a new religion, but neither are able to save us. Sometimes the marriage of traditional social realism and oneiric fantasy was British through and through. An appealing metaphor is that of the kaleidoscope: throw up the pieces and see where they fall. In all this wildness, with some spirits howling in the dark while others lurk on the edges of reason, Britain manages to retain its familiar landmarks: the Brits come across as eccentrics in a world where even the worst disasters usually bring out the stoical best in the people, whose humour, pessimism and pride are part of an essential survival kit. Maybe George Orwell was right: in these plays, the Brits seem able to change out of all recognition and yet still remain essentially the same.

CONCLUSION

Jeremy   And you are Jamaican? British? What do you guys call yourselves now?
Lavelle   (*ignores*) Whatever.

(Kwame Kwei-Armah, Seize the Day, 128)

In the 2000s, British new writing took a wide variety of forms, and grasped the opportunity to stage an ongoing conversation, often a debate, sometimes a polemic, about who we are and what we might become. All in all, playwrights didn't always agree on either the problem, or the solution. This is perfectly understandable: it would be odd indeed if the nation that playwrights imagined, whether English, Scottish, Welsh, Northern Irish or British, was always the same, and indeed it wasn't. In a world of multiple identities, diverse communities and conflicted individuals, a one-size-fits-all national identity is clearly a non-starter. Aptly enough, in *England People Very Nice* Richard Bean alludes to Daniel Defoe (14), who in his 1701 poem 'The True Born Englishman' concludes: 'A true-born Englishman's a contradiction, / In speech an irony, in fact a fiction.'[1] But it's precisely because national identity is a form of fiction that it is so suitable for fictional treatment. After all, in fiction you can imagine things that are difficult to realise in reality, and national identity is one of those things that stubbornly resist definition.

Everyone has their own idea of what being British means, and some even argue that to define what it means to be British is actually, er, very un-British. Of course, the God-blessed confidence of being born in England has traditionally meant that you didn't have to define anything. Yet sometimes an outsider would do it for you. In Ronald Harwood's *An English Tragedy* (Watford, 2008), a history play about the Second World War traitor John Amery, his Jewish father Leo Amery says: 'The English have never understood why anyone should be concerned with the mystery of identity. That's because they're so certain of their own. The notion of belonging or not belonging is alien to them because they belong' (62–3). The entire speech runs for more than a page, and successfully evokes the old certainties of an Imperial self-image, both internationalist and parochial. It is exactly these certainties that are now so uncertain.

In the postwar, post-Empire and edge-of-the-European Union era, notes of doubt, guilt and embarrassment have crept into the national psyche. Being English is still assumed to be a blessing, but now with an awareness of national decline, one of the stories the Brits constantly tell themselves. Gloom about decline is an emotional given: after listing a wide range of contemporary achievements by our happy breed, broadcaster Jeremy Paxman comments, 'And yet they remain convinced they're finished.'[2] English manners and customs are now objects of self-doubt and self-derision: Kate Fox lists 'social dis-ease', 'a shorthand term for all our chronic social inhibitions and handicaps', as top of her list of the characteristics of Englishness.[3] And British theatre agrees. In Mike Bartlett's *Cock*, a play full of typically awkward social interaction, John gives his lover a present, involving teddy bears. 'Very English,' remarks the lover (10). And sure enough, it's a present made in bad faith, to distract from an infidelity. Self-mockery, quiet evasiveness, social unease – this is the tone of voice that articulates the tensions between traditional and contemporary notions of identity, the whole subject being treated as a contested and contradictory territory.

Olde images of Britishness, or Englishness, are significant because they provide a stable fiction against which to define ourselves, and traditional images of the nation are not hard to find: for example, in the opening minute of Dennis Kelly's *Love and Money*, an Englishman asks a French woman: 'Are you missing our English food? If the pain gets too much my suggestion is have a look behind the fridge, find something brown, stick it between two slices of bread, et voila! The taste of England' (209). The tongue-in-cheek humour is as recognisable as the cuisine. For while some traditional notions of national identity are oppressive, they are also, at the same time, often enabling: when articulated on stage, they can be instantly parodied. So in David

Greig's *Pyrenees* when the hotel Proprietor asks, 'Do you think we [foreigners] all look the same, madam? Wogs begin at Calais?' (48), the satirical intent is clear. Similarly, in David Hare's *Stuff Happens* the line 'the English expression – "playing fair"' (74) is voiced not by a Brit, but by the French Foreign Minister, Dominique de Villepin. And when in Alan Bennett's *The Habit of Art* (National, 2009), W. H. Auden tells Benjamin Britten: 'This is England talking, isn't it, Ben? This is taste, modesty, self-restraint. The family virtues' (67), these traditional characteristics are seen through the lens of irony.

Most playwrights wrote against traditional and stereotypical images of Englishness. Although often overtaken by reality, such stereotypes still occur in culture and are still strong in the minds of overseas vistors to the UK. If the traditional image of the Englishman or woman was upper class and public school, then most playwrights explored society's lower depths; if the traditional English person was unemotional, most writers wrote characters who emoted freely; if the traditional English individual was moderate, most writers created bloody-minded extremists; if the traditional English family lived a happy suburban life, most writers penned stories of unhappy couples. If tradition was optimistic, most writers were the opposite. If the traditional view of the past was heroic and exceptional, playwrights such as Richard Bean and Jez Butterworth gave us lessons in alternative history, whether comic, mythic, or both. If national identity is based on stories we tell ourselves, then playwrights rewrote these stories in critical ways: the four corners of the UK that emerge from the plays of, for example, David Greig, David Harrower, Douglas Maxwell, Gary Owen, Gary Mitchell or Martin McDonagh, are not always traditional, or familiar. Against the sameness of steroetypes, British playwrights triumphantly provided evidence of individualism, non-conformity and flexible identity.

If national identity in the 2000s was increasingly fluid, dynamic and changeable, the country that playwrights described often seemed like a torn nation, not just divided but ripped and shredded. The violence of this image of a torn nation goes well beyond ordinary clichés about Broken Britain: it suggests a general mental state of acute dissatisfaction, and implies a desperate longing for change. Talking about the homegrown bombers of 7/7, Simon Stephens says, 'For me

England at the time felt like a country that was tearing.'[4] Similarly, in Tim Crouch's performance piece *England* the country is seen, in one critic's words, as 'a torn self that has barely even begun to really look at itself, despite its insistent demand to be seen'.[5] The same phrase could equally well be applied to controversies such as the one about *Behzti*, which showed a nation split between faith and secularity. Likewise, poverty tended to be portrayed as an emotionally fraught condition in which individuals were ripped apart. Not just social disadvantage, but human devastation. Little wonder that symbols of nationhood were similarly treated. Whenever a Union Jack or flag of St George appeared on stage, it was bound to be somehow defiled, or put into question. In Oladipo Agboluaje's *The Christ of Coldharbour Lane*, one scene shows sinner Maria Maudlin doing a pole dance dressed in a Union Jack bikini. The cover of Lucy Kirkwood's surreal *Tinderbox* featured a porky butcher with a Union Jack apron, while the flag is shown in flames on the cover of James Graham's 1950s history play *Eden's Empire* (Finborough, 2006). Even more provocatively, Cosh Omar's *The Great Extension* featured a Union Jack niqab on its cover, and, during the show, a Union Jack cushion was used to suffocate the traditional English character called Brown; throughout the play, the doorbell played the hymn 'Jerusalem'. At the start of Jez Butterworth's play of the same name, the cross of St George hangs faded and neglected.[6] In instances such as these, the subtext is the feeling of a decline from past glory. Less a New Jerusalem than a dark inferno.

Cultural hybrids

One of the changes in the way we imagine Britain comes from the notion of new hybrid identities. The idea of the hybrid is a model, an ideal which can both be aspired to and used to question the ownership, legitimacy and authenticity of received ideas of national identity. While many white English writers have been largely content with ironic asides or satirical swipes at traditional ideas of Englishness or Britishness, writers from the margin, whether they are Scottish or black, Irish or Asian, were better at imagining cultural hybrids. If genuine hybrid identities are rare, there are many examples of uneasy mixed identities, where different elements are in tension or contradiction. For example, Kofi Agyemang and Patricia Elcock's *Urban Afro Saxons* explored the relationship between skin colour, place of birth and cultural heritage. At one point, having been told that being born here makes her English, Patsy responds: 'So? Just 'cause you born in a stable, that don't make you a horse.' But when she visits Jamaica, the locals call her a 'foreigner'.[7] Hybridity can co-exist with rootlessness. Similarly, Henry Adam's *The People Next Door* includes the following: 'You dress like an American, you talk like a Jamaican, how can I know you? How can I know you if you don't know yourself?' (79). Several playwrights explored this question: in the work of Roy Williams, especially his *Clubland, Sing Yer Heart Out for the Lads* and *Little Sweet Thing*, white characters assume the language, attitudes and tastes of black urban street culture. Williams's work is an example of what Keith Peacock correctly calls 'the mixing of cultural identities to create not black-British (multicultural) but an altogether more complex identity'.[8] In Kwame Kwei-Armah's *Let There Be Love* a West Indian man shares the stage with a Polish woman, a sight that sums up one idea of a new Britain. Likewise, the stage image of the mixed-race child, whether in work by Gupta or Kwei-Armah, strongly argues for a hopeful future. Encouragingly, the new generation, led by playwrights such as Bola Agbaje, zestfully suggests that complexity is the face of the future.

Such hybrids are one result of decades of migration, and the heritage of Empire. On stage, the use of patois, creoles and other languages such as Hindi, Gujarati, Ibo or Yoruba challenges the idea that Britain is an exclusively English-speaking culture. Or one exclusively rooted in blood and soil. In Agbaje's *Detaining Justice*, the Zimbabwian Grace pointedly says, 'We are all immigrants in this land!' (242). Indeed, in opposition to the racist slogan that 'There ain't no black in the Union Jack', Gabriele Griffin argues 'that "black" is a constitutive part of the "Union Jack" as a metaphor for Britain'.[9] Blackness can, of course, refer to skin colour or language or culture, or all of these. In opposition to the traditional English stiff upper lip, a black character's annoyance might be expressed by means of 'teeth sucking or teeth kissing, simultaneously a bodily gesture and an utterance, which tend to occur in scripts by writers with a Caribbean or African background'.[10] In Kwame Kwei-Armah's *Elmina's Kitchen*, to use another example, '**Digger***'s accent swings from his native Grenadian to hard-core Jamaican to authentic black London*' (6).

In play after play, the culture of black and Asian Britons was asserted and reasserted, often in defiance of criticism: the work of Williams or Kwei-Armah or Agbaje has sometimes been attacked by black critics for its negative stereotyping of violent young black men. But there were plenty of other plays that showed the complex national mix, including Cosh Omar's *The Battle of Green Lanes*, about the Cypriot community, or Toby Whithouse's *Jump Mr Malinoff, Jump*, about Russian expats in Southend-on-Sea, or Charlotte Eilenberg's *The Lucky Ones*, about Jewish refugees from Germany, or Hassan Abdulrazzak's *Baghdad Wedding*, about Iraqis in London. In Mike Bartlett's *Artefacts*, the central character is part-Iraqi, part-British. In Adam's *The People Next Door*, the mixed-race Nigel comically redefines Scottish identity. Plays by writers such as Tanika Gupta, Gurpreet Kaur Bhatti or Shan Khan explored the influence of Asian heritage on today's identities. If the Other is often imagined as black in Britain, debbie tucker green's *Stoning Mary* challenges this assumption by using white characters to tell an African story. If you consider that plays such as Williams's *Sing Yer Heart Out for the Lads* or *Fallout* were some of the most exciting of the decade, you can readily agree with Andrew Wyllie when he says that 'the greatest vitality in British theatre in the early 2000s emerged from black writing'.[11]

Sport is central to our acting out of national identity, and football for example is a powerful arena for patriotic sentiment. It is also an area when national pride can degenerate into xenophobia. Oddly enough, there were few plays about sport in this decade, but memorable images include actor Nicholas Tennant as the screaming Tosser in Mike Packer's *A Carpet, a Pony and a Monkey*. But if Tosser is a white hooligan, the image of Barry, a black man with the cross of St George on his face in Roy Wiliams's *Sing Yer Heart Out for the Lads*, both encapsulates contradictions of race and offers a way of broadening the appeal of Englishness. And yes, there were other plays where stage images sometimes subverted expectation: for example, in Levi David Addai's *93.3FM* (Royal Court, 2006), young black men are not, in defiance of cliché, shown as gangstas. Director Dawn Walton says that 'the opening image [is] of two young Black men and what do we see them doing? We see them running a business. And that's an act of subversion.'[12] In drama, the gradual emergence of hyphenated-Britons (Anglo-Scottish, black-British, British-Asians) is just one step on the way to new ideas of the nation. What is clear, according to Josh Abrams, is that plays such as Alia Bano's *Shades* show people caught between assimilation and rejection – and refusing to choose either option.[13] Currently, the new Britishness is not a fixed identity, but a state of permanent tension. What's interesting about hybrids is not that they offer a solution to the puzzles of identity, but that they pose the question of who we are in such a clear way.

Fictional heroes

If every decade throws up a new type of fictional hero, someone who embodies the ambitions and anxieties of the age, who would fit the bill in 2000s new writing? The most obvious is the underclass yob, who was so popular a stage figure and so important an articulation of respectable fears about crime.[14] Often too poor, or too lacking in style, to aspire even to the trappings of chavdom, this foul-mouthed lowlife, with or without the trademark hood, appeared in play after play. Names include Lucy (Leo Butler's *Redundant*) or Shelley (April De Angelis's *Amongst Friends*), Liam (Dennis Kelly's *Orphans*) or Danny or Jamie (Simon Stephens's *Motortown* and *Country Music*), Deccy (Lin Coghlan's *Mercy*) or Daz (Gregory Burke's *On Tour*). As anti-heroes go, lager louts or petty crims are larger than life. As they run amok, we can vicariously enjoy the fantasy mayhem. At the same time, it's hard not to shudder. On the other hand, as Erkenwald in Che Walker's *The Frontline* opines: 'They're juss lonely li'l hooligan scumbag basstads really, thass all' (20). Occasionally, as in Simon

Stephens's *Herons*, which is a portrait of a shattered family, with shards of emotional agony flying in all directions, a playwright would prefer to express a sense of healing through metaphor rather than by offering political solutions: so the vision of a heron is a potent symbol of the desire to fly from a place which radiates danger.

In 2002, one critic asked:

> Our playwrights, from time to time, may shock us, but where are the plays that will challenge us? When playwrights deal with serious themes, they do so in a manner that allows us to distance ourselves from the social evils they portray, committed by characters who are mentally ill or not our class, dear.[15]

Her perception was that most playwrights portrayed untypically extreme characters who were either unusually vicious or mentally unbalanced, paedophiles or perverts. It's a good point. The shameless poor may not be 'bovvered', but their frequent stage appearances suggest that somehow we need them to people the nation's nightmares or to define ourselves as normal. That's the draw of fiction. As the poor stormed through plays, their writers were certainly vulnerable to the accusation of stereotyping, or of cultural tourism. Curiously enough, the marginal poor were more central to our imagined Britishness than ordinary citizens. Perhaps the popularity of the well-hard loser implies that middle-class Britain is inauthentic: the true Brits are the sons and daughters of the dole. Representations of the poor serve both to remind us of class divisions, and to imprint them even more strongly on our imaginations. By doing this, they also block our fantasies of social change.

One of the ways of asserting identity is by contrasting it with an Other, creating a neat separation between us and them. What is national is pitched against what is alien, whether this Other is German or American or Muslim or black. Mark Ravenhill's deliciously satirical *Product* showed how by creating an image of a fanatical terrorist Hollywood could reassert the identity of a Western audience. Often, identity is forged in war, when enemies can be demonised. Part of the success of Gregory Burke's *Black Watch* comes, surely, from the way the play reminds us of the central role that fighting enemies has had in the creation of Great Britain. In some audiences, this excites admiration rather than revulsion. National identity does change, but some things remain stubbornly the same. At home, the obsession with class distinctions; abroad, the desire for military glory. Traditionally, the Other, no matter where they were born, is always a bloody foreigner.

One common reaction to Others, to migration and to devolution, is resentful Englishness, often represented as an underclass neanderthalism, full of festering emotions and vicious acts. In the face of difference, resentful Englishness offers a hostility which aims to mask insecurity. From Joy Wilkinson's *Fair* to Roy Williams's *Days of Significance* or Ashmeed Sohoye's *Rigged* (Theatre Centre, 2009), the white working class was seen as a deep social problem. Resentful Englishness mirrored a recognisable social reality, and was pictured as both a national characteristic and a profound obstacle to change. Yet change continued apace. So as the variety of diasporas from ex-colonies was joined in the 2000s by migrants from the European Union, the result was a rich mix, although often a tense one. As Steve Blandford says, 'These welcome additions to the already highly diverse ways in which it is possible to be British' have been confronted by the ugly politics of xenophobia.[16] In the most asylum plays, Britain is not a friendly place: it is an unwelcoming fortress nation. But although such stage characters embodied our fears, did any embody our ambitions?

Not really. In British new writing, it was far easier to find losers than role models, crims than paragons, the unfaithful than the loyal. Celebrity cheats were more common than honest toilers. But some of the most memorable characters were eccentrics, a great British tradition. So Richard Bean's northern individualists, Jez Butterworth's rural fantasists, Philip Ridley's talk artists or Mike Packer's odd misfits could join Kay Adshead's strong women, Chloe Moss's soft teens, Mark Ravenhill's laconic ironists, debbie tucker green's agonised souls, Dennis Kelly's puzzled spirits, Gregory Burke's foul-mouthed males or the underclass losers of Chris O'Connell's *Street Trilogy*, in a panorama of the odd and unconventional. As ever, the national character involves humour – on stage, the Brits are usually, well, quite funny. But as well as laughter there was pain, lots of it. Along with the odd came all those desperate females and unsuitable couples, troubled teens and complicit victims, all suggesting a land being repeatedly made and remade in countless bedrooms and bars.

Although many playwrights rejoiced in humorous eccentricity, others pictured a diiferent side of the nation. The ordinary Englishman or woman became increasingly identified with hypocrisy and moral timidity. You can find the type in plays as varied as Joe Penhall's *Blue/Orange*, Charlotte Jones's *Humble Boy*, Michael Wynne's *The People Are Friendly*, Moira Buffini's *Dinner*, Simon Mendes da Costa's *Losing Louis*, or Kevin Elyot's *Forty Winks*. Their basic reflex is humorous evasiveness, or false courtesy. Real feelings hide behind self-control. Mired in failure, farce and delusion, the class-conscious English increasingly become figures who know not how to live, hard of heart and duplicitous: self-effacing, sorry-saying and fair-smiling. And old feelings of arrogant superiority remain safe behind a facade of benign self-disparagement.

Although the Thatcherite man or woman is well documented, was there such a fictional being as the New Labour person? Occasionally, in the satires of Alistair Beaton or the dramas of David Hare, New Labour politicians came across as the inheritors of Thatcherism, firm believers in market principles and spin. But, in British theatre, there were no major fictional New Labourites: no memorable politicians. And no memorable investment bankers, newspaper owners, estate agents or credit-card managers riding the long boom; writers looked not at the protagonists of turbocharged capitalism but at its victims. The one exception, Lucy Prebble's compelling portrait of the American Jeffrey Skilling in *Enron*, simply proves the rule. It is also true that there were precious few major oppositional characters who were able to reinvent the old radical spirit of anger. Who can name this decade's Jimmy Porter? Jez Butterworth's Rooster Byron perhaps, although he is, tellingly, a Romany, an outsider, a fantasist. Most playwrights preferred the traditional response of jokiness to the risks of outspoken dissent. And, in the onward march of verbatim theatre, overt political fictions shrivelled in front of political fact. On the other hand, moral conflict was often successfully articulated, as in the repeated clashes between ethical individuals and compromised pragmatists in, say, David Eldridge's *Under the Blue Sky* or Joe Penhall's *Blue/Orange* and *Landscape with Weapon*.

One tendency worth noting is a slight relaxation of the boundaries that in the recent past dominated our thinking about drama. Although people still talk of women's writing, gay theatre, black and Asian theatre, divisions such as these – which include the historic divisions between commercial and subsidised, mainstream and fringe – are gradually weakening. One of the great advances in audience receptiveness over the past twenty years is the acceptance of the gay play as a piece of drama, a play like any other. This not only reflects a wider cultural familiarity with gay people, but also shows how theatre can take a lead in social change. No one refers to Mark Ravenhill as a gay playwright, or a queer one. He's simply a writer. Similarly, a so-called Asian writer, such as Tanika Gupta, can now write a play (*Sugar Mummies*) in which there are no Asian characters. A so-called black writer, Roy Williams, can write a play (*Sing Your Heart Out for the Lads*) in which most of the characters are white. But these are rare instances of cultural crossover – most black and Asian writers seem stuck in the ghetto of their own heritage. But, in other areas, the question has been raised more acutely: when a Scottish writer no longer writes about Scotland, how and why should we talk about them as a Scottish playwright?

Rewriting politics

If British theatre in the 2000s has been successful in articulating social anxieties, did it also offer new images of how to change the nation? Chris Rojek argues that 'the theme of "another Britain", a golden land untainted by corruption, is seminal in British culture', and this mythical place, another country, provides the mythic undertow of plays such as *Jerusalem*, where it is located in tall tales that refer to the past.[17] But, in general, this golden land was scarcely glimpsed in 2000s drama. Why so? By the middle of the decade, many younger writers were arguing that the problem was that, in Fin Kennedy's words, 'Yes, we are very cool. But we have been depoliticized.'[18] After all, it took a global event such as 9/11 and the War on Terror to shock playwrights into rediscovering overtly political themes, yet there were very few plays about young people actually engaged in changing the world – despite the fact that there was much to change. This both reflected and perpetuated a climate of apathy, a lack of engagement with real issues. Critic Michael Billington put it well when he wrote:

> Our whole postwar history is one of unresolved national conflicts. We have spent years trying to reconcile our super-power pretentions with our economic under-performance, our love of tradition with our commitment to modernity, our attachment to America with our tentative affiliation to Europe. One could add a whole list of issues – class, race and monarchy – on which the nation remains deeply divided.[19]

Given these political divisions, and the way they shape national identity, it is surprising that theatre had so little to say about some of the topics that people actually argue about. Before we get too complacent about how contemporary new writing is, it might be worth noting there were no major plays about the house-price boom, the ethics of choosing schools or, with only one or two exceptions, global warming. Who spoke up for ordinary middle-class couples doing ordinary middle-class things? Old people were rarely of interest to young playwrights. Nor was the widening gulf between generations. The Baby Gap was not explored. The monarchy remained virtually undiscussed. Few plays featured Conservative politicians; few examined our ideas about Europe. Honour killing and mercy killing were mentioned, but where was the major play that examined either? White writers practically never wrote about black or Asian characters. The Chinese community in Britain had no voice in the theatre. Although frequently invited, the fabled right-wing play failed to arrive. There was a lack of engagement with moral values; instead, there was an assumption that we all share liberal ideals, which were usually unspoken.[20] The growth in religious feeling was of no concern to playwrights. In fact, one of the most charming plays on the subject,

Catherine Trieschmann's *Crooked* (Bush, 2006), was by an American author. In 2003, and again in 2008, most of the energy in new writing seemed to be coming from American or Irish playwrights. Over the decade, there were plenty of British plays about the War on Terror but none about the rise of China. South America was of no interest to playwrights. Politically, the world of 2000s British drama was a curiously shrunken place.

If you can blame playwrights for failing to write these kinds of plays, you also have to hold theatres to account for neither commissioning them, nor taking steps to widen their rather narrow repertoire of plays. Women writers, while more visible than in previous decades, still fared less well than men. Despite all the variety of the decade, artistic directors and literary managers showed precious little interest in boldly broadening their repertoires beyond standard naturalistic and realistic fare. So plays written in a more absurdist or surreal aesthetic got short shrift. Difficult foreign work was rare. Scared of the effect that new, or radically different, plays might have on audience attendance, most theatres played safe. Likewise, audiences did the same, often preferring the known to the unknown, the familiar to the unfamiliar. And if new writing aspires to be daring, it rarely delivers the goods. The irony is that, in the final analysis, those theatres that were so proud of being cutting edge were often offering something very like escapism: gritty plays about poor people set on council estates could be as unchallenging as a feelgood musical. One report which surveys much of the decade praises Arts Council England for promoting new writing, this being 'a major success story'.[21] True, the British new writing system delivered an absolute record amount of new work, but its overall quality was no better than in previous decades.

Indeed, the record of individual theatres has been mixed. The Royal Court, with its high-definition production values and its enviable ability to programme about sixteen plays a year on two stages, along with its annual Young Writers Festival and vigorous International Department, was at the top of the new writing establishment. But while it aspired to be contemporary, with its finger on every pulse, its critics pointed out that often it was merely fashionable, staging headline-grabbing work and chasing after novelty. Artistic director Ian Rickson admitted that 'he would like to be more strategic sometimes', but in practice was opportunistic.[22] When Scottish playwright Simon Farquhar stated that his *Rainbow Kiss* was originally called *Fuck Off* but had its title changed because it 'was in danger of causing the play to be misperceived' (16), it was hard to resist raising a sceptical eyebrow: the venue was no stranger to expletive-rich titles, and this tendency was parodied in Nicholas Craig's *I, An Actor*, a spoof memoir which talks of 'wading through a sea of syringes and crème fraiche as I did in *Fist F***ing* at the Royal Court'.[23] Rickson did consolidate the achievements of the 1990s, a good decade for the Court, but David Greig points out that the trendy, distressed look of the newly refurbished theatre in 2000 created a deliberate illusion of risk and change, while in reality the building was 'safe' and everything remained 'the same'.[24] In 2006, celebrations of the theatre's fiftieth anniversary were disrupted by a controversy over the programming of Tom Stoppard's *Rock 'N' Roll*, directed by Trevor Nunn, neither of whom had ever been associated with the venue. Under Dominic Cooke, Rickson's successor, programming was focused on a smaller number of new playwrights, most notably Polly Stenham, Bola Agbaje and Mike Bartlett. But Cooke spent most of his first year reviving the Court's tradition of staging international work. Unintentionally perhaps, this focus on foreign writers, followed by several American plays, suggested that British playwrights had little to offer. What Cooke did succeed in doing was mixing plays about middle-class experience with slices of dirty-realist low-life.

At the Traverse, critic Steve Cramer assesses Philip Howard's regime: 'His presence has created a particular "big play" ethos at the Traverse, taking the company much further down the line of less whimsical experiment and more major productions than his predecessor Ian Brown.'[25] His successor, Dominic Hill, began with a 2008 season, called *Manifesto*, which featured new political plays by Zinnie Harris and Simon Stephens. Hill also hosted Irish playwrights such as Mark O'Rowe and Enda Walsh, but, despite such successes, there is a feeling that the good, old Traverse has been partially eclipsed by the new kid on the block: the National Theatre of Scotland. At the Bush, under Mike Bradwell, work tended to fall into one of two categories: either quiet slice-of-life plays by writers such as Richard Cameron and Chloe Moss or screaming shockfests by writers such as Anthony Neilson and Mike Packer. Bradwell also ran a cottage industry in teen angst plays. But although he produced a number of highly memorable evenings, and his theatre was more consistent in its programming than its bigger rivals, the Bush never solved the problem of having a tiny auditorium and poor Arts Council support. In December 2007, Josie Rourke, Bradwell's successor, had to contend not only with a badly leaking roof, which disrupted programming, but also with the threat of a 40 per cent cut in her grant. In the end, the Arts Council relented but the fight over funding was an unwelcome distraction. The problem with the Soho under Abigail Morris was not only that her biggest successes – Diane Samuels's *Kindertransport* (1993) and Amanda Whittington's *Be My Baby* (1998) – had premiered in the previous decade, but also that her theatre's mission to stage exclusively first-time playwrights resulted in a repertoire of newcomers, most of whom soon vanished. While her successor, Lisa Goldman, brought in older, more experienced writers, the venue never really found the big, decade-defining political drama it seemed to be looking for. At the Hampstead, despite the fact that Jenny Topper staged plays by provocative writers such as Philip Ridley and debbie tucker green, her venue had a middle-class reputation, staging well-made but safe plays of ideas whose action often took place in studies and on patios. Too often, this was New Writing Lite. Although Anthony Clark, her successor, did much to extend the repertoire beyond youthful new writing, his programming attracted critical disdain. Over at the National, Nicholas Hytner has generally been successful in this mission to represent the various voices of the nation, staging powerful plays by black playwrights such as Kwame Kwei-Armah and provocative plays by writers such as Mark Ravenhill. But his tendency to select big history plays, especially in the National's two largest auditoriums, panders much too much to the nostalgia inherent in English culture. It's the safe option.

Backed by generous state subsidies, New Labour policies attempted to use theatre as a way of broadening audiences, encouraging ethnic diversity and stimulating innovation. But the results were mixed: while black and Asian playwrights flourished as never before, the diverse audiences they brought in tended not to return for other plays by writers from other backgrounds. Theatre audiences would occasionally get a shot of new arrivals, often university students, but the main body remained stubbornly middle-class, middle-aged and white. New writing did become more popular in the 2000s, with many more new plays staged outside London and more West End transfers, but it often preferred to pat audiences on the back rather than challenge them. Likewise, genius proved too wayward to respond to policy. While there were very many mediocre plays, there were only a handful of really good ones. The decade failed to find a new Sarah Kane. Nor did writers, with a handful of exceptions outside London, have much success in convincing theatres to allow them access to their biggest stages. Despite the publicity generated by the Monsterists, few playwrights enjoyed seeing their work in theatres with more than 500 seats. Although more medium-sized theatres put on new plays, very few theatres risked backing new plays with big casts on the largest stages. When the National finally put the first play by a living woman playwright on its huge Olivier arena, it was Rebecca Lenkiewicz's *Her Naked Skin* (2008), a history play about the suffragettes. Olivier plays eschewed the contemporary. In general, most New Writing Pure remained confined to smaller stages, and away from public scrutiny: it's easy for coterie audiences to be snobbish about cutting-edge drama in the safety of a tiny studio theatre.

Despite this, by 2009 some commentators were celebrating a new golden age of contemporary British theatre.[26] True, there had been some problems at the start of the decade: in 2000, the *Evening Standard* complained that the London stage was 'as placid as a neutered old tomcat basking in the sun', and neither the 1999 *Evening Standard* Award for Best Play nor the 2002 Verity Bargate Award for work by a first-time writer were awarded because the judges thought that none of the plays submitted were good enough.[27] In 2002, Michael Billington complained that although 'new plays poured out in abundance', 'there was something missing: a strange dearth of plays that grappled with public issues or portrayed what it is like to live in Britain today'.[28] Over the decade, such problems were partially overcome, but new ones arose. Increasingly, theatres affirmed their status as commercial institutions, with a full array of support staff (marketing, fundraising and outreach), but with a risk-averse attitude to programming. And this eventually raised the question of whether it is better to spend money on office staff or on artists?

Images of national identity are always a political statement, and politics is about changing things. But before you can change anything, you have to be able to imagine it differently. Playwrights rewrite the nation when they come up with metaphors, whether deadly serious or wryly funny (or both), which reimagine reality.

Although this happened very rarely in the 2000s, some examples suggest that this might become more common in the future. For instance, Kwame Kwei-Armah's *Seize the Day* dares to fantasise about a campaign for a black mayor of London – and it ends on a joke about a black prime minister! Clearly an example of the Obama effect. In the domestic sphere, by simply offering a glimpse of normal family life, Matt Charman's *The Five Wives of Maurice Pinder* (National, 2007) makes a case for thinking about the possibilities of polygamy, which straight society considers 'abhorent' (70). On a bigger canvas, the way playwrights have seen Britain's relationship with the USA has often been a protest against government policies in the War on Terror. Each play on this subject implicitly envisions a different relationship. Finally, plays about imaginary national emergencies tend to show us at our best. The Blitz spirit might be a self-regarding fantasy, but in the collective imagination it remains a strong cultural force.

By contrast, most plays about dystopias, whether by Mark Ravenhill or Philip Ridley, warn us of fearful change. At its most visionary, new writing seemed to be both reflecting social unease and grooming us for catastrophe. In the work of Britain's finest playwrights, Caryl Churchill, Martin Crimp, Ridley or Ravenhill, there were images aplenty of apocalypse. Motivated by an anger at social injustice and a dismay about the political order, such playwrights allowed their imaginations free rein through the twisting labyrinths of human horror. These warnings, in the safety of the fictional world, could be a dress rehearsal for tragedies that have not yet occurred. In the process, sometimes black humour was a statement of national self-awareness, substituting a comic streak for a political programme. The plays of Martin McDonagh or Anthony Neilson showed that darkness could be endured with a laugh, even if it was a grim one. Surely this was a typical way of being British.

In the slow creation of a compromise Britland, a new if uncertain notion of national identity, dialogue is central. As Declan Kiberd says, 'Since all identity is dialogic, "England" is more likely to achieve a satisfying definition in endless acts of negotiation with those of other identities', whether these are Scottish, Welsh, Irish, black or Asian.[29] Plays such as David Edgar's *Playing with Fire* and *Testing the Echo* showed the struggle to create this dialogue. Over the decade, a strong sense emerged that a finalised identity held little attraction. Instead, playwrights either questioned old stories about national identities or showed a process of becoming. The nation emerged as a work in progress. As Patrick Lonergan says, '[national] identity is not a brand arbitrarily imposed upon us, but a process to which we contribute'.[30] Playwrights were among those who contributed, taking the role of agents of our changing collective imagination, engineers of the 'imagined' community that is us.[31] One conclusion is that we are not only a mongrel nation, but a mongrel nation in constant change. Less of animal than a landscape forever altering. A few playwrights, led by Richard Bean, returned again and again to this idea of a mongrel Britain.

British theatre in the 2000s has been better at showing the hierarchies of class and race, and the cultural hybrids that already exist, or having visions of dystopic futures, than at suggesting practical new possibilities. It was better at criticising existing forms of identity rather than imagining different ones. New conceptions of who we are were rarely glimpsed. Perhaps this is not surprising. Playwrights are not, after all, policy-makers. Their failure to articulate idealistic views of human potential might just reflect the cynicism that infects all culture in the new millennium. And if most of the Britons shown on stage have remained the same, despite all the changes going on around them, it is because the contradictions they live with are slow to change: tradition versus modernity, class division versus mobility, segregation versus assimilation, conservatism versus reform. The list could go on, but these are the tensions that writers have been so good at showing in the past decade.

Still, the best British theatre did cross the landscape of the imagination. And perhaps its finest hours were when it encouraged the national characteristic of scepticism while challenging the traditional notion of restraint. And, so often, it was the outsider who brought the best news. In David Greig's *Damascus*, it is an Arab character who advises:

> Doubt, hesitancy, timidity, uncertainty – these are the ways we go towards the truth. Slowly. Unsure of ourselves. 'Is this the right way?' 'Are you OK?' 'How is it for you?' And through the darkness we go. Slowly we walk forward putting out our hands to feel the damp walls of the cave. Looking for the light. (94)

If a new national identity is a work in progress, one we are all slowly inching towards, the great thing about British new writing during the first decade of the new millennium has been its ability not only to reflect reality, but also to take part in the ongoing conversation by means of which we are all rewriting the nation.

NOTES

Introduction

1. S. E. Wilmer, *Theatre, Society and the Nation*, p. 1.
2. Tessa Jowell, *Government and the Value of Culture*, pp. 16–17; see also David Edgar, 'Where's the Challenge?', *Guardian*, 22 May 2004.
3. Steve Blandford, *Film, Drama and the Break-Up of Britain*, p. 9.
4. Eddie Izzard, *Mongrel Nation: Invasion, Immigration and Infusion*, Discovery Channel, 3 parts: 4, 11 and 18 June 2003.
5. '[Foreign Secretary] Robin Cook's Chicken Tikka Masala Speech', *Guardian*, 19 April 2001. For a dramatised version of this rewritten national myth, see Richard Bean, *England People Very Nice* (86–7). Chicken tikka masala also features in Nick Payne, *If There Is I Haven't Found It Yet* (69).
6. Kate Fox, *Watching the English*, pp. 14–15; cf. David Edgar, *Testing the Echo* (40–3). See also Dan Rebellato, *Theatre & Globalization*.
7. George Orwell, *The Lion and the Unicorn*, p. 70. Identity, as T. S. Eliot pointed out, embraces all of cultural life: in his list of thirteen characteristics of Englishness, eight were about sport, and three food (Eliot, *Notes Towards a Definition of Culture*, p. 31).
8. Jen Harvie, *Staging the UK*, p. 2.
9. Clare Wallace, *Suspect Cultures*, p. 5. As ever, reality plays a wicked game with any attempt to impose a rigid taxonomy: Martin McDonagh writes about Ireland, but was born in south London; Colin Teevan lives and works in Britain, but was born in Dublin; Conor McPherson lives in and writes about Ireland, but has built his career in London. Similarly, British-born Rebecca Lenkiewicz has written about Irish characters while Irish-born Stella Feehily and Lin Coghlan write British ones.
10. Mary Luckhurst, *A Companion to Modern British and Irish Drama*, p. 1; see also Declan Kiberd, 'Reinventing England'.
11. Krishan Kumar, *The Making of English National Identity*, p. 235.
12. Quoted in Harriet Devine, *Looking Back*, p. 263.
13. Aleks Sierz, 'What Kind of England Do We Want?', p. 120.
14. Moira Buffini, 'Introduction', *Plays One*, p. ix.
15. Leo Butler, 'Introduction', *Plays One*, p. viii.
16. Aleks Sierz, 'As Long as the Punters Enjoy It', p. 268; see also debbie tucker green on *Stoning Mary* in Ruth Little and Emily McLaughlin, *The Royal Court*, p. 425.
17. Emily McLaughlin, 'Interview with debbie tucker green', p. 4.
18. Quoted in Peter Billingham, *At the Sharp End*, p. 173.
19. Simon Stephens, 'Introduction', *Plays Two*, p. xvii.

20. Benedict Anderson, *Imagined Communities*, pp. 5–7, 204–6. For a discussion of the politics of Anderson's *Imagined Communities* see Jen Harvie, *Staging the UK*, pp. 3–4.

21. See Nikolaus Pevsner, *The Englishness of English Art*, p. 35.

22. Michael Kustow, *theatre@risk*, p. 194. I am indebted to the work of Andy Lavender, Laura Bonamici and Andrea Pitozzi.

23. Steve Dixon, *Digital Performance*, p. 3.

24. Interview with Aleks Sierz, London, 22 September 2005.

1 Cult of the New?

1. Harriet Devine, *Looking Back*, p. 3.

2. Lilli Geissendorfer, 'New Writing: More Sex, Less Foreplay', *Guardian* theatre blog, 8 April 2007, blogs.guardian.co.uk/theatre/2007/04/new_writing_more_sex_l ess_fore.html. Similarly, playwright Mark Ravenhill has argued, no doubt tongue in cheek, that there is too much new writing (Ravenhill, 'Theatres Must Stop Producing So Many New Plays and Focus More on the Classics', *Guardian*, 17 October 2005).

3. Michael Billington, 'Hampstead Theatre's Future Lies in Plays from the Past', *Guardian* theatre blog, 1 July 2009, www.guardian.co.uk/stage/theatreblog/2009/jul/01/anthony-clark-quits-hampstead-theatre.

4. British Theatre Consortium, *Writ Large*, pp. 6, 8, 13–14; see also Anne Millman and Jodi Myers, *Theatre Assessment*, p. 77.

5. John Russell Taylor, *Anger and After*, pp. 14, 28; Irving Wardle, *George Devine*, p. 180; John Elsom, *Post-War British Theatre*, p. 75; see also Aleks Sierz, *John Osborne's Look Back in Anger*, and Peter Gill, *Apprenticeship*, pp. 32–9.

6. Quoted in Ruth Little and Emily McLaughlin, *The Royal Court*, p. 17; cf. Harriet Devine, *Looking Back*, p. 3.

7. Stephen Lacey, *British Realist Theatre*, pp. 7–8.

8. Quoted in Dominic Sandbrook, *Never Had It So Good*, p. 173.

9. David Greig, 'A Tyrant for All Time', Guardian, 28 April 2003.

10. John Osborne, *Damn You, England*, pp. 255–8; see also Dan Rebellato, *1956 and All That*, pp. 156–223.

11. Quoted in Sandbrook, *Never Had It So Good*, p. 194.

12. Dominic Dromgoole, *The Full Room*, p. xiii.

13. David Edgar, *State of Play*, pp. 5–8, 18–19, 26–31; see also Aleks Sierz, *In-Yer-Face Theatre*.

14. David Edgar, *State of Play*, pp. 18–19.

15. David Edgar, 'The Canon, the Contemporary and the New', p. 31; see also Aleks Sierz, 'Art Flourishes in Times of Struggle', pp. 35–6, and Dominic Dromgoole, *The Full Room*, p. ix.

16. Dan Rebellato, *1956 and All That*, pp. 225–6; see also Ben Payne, 'In the Beginning', pp. 11, 23, 47.

17. Quoted in Fiachra Gibbons, 'Angry Young Men Under Fire from Gay Writer', *Guardian*, 8 November 1999.

18. Robert Leach, *Theatre Workshop*, p. 140.

19. Quoted in Ruth Little and Emily McLaughlin, *The Royal Court*, p. 61.

20. Stage Society quoted in Ian Clarke, *Edwardian Drama*, p. 16; see also pp. 12–21. The Court was later renamed Royal Court.

21. Stephen Lacey, *British Realist Theatre*, p. 3.

22. Richard Eyre and Nicholas Wright, *Changing Stages*, p. 130.

23. Christopher Innes, *Modern British Drama*, p. 251.

24. John Bull, *Stage Right*, p. 36.

25. 'Monsterist Manifesto', London, 2002; see Aleks Sierz, 'Big Ideas', Colin Teevan, 'Free the Playwrights!' and Sierz, 'New Writing 2006'; see also Sierz, 'Why Size Matters', *Plays International*, vol. 20, no. 1/2 (October/November 2004), pp. 16–17; Maddy Costa, 'Where Have All the Playwrights Gone?', *Guardian*, 7 October 2004, and David Eldridge, 'Massive Attack', *Guardian*, 27 June 2005.

26. Lyn Gardner, 'At Last, Theatre Is Shedding More Light on Feminism', *Guardian* theatre blog, 25 May 2009, www.guardian.co.uk/stage/theatreblog/2009/may/24/theatremore-light-feminism; see also Jane Edwardes, 'A Woman's Touch', *Time Out*, 28 June–5 July 2006.

27. Tim Fountain, *So You Want To Be a Playwright?*, p. 80.

28. Jane Edwardes, 'In Good Stead', *Time Out*, 17–24 September 2003, p. 159.

29. See Mary Luckhurst, *Dramaturgy*, pp. 200–62.

30. Theodore Shank, 'The Playwriting Profession', p. 184.

31. Interview with Aleks Sierz, London, 26 April 2002; Lyn Gardner, 'Raising the Roof', *Guardian Weekend*, 6 July 2002, p. 24.

32. Jane Edwardes, 'Playing with Figures', *Time Out*, 17–24 July 2002, p. 145.

33. Baz Kershaw, 'British Theatre, 1940–2002', p. 317.

34. Quoted in Robin Johnson, *New Theatre – New Writing?*, p. 14; see also Aleks Sierz, 'Art Flourishes in Times of Struggle'.

35. Quoted in Harriet Devine, *Looking Back*, p. 329.

36. Quoted in Kate Stratton, 'Please Be Seated', *Time Out*, 25 October–1 November 2000, p. 155.

37. Quoted in Aleks Sierz, 'Curtain Up for Act Two', *Independent*, 12 February 2003.

38. Quoted in Max Roberts, 'Introduction', p. xiii.

39. Quoted in Mark Brown and Maev Kennedy, 'New Director To Satirise Audience', *Guardian*, 7 February 2007; see also David Lister, 'Where Are the Playwrights in This Hour of Need?', *Independent*, 3 May 2008.

40. Quoted in Maxie Szalwinska, 'The New Man in Swiss Cottage', *Plays International*, vol. 19, no. 1 (November/December 2003), p. 16; Aleks Sierz, 'In His Own Footsteps', *The Stage*, 11 September 2003; see also 'Interview: Anthony Clark', theatreVOICE website, 22 June 2007, www.theatrevoice.com/listen_now/player/?audioID=492.

41. Mark Shenton, 'Putting Hampstead Theatre on the Map . . .', *The Stage* blog, 7 July 2009, blogs.thestage.co.uk/shenton/2009/07/putting-hampsteadtheatre-on-the-map.

42. 'Introduction to Producing Companies', Writernet website, 2003, www.writernet. co.uk/professional_development/producing_theatre_companies/introduction_to_pro ducing_theatre_companies.ph tml.

43. Nicholas Hytner, 'Sense of National Pride', *Evening Standard*, 26 September 2001; see also Ian Herbert, 'How It Was for Us', p. 201, and Aleks Sierz, 'To Market, to Market', *Sunday Times*, 28 April 2002.

44. Patrick Marmion, 'Coming in from the Fringe', *Evening Standard*, 14 December 2000; see also Aleks Sierz, 'Alternative or Mainstream?'

45. Jane Edwardes, 'On the Edge', *Time Out*, 18–25 February 2004, p. 139.

46. Aleks Sierz, 'Back in the Front Line', *Independent*, 8 July 2004; see also Jeremy Malies, 'Fighting for Finborough', *Plays International*, vol. 21, no. 3/4 (Winter, 2006), p. 19.

47. Dominic Dromgoole, *The Full Room*, p. 59.

48. Fiona Mountford, 'Spirit of the Fringe at the Latchmere', *Evening Standard Metro* magazine, 15/21 November 2002, p. 36.

49. Ben Payne, interview with Aleks Sierz, London, 16 April 2002; see also Mary Luckhurst, *Dramaturgy*, pp. 200–62.

50. Adrienne Scullion, 'Contemporary Scottish Women Playwrights', p. 115; see also Lyn Gardner, 'The Bold, the Old and the Obsolete', *Guardian*, 27 April 2009.

51. Trish Reid, 'From Scenes Like These', p. 201; see also Jan McDonald, 'Towards National Identities', and Robert Leach, 'The Short, Astonishing History of the National Theatre of Scotland'.

52. Publicity leaflet, *This Other England*, Paines Plough, January 2005. The plays were Walsh's *The Small Things*, Ridley's *Mercury Fur*, Greig's *Pyrenees* and Maxwell's *If Destroyed True*.

53. See Aleks Sierz, 'Headlong Cavalier', *Plays International*, vol. 22, no. 11/12 (Autumn, 2007), p. 13.

54. Howard Barker, 'The Olympics Killed My Theatre Company', *Guardian* theatre blog, 5 June 2007, blogs.guardian.co.uk/theatre/2007/06/the_olympics_killed_my _theatre .html; see also Aleks Sierz, 'The Art of the Matter', *The Stage*, 1 October 2009.

55. See Andrew Haydon, 'The Rise (and Possible Fall) of the Short Play', *Guardian* theatre blog, 25 October 2007, www.guardian.co.uk/stage/theatreblog/2007/oct/25/theriseand possiblefallof; see also 'Debate: A Crisis in New Writing?', theatreVOICE website, 24 November 2006, www.theatrevoice.com/listen_now/player/?audioID=441, Writernet website, www.writernet.co.uk, and Sean Aita, 'A Changing Landscape', *The Stage*, 15 October 2009.

56. Quoted in Aleks Sierz, 'Second Helpings', *Plays International*, vol. 20, no. 9/10 (Summer 2005), p. 17; see also Sierz, 'The Fight for Revival', *The Stage*, 26 May 2005.

57. Fin Kennedy, 'We're Taking a Risk Just by Writing for the Stage', *Guardian*, 15 March 2006.

58. Theodore Shank, 'The Multiplicity of British Theatre', p. 4.

59. Matthew Hemley, 'Ravenhill: Theatre Is Failing Playwrights Because It Is Obsessed with New Writers', *The Stage*, 12 November 2009.

2 What Is New Writing?

1. Chris Wilkinson, 'Noises Off: When Is a New Writer Not a New Writer?', *Guardian* theatre blog, 23 September 2009, www.guardian.co.uk/stage/theatreblog/2009/sep/23/ steinberg trust-new-writers; see also 'Debate: A Crisis in New Writing?', theatreVOICE website, 24 November 2006, www.theatrevoice.com/listen_now/player/?audioID=441.

2. Chris Goode, 'What's Wrong with UK Drama?', *Guardian*, 7 January 2004; see also Aleks Sierz, 'Rewrite the Script', *The Times*, 25 April 2001.

3. Colin Chambers, *Inside the Royal Shakespeare Company*, p. 132.

4. David Edgar, *How Plays Work*, p. 202.

5. H. Porter Abbott, *The Cambridge Introduction to Narrative*, p. 153.

6. Dominic Dromgoole, *The Full Room*, p. 306.

7. Tim Fountain, *So You Want To Be a Playwright?*, p. 23. In Martin Crimp's adaptation of Ferdinand Bruckner's *Pains of Youth*, there's an ironic moment: 'Your writing's terrible. But sometimes, for just a few lines, you can suddenly hear an individual voice' (27).

8. Phyllis Nagy, 'Hold Your Nerve: Notes for a Young Playwright', in David Edgar, *State of Play*, p. 131.

9. Interview with Aleks Sierz, London, 21 February 2006.

10. Jen Harvie, *Staging the UK*, pp. 114–15.

11. Michael Billington, *State of the Nation*, pp. 404, 411; see also Michael Kustow, *theatre@risk*, p. 209.

12. Kate Dorney, *The Changing Language of Modern English Drama*, pp. 7–8; see also pp. 110, 122–5, 148–9, 215–19.

13. Quoted in Harriet Devine, *Looking Back*, p. 328.

14. Interview with Aleks Sierz, London, 15 April 2009.

15. *Fight Club* was the first novel by American author Chuck Palahniuk, 1996; film version by David Fincher, 1999. 'The first rule about fight club is you don't talk about fight club' (Palahniuk, *Fight Club*, pp. 48, 96, 100, 134, 140, 157).

16. Tim Fountain, *So You Want To Be a Playwright?*, p. 40.

17. Terry Johnson, 'Introduction', Joe Penhall, *Plays One*, p. ix.

18. Dominic Dromgoole, *The Full Room*, p. xiii.

19. For satire on *Star Wars*, see Roy Williams, *Category B* (15).

20. Caroline McGinn, *Time Out*, 20–26 March 2008; *Theatre Record*, vol. XXVIII, no. 6 (2008), p. 296.

21. Kwame Kwei-Armah, 'Introduction', *Plays One*, p. xiii.

22. Example of mobile phone in Graham Saunders, *Closer*, p. 8; see also Roy Williams, *Little Sweet Thing* for latest mobile phone (26), Charlotte Jones, *Humble Boy* for mini-

disc player (12), and Mark Ravenhill, *Shoot/Get Treasure/Repeat* for iPod (5) and Xbox (93). When Fin Kennedy did some rewrites of *How To Disappear Completely and Never Be Found* for its 2008 revival, he added a reference to Facebook.

23. Interview with Aleks Sierz, London, 26 September 2003.

24. Interview with Aleks Sierz, London, 29 August 2003; see also Sierz, 'Can Old Forms Be Reinvigorated?'

25. Neil LaBute, 'How American Theatre Lost It', *Guardian*, 15 January 2008.

26. Peter Billingham, *At the Sharp End*, p. 16.

27. Mark Fisher, 'The Plays That Change the World', *Guardian* theatre blog, 16 September 2008, www.guardian.co.uk/stage/theatreblog/2008/sep/16/theatre.

28. 'It Was Officers v Inmates', *Guardian*, 14 November 2005; reprinted in the playtext, p. 9.

29. Steve Waters, 'The Truth Behind the Facts', *Guardian*, 11 February 2004. For political theatre, see Fiachra Gibbons, 'Fringe Favourites Take Aim at Politics', *Guardian*, 7 August 2003; Johann Hari, 'The Left Isn't Always Right', *Independent*, 21 August 2003; 'Political Theatre Special', *Front Row*, BBC Radio 4, 21 April 2003; Lisa Goldman and Joyce McMillan, 'Staging Our Protests', *Guardian*, 2 August 2003; and 'Debate: Political Theatre', TheatreVOICE website, 26 September 2003, www.theatrevoice.com/listen_now/player/?audioID=62.

30. Peter Billingham, *At the Sharp End*, p. 245. He also notes the significance of young people in the audience at Stratford East.

31. See Aleks Sierz, *The Theatre of Martin Crimp*, pp. 49–56, 67, 169, 170.

32. David Edgar, *How Plays Work*, p. 99.

33. See Aleks Sierz, *The Theatre of Martin Crimp*, pp. 67–9; see also Sierz, 'Form Follows Function'.

34. John Stokes, 'The City Inside Me', *TLS*, 10 April 2009, p. 17.

35. Quoted in Heidi Stephenson and Natasha Langridge, *Rage and Reason*, p. 130.

36. Elaine Aston, *Feminist Views on the English Stage*, p. 19; see also 'Interview: James Macdonald (2/2)', theatreVOICE website, 23 May 2008, www.theatrevoice.com/listen_now/player/?audioID=571.

37. Dan Rebellato, 'From the State of the Nation to Globalization', p. 259.

38. 'Interview: Simon Stephens', theatreVOICE website, 20 October 2008, www.theatrevoice.com/listen_now/player/?audioID=620; Andrew Haydon, 'When It Comes to Staging, We Play It Way Too Safe', *Guardian* theatre blog, 9 October 2008, www.guardian.co.uk/stage/theatreblog/2008/oct/09/theatre.

39. Michael Billington, 'Short Shrift', *Guardian*, 16 April 2005; David Eldridge, 'Oh, Throw Away Your Stopwatch', *Guardian*, 27 April 2005; Ian Rickson, 'Brief Is Beautiful', *Guardian*, 20 April 2005.

40. Lloyd Evans, *Spectator*, 13 January 2007; *Theatre Record*, vol. XXVII, no. 1/2 (2007), p. 13. Compare the much more contemporary dialogue of the middle-class schoolkids in Simon Stephens's *Punk Rock*. Note also Stephens's description of his play as 'The History Boys on crack' (quoted in Kate Muir, 'Roll Up! It's the School Shooting Play', *The Times*, 12 September 2009).

41. Keith Miller, 'A Little Bit Extra-Curricular', *TLS*, 1 June 2004, p. 16.

42. Interview with Aleks Sierz, London, 7 May 2008.

43. Harriet Devine, *Looking Back*, p. 3.

44. 'Theatre Forum Ireland 2006: Asking for Trouble (1/3)', theatreVOICE website, 16 June 2006, www.theatrevoice.com/listen_now/player/?audioID=423. 'Eventually Madhav Sharma who is a very experienced actor agreed to play the main role of Mr Sandhu, who is the rapist in the piece – the homosexual and the rapist' (ibid.).

45. Ash Kotak, 'Not in Our Gurdwaras [Sikh temples]', *Guardian*, 21 December 2004. His play about cross-dressing hijras has gay references which shocked the older generation of Asians in the audience when I saw it at the Bush on 18 November 2000.

46. Aleks Sierz, 'Richard Bean in Conversation', p. 359.

47. 'Interview: Ryan Craig', theatreVOICE website, 11 December 2006, www.theatrevoice.com/ listen_now/player/?audioID=443.

48. Steve Blandford, *Film, Drama and the Break-Up of Britain*, p. 180.

49. Quoted in Harriet Devine, *Looking Back*, p. 326.

3 Global Roaming

1. Tony Benn, *More Time for Politics*, p. 7 (13 September 2001).

2. Frank Furedi, *Culture of Fear Revisited*, p. vii. For example, the starting point of verbatim-theatre writer Alecky Blythe's *Come Out Eli* (Arcola, 2003) was 'to interview people about their fears' (Blythe, 'Introduction', *Cruising*, p. 3).

3. Richard Boon, *About Hare*, pp. 6, 26. Hare's *The Vertical Hour* is a companion piece to *Stuff Happens*, but its main focus is on the personal rather than the political.

4. David Hare, 'Author's Note', *Stuff Happens*, no page number.

5. David Hare quoted in [Lyn Hail (ed.)], *Faber Playwrights*, p. 24.

6. Polly Toynbee and Max Hastings, *Guardian*, 3 September 2004; *Theatre Record*, vol. XXIV, no. 19 (2004), pp. 1160, 1162.

7. Clive Davis, *The Times*, 6 September 2004; Michael Billington, *Guardian*, 11 September 2004; *Theatre Record*, vol. XXIV, no. 19 (2004), pp. 1163, 1153.

8. Peter Ansorge, 'Stopping for Lunch', p. 93. Kate Bassett, *Independent on Sunday*, 12 September 2004; *Theatre Record*, vol. XXIV, no. 19 (2004), p. 1152.

9. Michael Billington, *State of the Nation*, p. 390.

10. Michael Coveney, 'The National Theatre and Civic Responsibility', p. 182.

11. Simon Stephens, 'Debate: New Writing (2/3)', theatreVOICE website, 28 May 2004, www.theatrevoice.com/listen_now/player/?audioID=168; see also Philip Roberts, *About Churchill*, pp. 145–50.

12. Irving Wardle, *Sunday Telegraph*, 3 December 2000; *Theatre Record*, vol. XX, no. 24 (2000), p. 1575.

13. Dominic Dromgoole, *The Full Room*, p. 54; Michael Billington, *State of the Nation*, p. 375.

14. Elaine Aston, *Feminist Views*, p. 36.

15. Mark Ravenhill, 'Introduction', *Plays Two*, p. x.

16. Peter Billingham, *At the Sharp End*, p. 144.

17. Dan Rebellato, 'Introduction', Mark Ravenhill, *Plays One*, pp. xiii–xiv.

18. Quoted in Billingham, *At the Sharp End*, p. 127.

19. Nicholas de Jongh, *Evening Standard*, 1 March 2006; Michael Billington, *Guardian*, 1 March 2006; *Theatre Record*, vol. XXVI, no. 5 (2006), pp. 229, 228.

20. Ravenhill, 'Introduction', *Shoot/Get Treasure/Repeat*, p. 5.

21. Caroline McGinn, 'Get Treasure Hunt', *Time Out*, 3–9 April 2008, p. 147; see also Margherita Laera, 'Mark Ravenhill's *Shoot/Get Treasure/Repeat*'.

22. Mark Ravenhill, 'Introduction', *Plays Two*, p. xi.

23. Leo Butler, 'Introduction', *Plays One*, p. xi.

24. Roxana Silbert, interview with Aleks Sierz, London, 5 August 2003; Joyce McMillan, *Scotsman*, 2 August 2003; *Theatre Record*, vol. XXIII, no. 18, Edinburgh Supplement (2003), p. 1097.

25. Mark Fisher, *The List*, 7 August 2003; *Theatre Record*, vol. XXIII, no. 18, Edinburgh Supplement (2003), p. 1096.

26. See David Greig, 'Rough Theatre'.

27. Published as Nicolas Kent (ed.), *The Great Game: Afghanistan*.

28. BBC Radio 3, 11 July 2004.

29. Quentin Letts, *Daily Mail*, 17 January 2007; Charles Spencer, *Daily Telegraph*, 18 January 2007; *Theatre Record*, vol. XXVII, no. 1/2 (2007), pp. 80, 81. Another play that anatomised the white working class was Ashmeed Sohoye's *Rigged* (Theatre Centre, 2009); see 'White Working-class Special' [Roy Williams and Ashmeed Sohoye], theatreVOICE website, 21 August 2009, www.theatrevoice.com/listen_now/player/?audioID=732.

30. Ian Jack, 'It's in the Blood', *Guardian*, 14 June 2008; see also *Black Watch*, DVD of NTS stage play, BBC, JW477 (2008), which includes *Black Watch: A Soldier's Story*, a BBC Scotland documentary, August 2007.

31. John Tiffany, 'Introduction', Gregory Burke, *Black Watch*, p. xii.

32. Euan Ferguson, 'The Real Tartan Army', *Observer*, 13 April 2008.

33. Quoted in Dan Rebellato, 'National Theatre of Scotland', p. 216.

34. Ibid.

35. John Stokes, 'Saviours of Theatre', *TLS*, 8 February 2008, p. 17.

36. See Dan Rebellato, 'The Personal Is Not Political'; Philip Roberts, *About Churchill*, pp. 157–62; 'Interview: James Macdonald (2/2)', theatreVOICE website, 23 May 2008, www.theatrevoice.com/listen_now/player/?audioID=571.

37. Sam Marlowe, *The Times*, 3 June 2003; *Theatre Record*, vol. XXIII, no. 11/12 (2003), p. 769.

38. Quoted in Aleks Sierz, 'Debbie Tucker Green: If You Hate the Show, at Least You Have Passion', *Independent on Sunday*, 27 April 2003; see also Lynette Goddard, 'debbie tucker green', and Ruth Little and Emily McLaughlin, *The Royal Court*, pp. 422–5.

4 Market Forces

1. 'Essential Margaret Thatcher: Biography', the Margaret Thatcher Foundation website, 2009, www.margaretthatcher.org/essential/biography.asp#logo.

2. Stuart Hall, 'New Labour Has Picked up Where Thatcherism Left Off', *Guardian*, 6 August 2003; see also Hall, 'Labour's Double-Shuffle'.

3. 'Interview: David Eldridge', theatreVOICE website, 9 June 2006, www.theatrevoice.com/ listen_now/player/?audioID=400; see also Graham Saunders, 'Under Redevelopment'. For the effect of Thatcher's legacy on one playwright see Rebecca D'Monté, 'Thatcher's Children: Alienation and Anomie in the Plays of Judy Upton'.

4. Quoted in Aleks Sierz, *In-Yer-Face Theatre*, p. 212; see also Mireia Aragay, *British Theatre*, pp. 80, 84–6.

5. 'Interview: Joe Penhall (1/2)', theatreVOICE website, 31 January 2005, www.theatrevoice. com/listen_now/player/?audioID=264.

6. Quoted in Roger Foss, '(Not So) Strange Fruit', *What's On in London*, 12 April 2000, p. 59.

7. Michael Coveney, *Daily Mail*, 14 April 2000; Charles Spencer, *Daily Telegraph*, 17 April 2000; *Theatre Record*, vol. XX, no. 8 (2000), pp. 482–3.

8. Amelia Howe Kritzer, *Political Theatre*, p. 50.

9. David Eldridge, 'Introduction', *Plays One*, p. xii.

10. 'Interview: David Eldridge (1/2)', theatreVOICE website, 30 July 2008, www.theatrevoice.com/listen_now/player/?audioID=593; see also Ruth Little and Emily McLaughlin, *The Royal Court*, pp. 401–2.

11. Kate Stratton, 'True Blue', *Time Out*, 13–20 September 2000, p. 154.

12. 'Interview: David Eldridge (1/2)', ibid.

13. Quentin Letts, *Daily Mail*, 22 November 2006; Sam Marlowe, *The Times*, 23 November 2006; Charles Spencer, *Daily Telegraph*, 23 November 2006; *Theatre Record*, vol. XXVI, no. 24 (2006), pp. 1414–15.

14. Quoted in Aleks Sierz, 'Planned Offensive', *The Stage*, 4 January 2001.

15. Peter Billingham, *At the Sharp End*, p. 160; see also Scott Graham and Steven Hoggett, *The Frantic Assembly Book*, pp. 72–5.

16. Toby Lichtig, 'Escape to the Theatre', *TLS*, 17 September 2004, p. 19.

17. Hare rewrote the play for BBC Two TV in 2008. The new version is David Hare, *Plays Three*, pp. 371–463. References here are to the original edition.

18. See Amelia Howe Kritzer, *Political Theatre*, pp. 200–4, Elaine Aston, 'The Bogus Woman' and Kathleen Stark, 'I Believe', pp. 137–8.

19. Kay Adshead, 'Author's Note', *The Bogus Woman*, p. 15.

20. Gabriele Griffin, *Contemporary Black and Asian Women Playwrights*, p. 230.

21. Amelia Howe Kritzer, *Political Theatre*, p. 195; cf Gabriele Griffin, *Contemporary Black and Asian Women Playwrights*, p. 231.

22. Toby Lichtig, 'Tings Ain't What They Used To Be', *TLS*, 18/25 August 2006, p. 22.

23. Aleks Sierz, 'As Long as the Punters Enjoy it', p. 268. See also Peter Billingham, *At the Sharp End*, p. 247, and 'Asian Voices: Tanika Gupta', theatreVOICE website, 7 June 2009, www.theatrevoice.com/listen_now/player/?audioID=704.

24. The controversy is exemplified by Hussain Ismail, 'Why the National Theatre's New Play Is Racist and Offensive', *Guardian* theatre blog, 13 Feb 2009, www.guardian.co.uk/stage/theatreblog/2009/feb/13/nationaltheatre-play-racist. This blog attracted 138 comments in two days. See also John Bull, 'England People Very Nice'.

25. Mark Lawson, 'Interview with Richard Bean', *Front Row*, BBC Radio 4, 11 September 2009. The playtext of *The English Game* does have a reclining Labrador on the cover, but the dog does not appear in the play, and is certainly not called Mohammed.

26. Joshua Abrams, 'State of the Nation', p. 10.

27. Ian Shuttleworth, 'Prompt Corner', *Theatre Record*, vol. XXVI, no. 23 (2006), p. 1332.

28. Hare on *The Andrew Marr Show*, BBC One, 25 January 2009. The original scandal involved 'cash for peerages', the second alleged bribery of members of the House of Lords.

5 Two Nations

1. Polly Toynbee, *Hard Work*, p. 238.

2. David Cannadine, *Class in Britain*, p. 23.

3. Leo Butler, 'Introduction', *Plays One*, p. x.

4. Paul Taylor, *Independent*, 19 September 2001; Jane Edwardes, *Time Out*, 19–25 September 2001; *Theatre Record*, vol. XXI, no. 19 (2001), pp. 1209–10.

5. Polly Toynbee, *Hard Work*, p. 12.

6. Ian Herbert, 'Prompt Corner', *Theatre Record*, vol. XXI, no. 19 (2001), p. 1190.

7. Lyn Gardner, Guardian, 25 May 2006; Theatre Record, vol. XXVI, no. 9 (2006), p. 488.

8. 'Interview: Simon Stephens', theatreVOICE website, 28 April 2006, www.theatrevoice.com/listen_now/player/?audioID=394. Stephens was also influenced by the case of nineteen-year-old Private Gary Bartram, who was court-martialled in 2005 after he took a roll of film which showed him abusing Iraqi prisoners to a commercial developer.

9. Quentin Letts, *Daily Mail*, 28 April 2006; Paul Taylor, *Independent*, 28 April 2008; *Theatre Record*, vol. XXVI, no. 9 (2006), p. 489.

10. Ruth Little and Emily McLaughlin, *The Royal Court*, p. 436.

11. Chris O'Connell, *Street Trilogy* comprises *Car*, *Raw* and *Kid* (Theatre Absolute/Coventry, 1999, 2001, 2003).

12. Neil Dowden, 'Multiculturalism in the UK', *Plays International*, vol. 20, no. 11/12 (Autumn 2005), p.14.

13. Alfred Hickling, *Guardian*, 23 May 2006; *Theatre Record*, vol. XXVI, no. 10 (2006), p. 597.

14. Patrick Marmion, 'Play for Today', *Evening Standard*, 2 October 2001, p. 48.

15. Gregory Burke, 'Funny Peculiar', *Guardian*, 12 April 2003; and Burke, interview with Aleks Sierz, London, 21 October 2003.

16. Aleks Sierz, 'In Yer Face? in Bristol', p. 91.

17. 'Shan Khan's Office Politics', BBC news website, 16 August 2001, news.bbc.co.uk/1/hi/entertainment/arts/1493011.stm; see also Helen Chappell, 'Man at Work', *What's On in London*, 15 August 2001, p. 51.

18. Stephens quoted in Harriet Devine, *Looking Back*, p. 264.

19. John 8:32; see also Amelia Howe Kritzer, *Political Theatre*, p. 121, and Kathy Smith, 'A House Built on Mud'.

20. Quoted in Harriet Devine, *Looking Back*, p. 46.

21. As Richard Bean put it, 'The final scene, rather than being a misfit, is "the play". It is the roof on the house' (Bean, 'Right to Reply', *Guardian*, 21 September 2005); see also Aleks Sierz, 'Richard Bean in Conversation'.

22. Quoted in Aleks Sierz, 'Happily Counting His Chickens', *Daily Telegraph*, 27 February 2006.

23. Paul Kingsnorth, 'Oak, Ash and Thorn', programme, Jez Butterworth, *Jerusalem*, Apollo Theatre, February 2010.

24. Joshua Abrams, 'State of the Nation', p. 11; John Stokes, 'Country Matters', *TLS*, 7 August 2009, p. 21.

25. See Dominic Cavendish, 'Jerusalem: Why No Fuss about This Radical Play?', *Daily Telegraph*, 23 February 2010.

26. For the controversial use of a petrol smell in the last scene see Matt Trueman, 'Making a Stink about the Royal Court's Jerusalem', *Guardian* theatre blog, 20 July 2009, www.guardian.co.uk/stage/theatreblog/2009/jul/20/royalcourt-jerusalem.

27. Gurpreet Kaur Bhatti's account of the affair took the form of an imaginative play, *Behud* (Beyond Belief) (Coventry/Soho, 2010), with a playtext whose cover shows a gagged woman.

28. Dawinder Bansal, 'Review of Behzti', Asians in Media website, 13 December 2004, www.asiansinmedia.org.

29. Sunny Hundal, quoted in 'Give the Playwright Her Stage Back', Index on Censorship website, 23 December 2004, www.indexonline.org; see also Helen Freshwater, *Theatre Censorship*, pp. 139–58, and Geoffrey V. Davis and Anne Fuchs, *Staging New Britain*, pp. 121–6, 327–36.

30. Michael Billington, 'Lifting the Curtain', *Guardian*, 24 October 2007. The question wasn't really answered until 2009.

31. See 'Asian Voices: Pravesh Kumar', theatreVOICE website, 1 May 2010, www.theatrevoice.com/ listen_now/player/?audioID=842.

32. Quoted in Aleks Sierz, 'What Kind of England Do We Want?', p. 119.

33. Harry Derbyshire, 'Roy Williams', *Modern Drama*, pp. 423–4.

34. Deirdre Osborne, 'The State of the Nation', p. 89.

35. Brian Logan, *Time Out*, 25 June–1 July 2003; *Theatre Record*, vol. XXIII, no. 11/12 (2003), p. 759; see also Ruth Little and Emily McLaughlin, *The Royal Court*, pp. 417–19.

36. Quoted in Deirdre Osborne, 'Know Whence You Came', p. 257; see also Geoffrey Davis, 'This Is a Cultural Renaissance'.

37. Quoted in Peter Billingham, *At the Sharp End*, p. 34.

38. Interview with Aleks Sierz, London, 25 March 2004; see also Sierz, 'They Are Fighting for This Myth of Britain', *Financial Times*, 19 April 2004, and Sierz, 'What Kind of England Do We Want?'

39. At the 'How Was It for Us?' conference, London, 9 December 2007, another black playwright, Kwame Kwei-Armah, argued that 'he has no wish to write about racism, which he sees as "a white problem"' (Ian Herbert, 'Can You Hear Me in Britain', *Theatre Record*, vol. XXVII, no. 24 (2007), p. 1455).

40. John Stokes, 'Unofficial Rules of the Game', *TLS*, 6 November 2009.

41. Amelia Howe Kritzer, *Political Theatre*, p. 161.

42. Keith Peacock, 'The Question of Multiculturalism', p. 540.

43. See Joe Kelleher, *Theatre & Politics*, pp. 19–31.

44. Steve Blandford, *Film, Drama and the Break-Up of Britain*, p. 146.

45. Nadine Holdsworth, 'The Landscape of Contemporary Scottish Drama', p. 126.

46. Dan Rebellato, 'Introduction', to David Greig, *Plays One*, p. xxi.

47. Peter Billingham, *At the Sharp End*, p. 98; see also p. 88 for an account of *Victoria* as an example of the 'flowering of voice' in Scotland, plus pp. 110–18.

48. Nadine Holdsworth, 'Travelling Across Borders', p. 39. This article discusses the 1990s work of Greig and Stephen Greenhorn, but its conclusions apply equally to current Scottish drama.

49. David Pattie, 'Mapping the Territory', p. 144.

50. Heike Roms, 'Staging an Urban Nation', p. 117.

51. Steve Blandford, *Film, Drama and the Break-Up of Britain*, p. 172.

52. Ibid.

53. Heike Roms, 'Staging the Nation', p. 121.

54. Nadine Holdsworth and Wallace McDowell, 'A Legacy of Violence', p. 189. This article discusses his 1990s work, but its conclusions apply to these 2000s plays; see also Richard Rankin Russell, 'Loyal to the Truth'.

55. Amelia Howe Kritzer, *Political Theatre*, p. 164.

56. Benedict Nightingale, *The Times*, 12 April 2003; *Theatre Record*, vol. XXIII, no. 8 (2003), p. 468.

57. Tom Maguire, 'Northern Irish Drama', p. 67. For convictions, see also Jen Harvey, *Staging the UK*, pp. 53–67.

58. Mary Luckhurst, 'Martin McDonagh's Lieutenant of Inishmore', pp. 41, 35; Catherine Rees, 'The Good, the Bad, and the Ugly', p. 29; see also Patrick Lonergan, 'Commentary and Notes' and 'The Laughter Will Come of Itself'.

59. Steve Blandford, *Film, Drama and the Break-Up of Britain*, p. 137.

6 Love Hurts

1. Susie Orbach, *Bodies*, p. 116; Tim Fountain, *Rude Britannia*, p. 242.
2. Interview with Aleks Sierz, London, 23 February 2003; see also Robert Butler, *Humble Beginnings*, and Sierz, 'There's a Suicidal Astrophysicist at the National. Best Place for Him', *Independent on Sunday*, 5 August 2001.
3. Quoted in Jonathan Croall, *Buzz Buzz!*, p. 41.
4. Rachel Halliburton, *Evening Standard*, 18 August 2001; *Theatre Record*, vol. XXI, no. 16/17 (2001), p. 1017.
5. Amelia Howe Kritzer, *Political Theatre*, p. 101.
6. Quoted in Ruth Little and Emily McLaughlin, *The Royal Court*, p. 412.
7. Dan Rebellato, 'Simon Stephens', p. 176; the same is true of Stephens's *Harper Regan*.
8. John Mullan, 'You Can't Argue with That', *TLS*, 23 September 2005, p. 18; columnist Yasmin Alibhai-Brown made the implicit message clear when she compared this Jewish family with 'any number of middle-class Muslim homes, [where] exactly the same panic breaks out as their young suddenly embrace "true" Islam' (*New Statesman*, 10 October 2005, p. 8).
9. See Elaine Aston, *Feminist Views*, pp. 106–10.
10. Amelia Howe Kritzer, *Politcal Theatre*, p. 120.
11. 'Interview: Mike Bartlett', theatreVOICE website, 25 May 2007, www.theatrevoice.com/listen_now/player/?audioID=484.
12. The allusion is to George Orwell, *The Lion and the Unicorn*, pp. 53–5.
13. Jonathan Croall, *Buzz Buzz!*, p. 212; see also Aleks Sierz, 'Enter, Leftfield', *The Times*, 13 December 2003.
14. Email from Buffini, 25 February 2009. This discussion was stimulated by an email from Tom Boycott, 24 July 2007.
15. Lyn Gardner, *Guardian*, 11 December 2003; Benedict Nightingale, *The Times*, 11 December 2003; *Theatre Record*, vol. XXIII, no. 25/26 (2003), p. 1664.
16. The song is from the 1974 BBC children's programme *Bagpuss*.
17. Kathleen Stark, 'Battlefield Body', p. 177; I am also grateful for his insights to Christopher Gatt, director of the banned 2009 Maltese production of the play (Unifaun Theatre).
18. See Aleks Sierz, 'At Last I Get To Play a Proper Grown-up Woman', *Daily Telegraph*, 18 February 2006.
19. Publicity leaflet, David Harrower, *Blackbird*, Albery Theatre, February 2006.
20. Paul Taylor, *Independent*, 30 October 2003, Dominic Cavendish, *Daily Telegraph*, 23 October 2003; *Theatre Record*, vol. XXIII, no. 21 (2003), pp. 1414–15. The play's title refers to the idea that, during the Second World War, people used their food coupons for sweets, rather than meat, because 'they made you feel better instantly' (71).
21. Aleks Sierz, 'Putting a New Lens on the World', p. 115.
22. Rebecca D'Monté, 'Thatcher's Children', p. 86.
23. There are several allusions to the same song in Simon Stephens's *Pornography*, e.g. pp. 4, 14.

24. 'Simon Stephens on *Harper Regan*', programme, Simon Stephens, *Harper Regan*, National Theatre, April 2008.
25. David Hare, 'Introduction', *Plays Three*, p. ix.
26. Dominic Cavendish, *Daily Telegraph*, 27 February 2003; Sam Marlowe, *What's On in London*, 5 March 2003; *Theatre Record*, vol. XXIII, no. 4 (2003), pp. 214, 216.
27. Joyce McMillan, *Scotsman*, 19 October 2000; *Theatre Record*, vol. XX, no. 21 (2000), p. 1387.
28. Jack Bradley, 'Introduction', Richard Bean, *Plays Two*, p. 11.
29. Sam Marlowe, *What's On in London*, 31 July 2002; *Theatre Record*, vol. XXII, no. 15 (2002), p. 991.
30. Dan Rebellato, 'Simon Stephens', p. 176.
31. Muriel Zagha, 'Very Pastoral-Lyrical', *TLS*, 24 February 2006, p. 18.

7 Rival Realities

1. Munira Mirza, *Culture Vultures*, p. 19.
2. James Wood, *How Fiction Works*, p. 153; David Jays, 'Theatre's Landscape of the Mind', *Guardian* theatre blog, 12 March 2009, www.guardian.co.uk/stage/theatreblog/2009/mar/12/theatrelandscape-mind.
3. Graham Saunders, *'Love Me or Kill Me'*, p. 112; see also Saunders, *About Kane*, pp. 34–6, 80–1, and Clare Wallace, *Suspect Cultures*, pp. 185–235.
4. David Ian Rabey, *English Drama*, p. 208.
5. Quoted in Aleks Sierz, 'The Short Life of Sarah Kane', *Daily Telegraph*, 27 May 2000.
6. Christopher Innes, *Modern British Drama*, p. 536; see also Ruth Little and Emily McLaughlin, *The Royal Court*, pp. 399–401.
7. Dominic Cavendish, *Daily Telegraph*, 5 June 2000; *Theatre Record*, vol. XX, no. 13, (2000), p. 829.
8. 'Interview: Anthony Neilson', theatreVOICE website, 13 April 2007, www.theatrevoice.com/listen_now/player/?audioID=472.
9. Michael Billington, *Guardian*, 2 April 2007; Nicholas de Jongh, *Evening Standard*, 2 April 2007; *Theatre Record*, vol. XXVII, no. 7 (2007), pp. 384–5.
10. Trish Reid, 'Deformities of the Frame', p. 498.
11. See Aleks Sierz, *The Theatre of Martin Crimp*, pp. 218–20; see also Sierz, 'Form Follows Function', and Vicky Angelaki, 'Subtractive Forms and Composite Contents'.
12. David Ian Rabey, 'Ed Thomas: Jazz Pictures in the Gaps of Language', p. 549.
13. Patrick Marber, *Howard Katz*, no page number.
14. 'Interview: Philip Ridley', TheatreVOICE website, 4 March 2005, www.theatrevoice.com/listen_now/player/?audioID=275; see also Helen Chappell, 'State of Confusion', *New Statesman*, 21 March 2005, p. 42, and Aleks Sierz, 'Putting a New Lens on the World'.
15. Aleks Sierz, 'Putting a New Lens on the World', p. 114.

16. David Edgar, *Testing the Echo*, p. 59.

17. Vicky Featherstone, 'Introduction', Gary Owen, *Plays One*, p. xi.

18. Peter Ackroyd, *Albion*, p. 40.

19. See Scott Graham and Steven Hoggett, *The Frantic Assembly Book*, pp. 51, 67–9, 205–7, and Aleks Sierz, 'Frantic Assembly', *Theatre Forum*, 26, Winter/Spring 2005: pp. 3–9.

20. Quoted in Ruth Little and Emily McLaughlin, *The Royal Court*, p. 413, and Amelia Howe Kritzner, *Political Theatre*, p. 77.

21. Cf. D. Keith Peacock, 'Black British Drama and the Politics of Identity', p. 58.

22. Zinnie Harris, *Further than the Furthest Thing*, no page number.

23. Ravenhill, interview with Aleks Sierz, London, 18 July 2001; see also Jonathan Croall, *Inside the Molly House*, Mireia Aragay, *British Theatre*, pp. 99–101, and Caridad Svich, 'Commerce and Morality in the Theatre of Mark Ravenhill', pp. 93–5.

24. Ravenhill, interview with Aleks Sierz, London, 18 July 2001.

25. Michael Billington, *Guardian*, 5 September 2001; Benedict Nightingale, *The Times*, 6 September 2001; Alastair Macaulay, *Financial Times*, 6 September 2001; *Theatre Record*, vol. XXI, no. 18 (2001), pp. 1090–1; Andrew Wyllie, *Sex on Stage*, p. 144; see also p. 110.

26. David Rabey, *English Drama*, pp. 190, 189; see also 'Interview: Howard Barker (1/2)', TheatreVOICE website, 11 October 2004, www.theatrevoice.com/listen_now/player/?audioID=225, and Helen Iball, 'Dead Hands and Killer Heels'.

27. 'Focus on Youth Theatre (1/2)', theatreVOICE website, 26 March 2008, www.theatrevoice.com/listen_now/player/?audioID=559.

28. Catherine Rees, 'Postmodern Interrogations'; see also Hana Worthern and W. B. Worthern, 'The Pillowman and the Ethics of Allegory'.

29. See Ruth Little and Emily McLaughlin, *The Royal Court*, pp. 414–15.

30. It is surely significant that the British Library no longer resides in this traditional spot.

31. Programme, David Edgar, *Testing the Echo*, Out of Joint, January 2008, no page number.

32. 'A large proportion of Britain's Asian population fail to pass the cricket test. Which side do they cheer for? It's an interesting test. Are you still harking back to where you came from or where you are?' Trade minister Tebbit in 1990 *Los Angeles Times* interview (John Carvel, 'Tebbit's Cricket Loyalty Test Hit for Six', *Guardian*, 8 January 2004).

Conclusion

1. Extract quoted in the programme, Richard Bean, *England People Very Nice*, National Theatre, February 2009.

2. Jeremy Paxman, *The English*, p. 261.

3. Kate Fox, *Watching the English*, pp. 401, 410.

4. Simon Stephens, 'Keynote Address', p. 29.

5. Caridad Svich, 'The Looking Glass', Hot Reviews website, January 2009, www.hotreview. org/articles/thelookingglass.htm.

6. The passionate engagement with national identity in *Jerusalem* is due in part to the fact that Jez Butterworth is half-Irish.

7. Quoted in Victor Ukaegbu, 'Talawa Theatre Company', p. 144.

8. D. Keith Peacock, 'Black British Drama and the Politics of Identity', p. 49.

9. Gabriele Griffin, *Contemporary Black and Asian Women Playwrights*, p. 7.

10. Ibid., p. 21.

11. Andrew Wyllie, *Sex on Stage*, p. 7.

12. Quoted in Ruth Little and Emily McLaughlin, *The Royal Court Theatre*, p. 432.

13. Joshua Abrams, 'State of the Nation', p. 13.

14. Compare TV programmes such as the BBC's *Little Britain*, whose characters Chris Rojeck describes as 'a moronic inferno of welfare state scroungers [. . .] insularity, superiority and prejudice reign supreme' (Rojeck, *Brit-myth*, p. 120. See also p. 133).

15. Rhoda Koenig, 'What's Not on Stage', *Independent*, 4 September 2002. For the limiting aesthetics of new writing see Aleks Sierz, 'Reality Sucks', pp. 102–7.

16. Steve Blandford, *Film, Drama and the Break-Up of Britain*, p. 10.

17. Chris Rojek, *Brit-myth*, p. 55. Such utopian imaginings in the wider culture include evocations of Albion, Arthur and our Green and Pleasant Land. An example of using this utopian myth for political ends is Julian Mitchell's *Another Country* (1981).

18. Quoted in Anon, 'Ditch the Mumbling Smackheads!', *Guardian*, 7 January 2004.

19. Michael Billington, 'The Players', *Guardian Weekend* magazine, 6 July 2002, p. 16.

20. See Dominic Cavendish, 'Would an Enoch Powell Play Be Staged?', *Daily Telegraph*, 31 December 2007.

21. British Theatre Consortium, *Writ Large*, pp. 8, 13.

22. Quoted in Mireia Aragay et al., *British Theatre*, p. 21.

23. Nicholas Craig, *I, An Actor*, pp. xv, xxi, xxviii; see also Tim Crouch, *The Author*, which satirises the typical in-yer-face play.

24. David Greig, 'Rough Theatre', p. 212. See also Paul Taylor, 'London's Hottest Restoration Drama', *Independent*, 16 February 2000.

25. Steve Cramer, 'New Directions', *The List*, issue 561, 16 October 2006.

26. Mark Lawson, 'Is This a New Golden Age for British Theatre?', *Guardian*, 2 December 2009; cf. Dominic Dromgoole, 'We've Never Had It So Good', *Guardian*, 10 January 2001.

27. Nicholas de Jongh, 'The London Stage: It's Like a Neutered Old Tomcat', *Evening Standard*, 5 January 2000. I was one of the judges of the Verity Bargate Award in 2002.

28. Michael Billington, 'Modern Life Is Rubbish', *Guardian*, 18 December 2002.

29. Declan Kiberd, 'Reinventing England', p. 33.

30. Patrick Lonergan, *Theatre and Globalization*, p. 215.

31. Benedict Anderson, *Imagined Communities*, pp. 5–7, 204–6. For a discussion of the politics of Anderson's *Imagined Communities* see Jen Harvie, *Staging the UK*, pp. 3–4.

BIBLIOGRAPHY

Plays

All references to plays are to the editions listed below.

Abdulrazzak, Hassan, *Baghdad Wedding* (London: Oberon, 2007).

Adam, Henry, *Among Unbroken Hearts* (London: Nick Hern, 2001).

Adam, Henry, *The People Next Door* (London: Nick Hern, 2003).

Addai, Levi David, *93.2FM* (London: Methuen Drama, 2006).

Addai, Levi David, *Oxford Street* (London: Methuen Drama, 2008).

Adshead, Kay, *The Bogus Woman* (London: Oberon, 2001).

Adshead, Kay, *Animal* (London: Oberon, 2003).

Adshead, Kay, *Bites* (London: Oberon, 2005).

Adshead, Kay, *Bones* (London: Oberon, 2006).

Agbaje, Bola, *Gone Too Far!* (London: Methuen Drama, 2007).

Agbaje, Bola, *Detaining Justice*, in Nicolas Kent (ed.), *Not Black & White* (London: Methuen Drama, 2009).

Agboluaje, Oladipo, *The Christ of Coldharbour Lane* (London: Oberon, 2007).

Almond, Suzy, *School Play* (London: Oberon, 2001).

Bano, Alia, *Shades* (London: Methuen Drama, 2009).

Barker, Howard, *Dead Hands* (London: Oberon, 2004).

Bartlett, Mike, *My Child* (London: Methuen Drama, 2007).

Bartlett, Mike, *Artefacts* (London: Methuen Drama, 2008).

Bartlett, Mike, *Contractions* (London: Methuen Drama, 2008).

Bartlett, Mike, *Cock* (London: Methuen Drama, 2009).

Bayley, Clare, *The Container* (London: Nick Hern, 2009).

Bean, Richard, *Plays One: The Mentalists; Under the Whaleback; The God Botherers* (London: Oberon, 2005).

Bean, Richard, *Plays Two: Toast; Mr England; Smack Family Robinson; Honeymoon Suite* (London: Oberon, 2007).

Bean, Richard, *Plays Three: Harvest; In the Club; The English Game; Up on Roof* (London: Oberon, 2009).

Bean, Richard, *England People Very Nice* (London: Oberon, 2009).

Beaton, Alistair, *Feelgood* (London: Methuen Drama, 2001).

Bennett, Alan, *The History Boys* (London: Faber, 2004).

Bennett, Alan, *The Habit of Art* (London: Faber, 2009).

Bhatti, Gurpreet Kaur, *Behsharam (Shameless)* (London: Oberon, 2001).

Bhatti, Gurpreet Kaur, *Behzti (Dishonour)* (London: Oberon, 2004).

Bhim, Michael, *Pure Gold* (London: Methuen Drama, 2007).

Block, Simon, *A Place at the Table* (London: Nick Hern, 2000).

Blythe, Alecky, *Cruising* (London: Nick Hern, 2006.

Brace, Adam, *Stovepipe* (London: Faber, 2009).

Bruckner, Ferdinand, *Pains of Youth*, in a version by Martin Crimp (London: Faber, 2009).

Buffini, Moira, *Dinner* (London: Faber, 2002).

Buffini, Moira, *Plays One: Blavatsky's Tower; Gabriel; Silence; Loveplay* (London: Faber, 2006).

Bullmore, Amelia, *Mammals* (London: Methuen Drama, 2005).

Burke, Gregory, *Gagarin Way* (London: Faber, 2001).

Burke, Gregory, *On Tour* (London: Faber, 2005).

Burke, Gregory, *Black Watch* (London: Faber, 2007).

Burt, Simon, *Bottle Universe* (London: Nick Hern, 2005).

Butler, Leo, *Plays One: Made of Stone; Redundant; Lucky Dog; The Early Bird* (London: Methuen Drama, 2008).

Butler, Leo, *Faces in the Crowd* (London: Methuen Drama, 2008).

Butterworth, Jez, *The Night Heron* (London: Nick Hern, 2002).

Butterworth, Jez, *The Winterling* (London: Nick Hern, 2006).

Butterworth, Jez, *Parlour Song* (London: Nick Hern, 2009).

Butterworth, Jez, *Jerusalem* (London: Nick Hern, 2009).

Caldwell, Lucy, *Leaves* (London: Faber, 2007).

Cameron, Richard, *Gong Donkeys* (London: Methuen Drama, 2004).

Cannon, Glyn, *On Blindness* (London: Methuen Drama, 2004).

Chappell, In-Sook, *This Isn't Romance* (London: Oberon, 2009).

Charman, Matt, *A Night at the Dogs* (London: Faber, 2005).

Charman, Matt, *The Five Wives of Maurice Pinder* (London: Faber, 2007).

Charman, Matt, *The Observer* (London: Faber, 2009).

Churchill, Caryl, *Plays Four: Hotel; This Is a Chair; Blue Heart; Far Away; A Number; A Dream Play; Drunk Enough To Say I Love You?* (London: Nick Hern, 2008).

Cleugh, Grae, *Fucking Games* (London: Methuen Drama, 2001).

Coghlan, Lin, *Mercy* (London: Oberon, 2004).

Complicite, *A Disappearing Number* (London: Oberon, 2008).

Cooper, Helen, *Three Women and a Piano Tuner* (London: Nick Hern, 2004).

Coxon, Lucinda, *Happy Now?* (London: Nick Hern, 2008).

Craig, Ryan, *What We Did to Weinstein* (London: Oberon, 2005).

Craig, Ryan, *The Glass Room* (London: Oberon, 2006).

Crimp, Martin, *Plays Two: No One Sees the Video; The Misanthrope; Attempts on Her Life; The Country* (London: Faber, 2005).

Crimp, Martin, *Fewer Emergencies* (London: Faber, 2005).

Crimp, Martin, *The City* (London: Faber, 2008).

Crouch, Tim, *An Oak Tree* (London: Oberon, 2005).

Crouch, Tim, *England* (London: Oberon, 2007).

Crouch, Tim, *The Author* (London: Oberon, 2009).

Davies, Molly, *A Miracle* (London: Methuen Drama, 2009).

De Angelis, April, *Wild East* (London: Faber, 2004).

De Angelis, April, *Amongst Friends* (London: Faber, 2009).

Dipper, David, *Flush* (London: Nick Hern, 2004).

Dunster, Matthew, *You Can See the Hills*, rev. edn (London: Oberon, 2009).

Edgar, David, *The Prisoner's Dilemma*, rev. edn (London: Nick Hern, 2002).

Edgar, David, *Playing with Fire* (London: Nick Hern, 2005).

Edgar, David, *Testing the Echo* (London: Nick Hern, 2008).

Edmundson, Helen, *Mother Teresa Is Dead* (London: Nick Hern, 2002).

Eilenberg, Charlotte, *The Lucky Ones* (London: Methuen Drama, 2002).

Eldridge, David, *Plays One: Serving It Up; Summer Begins; Under the Blue Sky; M.A.D.* (London: Methuen Drama, 2005).

Eldridge, David, *Incomplete and Random Acts of Kindness* (London: Methuen Drama, 2005).

Elyot, Kevin, *Four Plays: Coming Clean; My Night with Reg; The Day I Stood Still; Mouth to Mouth* (London: Nick Hern, 2004).

Elyot, Kevin, *Forty Winks* (London: Nick Hern, 2004).

Evans, Fiona, *Scarborough* (London: Nick Hern, 2008).

Evans, Rob, *A Girl in a Car with a Man* (London: Faber, 2004).

Farquhar, Simon, *Rainbow Kiss* (London: Oberon, 2006).

Farr, David, *The Danny Crowe Show* (London: Faber, 2001).

Farr, David, *Night of the Soul* (London: Faber, 2002).

Feehily, Stella, *Dreams of Violence* (London: Nick Hern, 2009).

Fitch, Georgia, *I Like Mine with a Kiss* (London: Oberon, 2007).

Frost, Emma, *Airsick* (London: Nick Hern, 2003).

green, debbie tucker, *Dirty Butterfly* (London: Nick Hern, 2003).

green, debbie tucker, *Born Bad* (London: Nick Hern, 2003).

green, debbie tucker, *Stoning Mary* (London: Nick Hern, 2005).

green, debbie tucker, *Trade & Generations* (London: Nick Hern, 2005).

green, debbie tucker, *Random* (London: Nick Hern, 2008).

Greig, David, *Victoria* (London: Methuen Drama, 2000).

Greig, David, *Outlying Islands* (London: Faber, 2002).

Greig, David, *Plays One: Europe; The Architect; The Cosmonaut's Last Message to the Woman He Once Loved in the Former Soviet Union* (London: Methuen Drama, 2002).

Greig, David, *San Diego* (London: Faber, 2003).

Greig, David, *The American Pilot* (London: Faber, 2005).

Greig, David, *Pyrenees* (London: Faber, 2005).

Greig, David, *Damascus* (London: Faber, 2007).

Greig, David, and Gordon McIntyre, *Midsummer* (London: Faber, 2009).

Grosso, Nick, *Kosher Harry* (London: Methuen Drama, 2002).

Gupta, Tanika, *The Waiting Room* (London: Faber, 2000).

Gupta, Tanika, *Sanctuary* (London: Oberon, 2002).

Gupta, Tanika, *Gladiator Games* (London: Oberon, 2006).

Gupta, Tanika, *Sugar Mummies* (London: Oberon, 2006).

Gupta, Tanika, *White Boy* (London: Oberon, 2008).

Hare, David, *My Zinc Bed* (London: Faber, 2000).

Hare, David, *Stuff Happens* (London: Faber, 2004).

Hare, David, *Plays Three: Skylight; Amy's View; The Judas Kiss; My Zinc Bed* (London: Faber, 2008).

Hare, David, *The Vertical Hour* (London: Faber, 2008).

Hare, David, *Gethsemane* (London: Faber, 2008).

Hare, David, *The Power of Yes* (London: Faber, 2009).

Harris, Zinnie, *Further than the Furthest Thing* (London: Faber, 2000).

Harris, Zinnie, *Midwinter* (London: Faber, 2004).

Harrower, David, *Dark Earth* (London: Faber, 2003).

Harrower, David, *Blackbird* (London: Faber, 2006).

Harvey, Jonathan, *Out in the Open* (London: Methuen Drama, 2001).

Harwood, Ronald, *An English Tragedy* (London: Faber, 2008).

Hood, Kerry, *Meeting Myself Coming Back* (London: Oberon, 2002).

Horwood, Joel, *I Caught Crabs in Walberswick* (London: Nick Hern, 2008).

Hutchinson, Ron, *Head/Case* (London: Oberon, 2004).

Jeffreys, Stephen, *I Just Stopped by To See the Man* (London: Nick Hern, 2000).

Johnson, Terry, *Hitchcock Blonde* (London: Methuen Drama, 2003).

Johnson, Terry, *Piano/Forte* (London: Methuen Drama, 2006).

Jones, Charlotte, *Humble Boy* (London: Faber, 2001).

Kane, Sarah, *Complete Plays: Blasted; Phaedra's Love; Cleansed; Crave; 4.48 Psychosis; Skin* (London: Methuen Drama, 2001).

Kaye Campbell, Alexi, *The Pride* (London: Nick Hern, 2008).

Kaye Campbell, Alexi, *Apologia* (London: Nick Hern, 2009).

Kelly, Dennis, *Taking Care of Baby* (London: Oberon, 2007).

Kelly, Dennis, *Plays One: Debris; Osama the Hero; After the End; Love and Money* (London: Oberon, 2008).

Kelly, Dennis, *Orphans* (London: Oberon, 2009).

Kennedy, Fin, *Protection* (London: Nick Hern, 2003).

Kennedy, Fin, *How To Disappear Completely and Never Be Found* (London: Nick Hern, 2007).

Kent, Nicolas (ed.), *The Great Game: Afghanistan* (London: Oberon, 2009).

Kent, Nicolas (ed.), *Not Black & White* (London: Methuen Drama, 2009).

Khan, Shan, *Office* (London: Faber, 2001).

Kirkwood, Lucy, *Tinderbox* (London: Nick Hern, 2008).

Kirkwood, Lucy, *it felt empty when the heart went at first but it is alright now* (London: Nick Hern, 2009).

Kwei-Armah, Kwame, *Plays One: Elmina's Kitchen; Fix Up; Statement of Regret; Let There Be Love* (London: Methuen Drama, 2009).

Kwei-Armah, Kwame, *Seize the Day*, in Nicolas Kent (ed.), *Not Black & White* (London: Methuen Drama, 2009).

Langridge, Natasha, *Shraddha* (London: Oberon, 2009).

Laurens, Joanna, *Five Gold Rings* (London: Oberon, 2003).

Laurens, Joanna, *Poor Beck* (London: Oberon, 2004).

Lavery, Bryony, *Plays One: A Wedding Story; Frozen; Illyria; More Light* (London: Faber, 2007).

Lavery, Bryony, *Stockholm* (London: Oberon, 2007).

Leigh, Mike, *Two Thousand Years* (London: Faber, 2005).

Lenkiewicz, Rebecca, *Shoreditch Madonna* (London: Faber, 2005).

Leyshon, Nell, *Comfort Me with Apples* (London: Oberon, 2005).

Lucie, Doug, *The Green Man* (London: Methuen Drama, 2003).

Luscombe, Tim, *The Schuman Plan* (London: Nick Hern, 2006).

Marber, Patrick, *Howard Katz* (London: Faber, 2001).

Maxwell, Douglas, *Helmet* (London: Oberon, 2002).

Maxwell, Douglas, *If Destroyed True* (London: Oberon, 2005).

McDonagh, Martin, *The Lieutenant of Inishmore* (London: Methuen Drama Student Edition, 2009).

McDonagh, Martin, *The Pillowman* (London: Faber, 2003).

Mendes da Costa, Simon, *Losing Louis* (London: Methuen Drama, 2005).

Mitchell, Gary, *The Force of Change* (London: Nick Hern, 2000).

Mitchell, Gary, *Loyal Women* (London: Nick Hern, 2003).

Morgan, Abi, *Tiny Dynamite* (London: Oberon, 2001).

Morgan, Abi, *Tender* (London: Oberon, 2001).

Moore, D. C., *Alaska* (London: Methuen Drama, 2007).

Moss, Chloe, *How Love Is Spelt* (London: Nick Hern, 2004).

Moss, Chloe, *Christmas Is Miles Away* (London: Nick Hern, 2005).

Moss, Chloe, *This Wide Night* (London: Nick Hern, 2008).

Munro, Rona, *Iron* (London: Nick Hern, 2003).

Neilson, Anthony, *Stitching* (London: Methuen Drama, 2002).

Neilson, Anthony, *The Wonderful World of Dissocia; Realism* (London: Methuen Drama, 2007).

Neilson, Anthony, *Plays Two: Edward Gant's Amazing Feats of Loneliness!; The Lying Kind; The Wonderful World of Dissocia; Realism* (London: Methuen Drama, 2008).

Norfolk, Mark, *Wrong Place* (London: Oberon, 2003).

O'Connell, Chris, *Street Trilogy: Car; Raw; Kid* (London: Oberon, 2003).

Oglesby, Tamsin, *US and Them* (London: Faber, 2003).

Omar, Cosh, *The Battle of Green Lanes* (London: Oberon, 2004).

Omar, Cosh, *The Great Extension* (London: Oberon, 2009).

Oparei, DeObia, *Crazyblackmuthafuckin'self* (London: Royal Court, 2002).

Owen, Gary, *Plays One: Crazy Gary's Mobile Disco; The Shadow of a Boy; The Drowned World; Fags; Cancer Time* (London: Methuen Drama, 2005).

Packer, Mike, *A Carpet, a Pony and a Monkey* (London: Faber, 2002).

Packer, Mike, *The Dysfunckshonalz!* (London: Faber, 2007).

Pautz, Drew, *Someone Else's Shoes* (London: Nick Hern, 2007).

Payne, Nick, *If There Is I Haven't Found It Yet* (London: Faber, 2009).

Penhall, Joe, *Landscape with Weapon* (London: Methuen Drama, 2007).

Penhall, Joe, *Plays Two: Blue/Orange; Dumb Show; Wild Turkey* (London: Methuen Drama, 2008).

Pinnock, Winsome, *One Under* (London: Faber, 2005).

Pollard, Clare, *The Weather* (London: Faber, 2004).

Prebble, Lucy, *The Sugar Syndrome* (London: Methuen Drama, 2003).

Prebble, Lucy, *Enron* (London: Methuen Drama, 2009).

Priestley, J. B., *An Inspector Calls,* in *Time and the Conways and Other Plays* (Harmondsworth: Penguin, 1969).

Raine, Nina, *Rabbit* (London: Nick Hern, 2006).

Ravenhill, Mark, *Plays One: Shopping and Fucking; Faust Is Dead; Handbag; Some Explicit Polaroids* (London: Methuen Drama, 2001).

Ravenhill, Mark, *Plays Two: Mother Clap's Molly House; Product; The Cut; Citizenship; pool (no water)* (London: Methuen Drama, 2008).

Ravenhill, Mark, *Shoot/Get Treasure/Repeat* (London: Methuen Drama, 2008).

Rebellato, Dan, *Static* (London: Oberon, 2008).

Ridley, Philip, *Plays Two: Vincent River; Mercury Fur; Leaves of Glass; Piranha Heights* (London: Methuen Drama, 2009).

Roberts, Max (ed.), *Live Theatre: Six Plays from the North East* (London: Methuen Drama, 2003).

Sen Gupta, Atiha, *What Fatima Did . . .* (London: Oberon, 2009).

Silas, Shelley, *Falling* (London: Oberon, 2002).

Stafford, Nick, *Love Me Tonight* (London: Faber, 2004).

Stenham, Polly, *That Face* (London: Faber, 2007).

Stenham, Polly, *Tusk Tusk* (London: Faber, 2009).

Stephens, Simon, *Plays One: Bluebird; Christmas; Herons; Port* (London: Methuen Drama, 2005).

Stephens, Simon, *On the Shore of the Wide World* (London: Methuen Drama, 2005).

Stephens, Simon, *Plays Two: One Minute; Country Music; Motortown; Pornography; Sea Wall* (London: Methuen Drama, 2009).

Stephens, Simon, *Harper Regan* (London: Methuen Drama, 2008).

Stephens, Simon, *Punk Rock* (London: Methuen Drama, 2009).

Stephenson, Shelagh, *Mappa Mundi* (London: Methuen Drama, 2002).

Stephenson, Shelagh, *Plays One: The Memory of Water; Five Kinds of Silence; An Experiment with an Air Pump; Ancient Lights* (London: Methuen Drama, 2003).

Stephenson, Shelagh, *The Long Road* (London: Methuen Drama, 2008).

Stoppard, Tom, *Rock 'N' Roll* (London: Faber, 2006).

Taylor, Ali, *Cotton Wool* (London: Nick Hern, 2008).

Taylor, Ali, *Overspill* (London: Nick Hern, 2008).

Teevan, Colin, *How Many Miles to Basra?* (London: Oberon, 2006).

Thomas, Ed, *Stone City Blue* (London: Methuen Drama, 2004).

Thompson, Steve, *Damages* (London: Josef Weinberger, 2004).

Thompson, Steve, *Whipping It Up* (London: Nick Hern, 2006).

Thorne, Jack, *Stacy; Fanny and Faggot* (London: Nick Hern, 2007).

Thorne, Jack, *2nd May 2007* (London: Nick Hern, 2009).

Tregenna, Catherine, *Art and Guff* (London: Oberon, 2001).

Upton, Judy, *Sliding with Suzanne* (London: Methuen Drama, 2001).

Vinnicombe, Simon, *Cradle Me* (London: Methuen Drama, 2008).

Wade, Laura, *Breathing Corpses* (London: Oberon, 2005).

Wade, Laura, *Other Hands* (London: Oberon, 2006).

Walker, Che, *Flesh Wound* (London: Faber, 2003).

Walker, Che, *The Frontline* (London: Faber, 2008).

Waters, Steve, *World Music* (London: Nick Hern, 2003).

Waters, Steve, *The Contingency Plan: On the Beach* and *Resilience* (London: Nick Hern, 2009).

Wertenbaker, Timberlake, *Credible Witness* (London: Faber, 2001).

Whithouse, Toby, *Jump Mr Malinoff, Jump* (London: Faber, 2000).

Wilkinson, Joy, *Fair; Felt Effects* (London: Nick Hern, 2005).

Williams, Roy, *Plays Two: The Gift; Clubland; Sing Yer Heart Out for the Lads* (London: Methuen Drama, 2004).

Williams, Roy, *Plays Three: Fallout; Slow Time; Days of Significance; Absolute Beginners* (London: Methuen Drama, 2008).

Williams, Roy, *Category B*, in Nicolas Kent (ed.), *Not Black & White* (London: Methuen Drama, 2009).

Wright, Isabel, *Peepshow* (London: Oberon, 2002).

Wynne, Michael, *The People Are Friendly* (London: Faber, 2002).

Wynne, Michael, *The Priory* (London: Faber, 2009).

Zegerman, Alexis, *Lucky Seven* (London: Nick Hern, 2008).

Analysis and commentary

Books

Ackroyd, Peter, *Albion: The Origins of the English Imagination* (London: Chatto & Windus, 2002).

Anderson, Benedict, *Imagined Communities: Reflections on the Origins and Spread of Nationalism*, rev. edn (London: Verso, 1991).

Aragay, Mireia, Hildegard Klein, Enric Monforte and Pilar Zozaya (eds), *British Theatre of the 1990s: Interviews with Directors, Playwrights, Critics and Academics* (Basingstoke: Palgrave Macmillan, 2007).

Aston, Elaine, *Feminist Views on the English Stage: Women Playwrights, 1990–2000* (Cambridge: Cambridge University Press, 2003).

Benn, Tony, *More Time for Politics: Diaries 2001–2007*, ed. Ruth Winstone (London: Arrow, 2007).

Billingham, Peter, *At the Sharp End: Uncovering the Work of Five Contemporary Dramatists* (London: Methuen Drama, 2007).

Billington, Michael, *State of the Nation: British Theatre Since 1945* (London: Faber, 2007).

Blandford, Steve, *Film, Drama and the Break-Up of Britain* (Bristol: Intellect, 2007).

Boon, Richard, *About Hare: The Playwright and the Work* (London: Faber, 2003).

Boon, Richard (ed.), *The Cambridge Companion to David Hare* (Cambridge: Cambridge University Press, 2007).

Bradwell, Mike (ed.), *The Bush Theatre Book* (London: Methuen Drama, 1997).

British Theatre Consortium, *Writ Large: New Writing on the English Stage 2003–2009* (London: Arts Council England, 2009).

Bull, John, *Stage Right: Crisis and Recovery in British Contemporary Theatre* (London: Macmillan, 1994).

Butler, Robert, *Humble Beginnings* (London: National Theatre, 2001).

Cannadine, David, *Class in Britain* (London: Penguin, 2000).

Chambers, Colin, *Inside the Royal Shakespeare Company: Creativity and the Institution* (London: Routledge, 2004).

Clarke, Ian, *Edwardian Drama: A Critical Study* (London: Faber, 1989).

Craig, Nicholas [Christopher Douglas and Nigel Planer], *I, An Actor*, rev. edn (London: Methuen Drama, 2001).

Croall, Jonathan, *Inside the Molly House* (London: National Theatre, 2001).

Croall, Jonathan, *Buzz Buzz! Playwrights, Actors and Directors at the National Theatre* (London: Methuen Drama, 2008).

Davis, Geoffrey V. and Anne Fuchs (eds), *Staging New Britain: Aspects of Black and South Asian British Theatre Practice* (Brussels: Presses Interuniversitaires Européennes, 2006).

Devine, Harriet, *Looking Back: Playwrights at the Royal Court 1956–2006* (London: Faber, 2006).

D'Monté, Rebecca and Graham Saunders (eds), *Cool Britannia? British Political Drama in the 1990s* (Basingstoke: Palgrave Macmillan, 2008).

Dixon, Steve, *Digital Performance: A History of New Media in Theater, Dance, Performance Art, and Installation* (Cambridge, MA: MIT Press, 2007).

Dorney, Kate, *The Changing Language of Modern British Drama 1945–2005* (Basingstoke: Palgrave Macmillan, 2009).

Dromgoole, Dominic, *The Full Room: An A–Z of Contemporary Playwriting*, 2nd edn (London: Methuen Drama, 2002).

Edgar, David (ed.), *State of Play: Playwrights on Playwriting* (London: Faber, 1999).

Edgar, David, *How Plays Work* (London: Nick Hern, 2009).

Eliot, T. S., *Notes Towards a Definition of Culture* (London: Faber, 1962).

Elsom, John, *Post-War British Theatre* (London: Routledge and Kegan Paul, 1976).

Eyre, Richard and Nicholas Wright, *Changing Stages: A View of British Theatre in the Twentieth Century* (London: Bloomsbury, 2000).

Fountain, Tim, *So You Want To Be a Playwright? How To Write a Play and Get It Produced* (London: Nick Hern, 2007).

Fountain, Tim, *Rude Britannia: One Man's Journey around the Highways and Bi-Ways of British Sex* (London: Phoenix, 2009).

Fox, Kate, *Watching the English: The Hidden Rules of English Behaviour* (London: Hodder & Stoughton, 2004).

Freshwater, Helen, *Theatre Censorship in Britain: Silencing, Censure and Suppression* (Basingstoke: Palgrave Macmillan, 2009).

Furedi, Frank, *Culture of Fear Revisited: Risk-Taking and the Morality of Low Expectation*, 4th edn (London: Continuum, 2006).

Gill, Peter, *Apprenticeship* (London: Oberon, 2008).

Godiwala, Dimple (ed.), *Alternatives within the Mainstream: British Black and Asian Theatres* (Newcastle: Cambridge Scholars, 2006).

Graham, Scott, and Steven Hoggett, *The Frantic Assembly Book of Devising Theatre* (Abingdon: Routledge, 2009).

Griffin, Gabriele, *Contemporary Black and Asian Women Playwrights in Britain* (Cambridge: Cambridge University Press, 2003).

Gritzner, Karoline and David Ian Rabey (eds), *Theatre of Catastrophe: New Essays on Howard Barker* (London: Oberon, 2006).

[Haill, Lyn] (ed.), *Faber Playwrights at the National Theatre* (London: Faber, 2005).

Harvie, Jen, *Staging the UK* (Manchester: Manchester University Press, 2005).

Henke, Christoph and Martin Middeke (eds), *Drama and/after Postmodernism* (CDE 14) (Trier: Wissenschaftlicher Verlag Trier, 2007).

Holdsworth, Nadine and Mary Luckhurst (eds), *A Concise Companion to Contemporary British and Irish Drama* (Oxford: Blackwell, 2006).

Howe Kritzer, Amelia, *Political Theatre in Post-Thatcher Britain: New Writing 1995–2005* (Basingstoke: Palgrave Macmillan, 2008).

Innes, Christopher, *Modern British Drama: The Twentieth Century* (Cambridge: Cambridge University Press, 2002).

Johnson, Robin, *New Theatre – New Writing?*, Report by the International Theatre Institute on the first ITI forum, Soho Theatre, 25 February 2003 (London: ITI, 2003).

Jowell, Tessa, 'Government and the Value of Culture' (London: DCMS, 2004).

Kelleher, Joe, *Theatre & Politics* (Basingstoke: Palgrave Macmillan, 2009).

Kumar, Krishan, *The Making of English National Identity* (Cambridge: Cambridge University Press, 2003).

Kustow, Michael, *theatre@risk*, 2nd edn (London: Methuen Drama, 2001).

Lacey, Stephen, *British Realist Theatre: The New Wave in Its Context 1956–1965* (London: Routledge, 1995).

Leach, Robert, *Theatre Workshop: Joan Littlewood and the Making of Modern British Theatre* (Exeter: University of Exeter Press, 2006).

Little, Ruth and Emily McLaughlin, *The Royal Court Theatre Inside Out* (London: Oberon, 2007).

Lonergan, Patrick, *Theatre and Globalization: Irish Drama in the Celtic Tiger Era* (Basingstoke: Palgrave Macmillan, 2009).

Luckhurst, Mary (ed.), *A Companion to Modern British and Irish Drama 1880–2005* (Oxford: Blackwell, 2006).

Luckhurst, Mary, *Dramaturgy: A Revolution in Theatre* (Cambridge: Cambridge University Press, 2006).

Millman, Anne and Jodi Myers, *Theatre Assessment 2009* (London: Arts Council England, 2009).

Mirza, Munira (ed.), *Culture Vultures: Is UK Arts Policy Damaging the Arts?* (London: Policy Exchange, 2006).

Orbach, Susie, *Bodies* (London: Profile, 2009).

Orwell, George, *The Lion and the Unicorn: Socialism and the English Genius* (Harmondsworth: Penguin, 1982 [original edn 1941]).

Osborne, John, *Damn You, England: Collected Prose* (London: Faber, 1994).

Palahniuk, Chuck, *Fight Club* (London: Vintage, 2006).

Paxman, Jeremy, *The English: A Portrait of a People* (London: Penguin, 2007).

Pevsner, Nikolaus, *The Englishness of English Art* (Harmondsworth: Penguin, 1964).

Porter Abbott, H., *The Cambridge Introduction to Narrative*, 2nd edn (Cambridge: Cambridge University Press, 2008).

Rabey, David Ian, *English Drama since 1940* (Harlow: Longman, 2003).

Rebellato, Dan, *1956 and All That: The Making of Modern British Drama* (London: Routledge, 1999).

Rebellato, Dan, *Theatre & Globalization* (Basingstoke: Palgrave Macmillan, 2009).

Roberts, Philip, *About Churchill: The Playwright and the Work* (London: Faber, 2008).

Rojek, Chris, *Brit-myth: Who Do the British Think They Are?* (London: Reaktion, 2007).

Sandbrook, Dominic, *Never Had It So Good: A History of Britain from Suez to the Beatles* (London: Abacus, 2006).

Saunders, Graham, *'Love Me or Kill Me': Sarah Kane and the Theatre of Extremes* (Manchester: Manchester University Press, 2002).

Saunders, Graham, *About Kane: The Playwright and the Work* (London: Faber, 2009).

Shank, Theodore (ed.), *Contemporary British Theatre* (London: Macmillan, 1994).

Sierz, Aleks, *In-Yer-Face Theatre: British Drama Today* (London: Faber, 2001).

Sierz, Aleks, *The Theatre of Martin Crimp* (London: Methuen Drama, 2006).

Sierz, Aleks, *John Osborne's Look Back in Anger* (London: Continuum, 2008).

Stark, Kathleen, *'I Believe in the Power of Theatre': British Women's Drama of the 1980s and 1990s* (Trier: Wissenschafter Verlag Trier, 2005).

Stephenson, Heidi and Natasha Langridge, *Rage and Reason: Women Playwrights on Playwriting* (London: Methuen Drama, 1997).

Taylor, John Russell, *Anger and After: A Guide to the New British Drama*, 2nd edn (London: Eyre Methuen, 1969).

Toynbee, Polly, *Hard Work: Life in Low-Pay Britain* (London: Bloomsbury, 2003).

Tynan, Kenneth, *Theatre Writings*, ed. Dominic Shellard (London: Nick Hern, 2007).

Wallace, Clare, *Suspect Cultures: Narrative, Identity and Citation in 1990s New Drama* (Prague: Litteraria Pragensia, 2006).

Wardle, Irving, *The Theatres of George Devine* (London: Jonathan Cape, 1978).

Wilmer, S. E., *Theatre, Society and the Nation: Staging American Identities* (Cambridge: Cambridge University Press, 2002).

Wood, James, *How Fiction Works* (London: Vintage, 2009).

Wyllie, Andrew, *Sex on Stage: Gender and Sexuality in Post-War British Theatre* (Bristol: Intellect, 2009).

Chapters and articles

Abrams, Joshua, 'State of the Nation: New British Theatre', *PAJ: A Journal of Performance and Art* 95, vol. 32, no. 2 (May 2010): 8–16.

Angelaki, Vicky, 'Subtractive Forms and Composite Contents: Martin Crimp's Fewer Emergencies', in Ellen Redling and Peter Paul Schnierer (eds), *Non-Standard Forms of Contemporary Drama and Theatre* (Trier: Wissenschaftlicher Verlag Trier, 2008): 31–46.

Ansorge, Peter, '"Stopping for Lunch": The Political Theatre of David Hare', in Richard Boon (ed.), *The Cambridge Companion to David Hare* (Cambridge: Cambridge University Press, 2007): 92–106.

Aston, Elaine, 'The Bogus Woman: Feminism and Asylum Theatre', *Modern Drama*, vol. 46, no. 1 (Spring 2003): 5–21.

Bull, John, 'England People Very Nice: Intercultural Confusions at the National Theatre, London', in Werner Huber, Margarete Rubik and Julia Novak (eds), *Staging Interculturality* (Trier: Wissenschaftlicher Verlag Trier, 2010): 123–43.

Coveney, Michael, 'The National Theatre and Civic Responsibility in the British Isles', in S. E. Wilmer (ed.), *National Theatres in a Changing Europe* (Palgrave Macmillan, 2008): 180–6.

Crow, Brian, 'Issues in Multicultural Theatre: Birmingham Rep and Its Audiences', in Geoffrey V. Davis and Anne Fuchs (eds), *Staging New Britain*: 107–26.

Davis, Geoffrey, '"This Is a Cultural Renaissance": An Interview with Kwame Kwei-Armah', in Geoffrey V. Davis and Anne Fuchs (eds), *Staging New Britain*: 239–51.

Derbyshire, Harry, 'Roy Williams: Representing Multicultural Britain in Fallout', *Modern Drama*, vol. 50, no. 3 (Fall 2007): 414–34.

D'Monté, Rebecca, 'Thatcher's Children: Alienation and Anomie in the Plays of Judy Upton', in Rebecca D'Monté and Graham Saunders (eds), *Cool Britannia?*: 79–95.

Edgar, David. 'The Canon, the Contemporary and the New', in Bernhard Reitz and Heiko Stahl (eds), *What Revels Are in Hand? Contemporary Drama in English 8* (Trier: Wissenschafter Verlag Trier, 2001): 29–35.

Featherstone, Vicky, 'Introduction', in Gary Owen, *Plays One: Crazy Gary's Mobile Disco; The Shadow of a Boy; The Drowned World; Fags; Cancer Time* (London: Methuen Drama, 2005): ix–xiii.

Goddard, Lynette, 'debbie tucker green', *Contemporary Theatre Review*, vol. 15, no. 3 (August 2005): 376–81.

Greig, David, 'Rough Theatre', in Rebecca D'Monté and Graham Saunders (eds), *Cool Britannia?*: 208–21.

Hall, Stuart, 'Labour's Double-Shuffle', *Soundings*, no. 24 (Autumn 2003): 10–24.

Herbert, Ian, '"How It Was for Us" – at the British Theatre Conference', *New Theatre Quarterly*, 94 (May 2008): 201–2.

Holdsworth, Nadine, 'Travelling Across Borders: Re-Imagining the Nation and Nationalism in Contemporary Scottish Theatre', *Contemporary Theatre Review*, vol. 13, no. 2 (May 2003): 25–39.

Holdsworth, Nadine and Wallace McDowell, 'A Legacy of Violence: Representing Loyalism in the Plays of Gary Mitchell', in Rebecca D'Monté and Graham Saunders (eds), *Cool Britannia?*: 176–91.

Holdsworth, Nadine, 'The Landscape of Contemporary Scottish Drama: Place, Politics and Identity', in Nadine Holdsworth and Mary Luckhurst (eds), *A Concise Companion to Contemporary British and Irish Drama*: 125–45.

Iball, Helen, 'Dead Hands and Killer Heels', in Karoline Gritzner and David Ian Rabey (eds), *Theatre of Catastrophe*: 70–82.

Kershaw, Baz, 'British Theatre, 1940–2002: An Introduction', in Baz Kershaw (ed.), *The Cambridge History of British Theatre: Vol. 3, Since 1895* (Cambridge: Cambridge University Press, 2004): 291–325.

Kiberd, Declan, 'Reinventing England', in Mary Luckhurst (ed.), *A Companion to Modern British and Irish Drama*: 22–34.

Laera, Margherita, 'Mark Ravenhill's Shoot/Get Treasure/Repeat: A Treasure Hunt in London', *Theatre Forum*, no. 35 (Summer 2009): 3–9.

Leach, Robert, 'The Short, Astonishing History of the National Theatre of Scotland', *New Theatre Quarterly*, 90 (May 2007): 171–83.

Lonergan, Patrick, '"The Laughter Will Come of Itself. The Tears Are Inevitable": Martin McDonagh, Globalization, and Irish Theatre Criticism', *Modern Drama*, vol. 47, no. 4 (Winter 2004): 636–58.

Lonergan, Patrick, 'Commentary and Notes', in Martin McDonagh, *The Lieutenant of Inishmore* (London: Methuen Student Edition, 2009): v–lxi.

Luckhurst, Mary, 'Martin McDonagh's Lieutenant of Inishmore: Selling (-Out) to the English', *Contemporary Theatre Review*, vol. 14, no. 4 (November 2004): 34–41.

Maguire, Tom, 'Northern Irish Drama: Speaking the Peace', in Nadine Holdsworth and Mary Luckhurst (eds), *A Concise Companion to Contemporary British and Irish Drama*: 66–84.

McDonald, Jan, 'Towards National Identities: Theatre in Scotland', in Baz Kershaw (ed.), *The Cambridge History of British Theatre: Vol. 3, Since 1895* (Cambridge: Cambridge University Press, 2004): 195–227.

McLaughlin, Emily, 'Interview with debbie tucker green', *debbie tucker green: Stoning Mary Education Resources* (London: Royal Court Young Writers Programme, 2005).

Osborne, Deirdre, '"Know Whence You Came": Kwame Kwei-Armah in Conversation', *New Theatre Quarterly*, 91 (August 2007): 253–63.

Osborne, Deirdre, 'The State of the Nation: Contemporary Black British Theatre and the Staging of the UK', in Dimple Godiwala (ed.), *Alternatives within the Mainstream*: 82–100.

Pattie, David, '"Mapping the Territory": Modern Scottish Drama', in Rebecca D'Monte and Graham Saunders (eds), *Cool Britannia?*: 143–57.

Payne, Ben, 'In the Beginning Was the Word', in John Deeney (ed.), *Writing Live: An Investigation of the Relationship Between Writing and Live Art* (London: New Playwrights Trust, 1998): 9–50.

Peacock, D. Keith, 'The Question of Multiculturalism: The Plays of Roy Williams', in Mary Luckhurst (ed.), *A Companion to Modern British and Irish Drama 1880–2005*: 530–40.

Peacock, D. Keith, 'Black British Drama and the Politics of Identity', in Nadine Holdsworth and Mary Luckhurst (eds), *A Concise Companion to Contemporary British and Irish Drama*: 48–65.

Rabey, David Ian, 'Ed Thomas: Jazz Pictures in the Gaps of Language', in Mary Luckhurst (ed.), *A Companion to Modern British and Irish Drama 1880–2005*: 541–50.

Rebellato, Dan, 'Introduction', in Mark Ravenhill, *Plays One: Shopping and Fucking; Faust Is Dead; Handbag; Some Explicit Polaroids* (London: Methuen Drama, 2001): ix–xx.

Rebellato, Dan, 'Introduction', in David Greig, *Plays One: Europe; The Architect; The Cosmonaut's Last Message to the Woman He Once Loved in the Former Soviet Union* (London: Methuen Drama, 2002): ix–xxiii.

Rebellato, Dan, 'Simon Stephens', *Contemporary Theatre Review*, vol. 15, no. 1 (February 2005): 174–8.

Rebellato, Dan, 'National Theatre of Scotland: The First Year', *Contemporary Theatre Review*, vol. 17, no. 2 (May 2007): 213–8.

Rebellato, Dan, 'The Personal Is Not Political: Caryl Churchill's *Drunk Enough To Say I Love You?'*, *Western European Stages*, vol. 19, no. 1 (Winter 2007): 33–6.

Rebellato, Dan, 'From the State of the Nation to Globalization: Shifting Political Agendas in Contemporary British Playwriting', in Nadine Holdsworth and Mary Luckhurst (eds), *A Concise Companion to Contemporary British and Irish Drama*: 245–62.

Rees, Catherine, 'The Good, the Bad, and the Ugly: the Politics of Morality in Martin McDonagh's Lieutenant of Inishmore', *New Theatre Quarterly*, 81 (February 2005): 28–33.

Rees, Catherine, 'Postmodern Interrogations: Power Narratives in Martin McDonagh's The Pillowman', unpublished article, typescript, 2009.

Reid, Trish, '"From Scenes Like These Old Scotia's Grandeur Springs": The New National Theatre of Scotland', *Contemporary Theatre Review*, vol. 17, no. 2 (May 2007): 192–201.

Reid, Trish, '"Deformities of the Frame": The Theatre of Anthony Neilson', *Contemporary Theatre Review*, vol. 17, no. 4 (November 2007): 487–98.

Roberts, Max (ed.), 'Introduction', *Live Theatre: Six Plays from the North East* (London: Methuen Drama, 2003).

Roms, Heike, 'Staging an Urban Nation: Place and Identity in Contemporary Welsh Theatre', in Nadine Holdsworth and Mary Luckhurst (eds), *A Concise Companion to Contemporary British and Irish Drama*: 107–24.

Russell, Richard Rankin, '"Loyal to the Truth": Gary Mitchell's Aesthetic Loyalism in As the Beast Sleeps and The Force of Change', *Modern Drama*, vol. 48, no. 1 (Spring 2005): 186–201.

Saunders, Graham, '"Under Redevelopment": The Tradition of City Comedy in Contemporary British Drama', in Monika Pietrzak-Franger and Eckart Voigts-Virchow (eds), *Adaptations: Performing across Media and Genres* (Trier: Wissenschaftlicher Verlag Trier, 2009): 19–30.

Scullion, Adrienne, 'Contemporary Scottish Women Playwrights', in Elaine Aston and Janelle Reinelt (eds), *The Cambridge Companion to Modern British Women Playwrights* (Cambridge: Cambridge University Press, 2000): 94–118.

Shank, Theodore, 'The Multiplicity of British Theatre', in Theodore Shank (ed.), *Contemporary British Theatre* (London: Macmillan, 1994): 3–18.

Shank, Theodore, 'The Playwriting Profession: Setting Out and the Journey', in

Theodore Shank (ed.), *Contemporary British Theatre* (London: Macmillan, 1994): 181–204.

Sierz, Aleks, '"In Yer Face?" in Bristol', *New Theatre Quarterly*, 73 (February 2003): 90–1.

Sierz, Aleks, '"Art Flourishes in Times of Struggle": Creativity, Funding and New Writing', *Contemporary Theatre Review*, vol. 13, no. 1 (February 2003): 33–45.

Sierz, Aleks, '"Me and My Mates": The State of English Playwriting, 2003', *New Theatre Quarterly*, 77 (February 2004): 79–83.

Sierz, Aleks, '"Big Ideas" for Big Stages, 2004', *New Theatre Quarterly*, 81 (February 2005): 96–8.

Sierz, Aleks, '"Two Worlds Fighting Each Other": Roy Williams and Contemporary Black British theatre', in Geoffrey V. Davis and Anne Fuchs (eds), *Staging New Britain*: 177–88.

Sierz, Aleks, 'Alternative or Mainstream?: London Fringe Theatre in Image and Reality', in Thomas Rommel and Mark Schreiber (eds), *Mapping Uncertain Territories: Space and Place in Contemporary Theatre and Drama* (CDE 13) (Trier: Wissenschaftlicher Verlag Trier, 2006): 23–38.

Sierz, Aleks, '"What Kind of England Do We Want?": Roy Williams in Conversation', *New Theatre Quarterly*, 86 (May 2006): 113–21.

Sierz, Aleks, '"Can Old Forms Be Reinvigorated?" Radical Populism and New Writing in British Theatre Today', *Contemporary Theatre Review*, vol. 16, no. 3 (August 2006): 301–11.

Sierz, Aleks, 'New Writing 2006', *Contemporary Theatre Review*, vol. 16, no. 3 (August 2006): 371–3.

Sierz, Aleks, 'Richard Bean in Conversation', in Christoph Henke and Martin Middeke (eds), *Drama and/after Postmodernism* (CDE 14), Trier: Wissenschaftlicher Verlag Trier, 2007: 351–61.

Sierz, Aleks, '"Form Follows Function": Meaning and Politics in Martin Crimp's Fewer Emergencies', *Modern Drama*, vol. 50, no. 3 (Fall 2007): 375–93.

Sierz, Aleks, 'Reality Sucks: The Slump in British New Writing', *PAJ: A Journal of Performance and Art* 89, vol. 30, no. 2 (May 2008): 102–7.

Sierz, Aleks, '"As Long as the Punters Enjoy It": Tanika Gupta in Conversation', *New Theatre Quarterly*, 95 (August 2008): 260–9.

Sierz, Aleks, '"Putting a New Lens on the World": Philip Ridley in Conversation', *New Theatre Quarterly*, 98 (May 2009): 109–17.

Smith, Kathy, 'A House Built on Mud: Stages of Translation and the Theatre of Rona Munro', in Monika Pietrzak-Franger and Eckart Voigts-Virchow (eds), *Adaptations: Performing across Media and Genres* (Trier: Wissenschaftlicher Verlag Trier, 2009): 239–52.

Stark, Kathleen, 'Battlefield "Body": Gregory Burke's Gagarin Way and Anthony Neilson's Stitching', in Hans-Ulrich Mohr and Kerstin Machler (eds), *Extending the Code: New Forms of Dramatic and Theatrical Expression* (Trier: Wissenschaftlicher Verlag Trier, 2004): 171–9.

Stephens, Simon, 'Keynote Address: Writing Black People', in Werner Huber, Margarete Rubik and Julia Novak (eds), *Staging Interculturality* (Trier: Wissenschaftlicher Verlag Trier, 2010): 19–36.

Svich, Caridad, 'Commerce and Morality in the Theatre of Mark Ravenhill', *Contemporary Theatre Review*, vol. 13, no. 1 (February 2003): 81–96.

Teevan, Colin, 'Free the Playwrights! A Brief Introduction to Monsterism', *Contemporary Theatre Review*, vol. 16, no. 2 (May 2006): 239–45.

Ukaegbu, Victor, 'Talawa Theatre Company: The "Likkle" Matter of Black Creativity and Representation on the British Stage', in Dimple Godiwala (ed.), *Alternatives within the Mainstream*: 123–52.

Worthern, Hana, and W. B. Worthern, 'The Pillowman and the Ethics of Allegory', *Modern Drama*, vol. 49, no. 2 (Summer 2006): 155–73.

Video recordings

The following can be found in The National Video Archive of Performance recordings, V&A Theatre and Performance Collections.

Blue/Orange by Joe Penhall, Duchess, July 2001.

Days of Significance by Roy Williams, Tricycle, March 2008.

Far Away by Caryl Churchill, Albery, January 2001.

Feelgood by Alistair Beaton, Hampstead, October 2001.

Five Gold Rings by Joanna Laurens, Almeida, January 2004.

The Great Game: Afghanistan by various, Tricycle, May 2009.

Humble Boy by Charlotte Jones, National Theatre, November 2001.

Jerusalem by Jez Butterworth, Royal Court, August 2009.

The Lieutenant of Inishmore by Martin McDonagh, Barbican, January 2002.

A Number by Carl Churchill, Royal Court, October 2002.

Product: World Remix by Mark Ravenhill, Bush, January 2007.

Tusk Tusk by Polly Stenham, Royal Court, April 2009.

Websites

The British Theatre Guide: www.britishtheatreguide.info.

Guardian theatre blog: www.guardian.co.uk/stage/theatreblog.

In-Yer-Face Theatre: www.inyerface-theatre.com.

TheatreVOICE: www.theatrevoice.com.

Whatsonstage: www.whatsonstage.com.

INDEX

Note: only plays, playwrights, theatre companies and theatres are listed in the index. Plays are entered directly under their titles.